Migrant Longing

Migrant Longing

Letter Writing across the U.S.-Mexico Borderlands

Miroslava Chávez-García

University of North Carolina Press CHAPEL HILL

This book was also published with the assistance of a grant from the Department of History at the University of California, Santa Barbara.

Set in Espinosa Nova by Westchester Publishing Services
Manufactured in the United States of America

The University of North Carolina Press has been a member of the Green Press Initiative since 2003.

Library of Congress Cataloging-in-Publication Data
Names: Chávez-García, Miroslava, 1968– author.
Title: Migrant longing : letter writing across the U.S.-Mexico borderlands / Miroslava Chávez-García.
Other titles: David J. Weber series in the new borderlands history.
Description: Chapel Hill : University of North Carolina Press, [2018] | Series: The David J. Weber series in the new borderlands history | Includes bibliographical references and index.
Identifiers: LCCN 2017044539| ISBN 9781469641027 (cloth : alk. paper) | ISBN 9781469641034 (pbk : alk. paper) | ISBN 9781469641041 (ebook)
Subjects: LCSH: Mexicans—United States—Correspondence. | Immigrants—United States—Correspondence. | Mexicans—United States—Social conditions—Correspondence. | Mexico—Emigration and immigration—Social aspects—Correspondence. | Mexico—Emigration and immigration—Social aspects—Sources.
Classification: LCC E184.M5 C3838 2018 | DDC 305.868/72073—dc23
LC record available at https://lccn.loc.gov/2017044539

Cover illustration: Photograph and text from letter sent by José Chávez Esparza to María Concepción Alvarado, 1965 (author's collection).

Portions of chapters one and two were previously published as "Migrant Longing, Courtship, and Gendered Identity in the U.S.-Mexico Borderlands," *Western Historical Quarterly* 47:2 (Summer 2016): 137–60. Used here with permission.

In loving memory of my tía Beatríz Chávez and with gratitude to her and my tío Paco Chávez for their continuous support throughout the years.

Contents

Illustrations

A Note on Sources

Quotes that appear in the text—in the narrative—are my translations of the original Spanish-language writings found in the letters. I have lightly edited those quotes when using phrases that come from complete sentences found in the letters by capitalizing the first word of the sentence and adding a period at the end of the phrase, thereby transforming it into a complete sentence. This allowed me to quote phrases without having to insert brackets at the beginning and end and without disrupting the narrative. Rarely, if ever, are words "corrected" in the English translation or the Spanish original.

Quotes that appear in the notes are the Spanish-language originals found in the letters. Those quotes are transcribed verbatim, with any slight changes noted in brackets. In most instances, the only changes are added capital letters and periods. Rarely are other changes made. This allows the reader to see the original text, which is important, as interpretations and translations vary from speaker to speaker. I am a native Spanish speaker and used my skills as well as the insights of family members and online translation services in translating phrases, *dichos* (sayings), and colloquial expressions. Paco Chávez, "the keeper of the letters," also reviewed the entire manuscript and offered minor corrections.

I have deposited the original letters at the Huntington Library, San Marino, California, where they now constitute the Chávez Family Papers. I retain the digital scans.

Migrant Longing

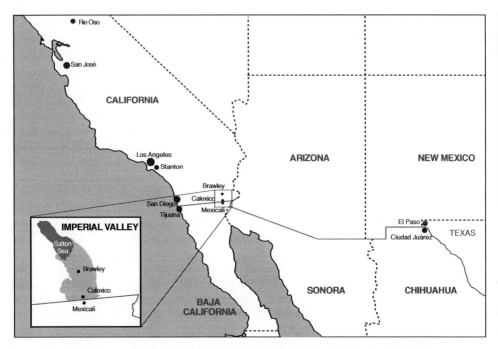

The U.S.-Mexico border region with prominent cities and locales highlighted,
demonstrating the various rural and urban spaces migrants central to this
narrative traversed, inhabited, and eventually settled.

Map created by Ebers García.

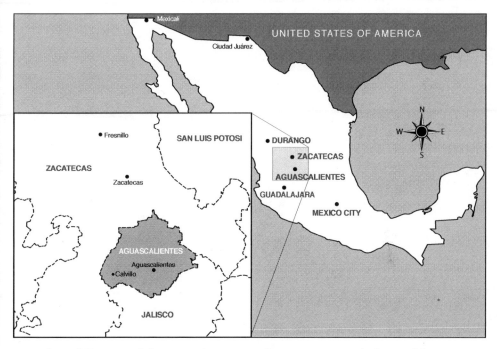

Central Mexico and the geographic origins of most migrants at the heart of this study, namely, Calvillo, Aguascalientes, as well as key cities and regions they visited in their daily travels and on their way to and from *el norte*.
Map created by Ebers García.

Introduction
An Archive of Intimacy

Until recently, at the bottom of my closet sat a neatly organized treasure trove of over 300 personal letters written in the 1960s and early 1970s and exchanged among family members across the U.S.-Mexico borderlands. Written in Spanish with sprinklings of English, they contain a wealth of insight about the social, familial, and intimate relations built, sustained, and sometimes lost across the vast divide. They underscore that the decision to immigrate to the United States was not without personal and emotional pain, although it could also elicit excitement and eager anticipation. Indeed, migrating invited a host of challenges as well as rewards. The writings depict longing, isolation, and restlessness living between here (*aqui*) and there (*allá*) and demonstrate moments of discovery, deep satisfaction, and joy in having made the move, albeit often temporarily. They reveal, too, the creative coping mechanisms and cultural resources migrants devised, adapted, and drew upon to negotiate the daily reality of living relatively alone and facing a host of gender, racial, ethnic, class, and cultural constraints in the new environment.

More than a collection of deeply personal, emotional, and individual self-expressive experiences, the missives provide a window onto the social, economic, cultural, and political developments of the day in and across Mexico and the United States. The letters, as I have found in my effort to map my family's history on a broader genealogy of migration across the borderlands, are versatile, open to multiple interpretations, and reflect the hopes and dreams as well as *fracasos* (failures) of those who sought to improve their lives—and the lives of those they left behind—by migrating to *el norte* (the United States; literally, the north). Like all sources, the letters are biased, inconsistent (some are missing, undated, illegible, incomplete, or penned sporadically), manipulative, formulaic, and mundane. Without a richly textured historical framework animating and breathing life into them, the missives are anecdotal, irrelevant, and cut off from the ebbs and flows of that region of the globe.

My effort to make meaning of the letters began in 2012, shortly after my tío Paco, my father's youngest brother, who raised my only brother and me,

1

rediscovered the letters and placed them in my hands. My uncle had found the letters in the basement of his house, where they had been stored ever since my brother and I had moved into his home and that of his wife, Beatríz Chávez, in 1981, after a horrific car accident early that year, on our way home from Mexico, took the lives of my parents and my paternal grandmother. My brother and I, who were thirteen and twelve years of age, respectively, were also in the wreck but fortunately survived with few serious injuries. In the process of adjusting our lives to the new household, we got rid of most of my family's belongings, save for family albums, heirlooms, and random knickknacks. Thankfully, we hung onto the surviving eighty letters my parents had exchanged: forty-five from my father written in the United States, thirty-five from my mother based in Mexico.[1] I was familiar with the letters when my uncle found them. I had discovered them when I was an undergraduate in the late 1980s, but had been unable and, admittedly, unwilling to decipher the mostly handwritten Spanish-language notes. Later, over the years, I thought about them and their location but, unable to find them, I figured I had lost them. I was elated, then, when my uncle passed them to me.

I spent the rest of that year organizing, transcribing, and translating the letters and formulating analyses. At the heart of the communication was my father's desire to court and eventually wed my mother, whom he had met briefly in December 1962 during one of his visits home to Mexico during the holidays. At the time, my father was a single, thirty-year-old farm-worker in Imperial Valley, one of California's most productive agricultural zones, situated across the border from the Mexicali Valley in Baja California, Mexico. He had migrated there a few years earlier, in 1957, as a means of surviving the growing impoverishment of the Mexican countryside, de-spite the purported gains of Mexico's rapid industrialization, moderniza-tion, and integration into the global economy in during World War II and the postwar era. Rather than face bleak prospects in his pueblo or try his luck in Mexico City, as many rural Mexicans did, he took advantage of the employment opportunities offered by the bracero program. A contract-labor importation accord negotiated through a series of agreements between Mex-ico and the United States, the bracero program was initiated as a wartime strategy for the northerly neighbor's need for inexpensive agricultural workers. Launched in 1942 as part of the effort to ease a so-called labor shortage in farmwork resulting from World War II and, later, the Korean War, that program would go on to last for twenty-two years, until 1964, after repeated calls for the continued need and desire for a cheap (read: controllable and dispensable) labor force. Mexico benefited, too, because the program relieved some of the poverty and misery in the rural zones and in the growing urban areas through the employment of landless Mexican males in el norte as well as through remittances (*remesas*). As early as the 1950s, according to Deborah Cohen, remittances made up "Mexico's third-largest source of hard currency." By the late 1970s, remesas would serve as an increasingly indispensable component of Mexico's sources of foreign income.[2] Agricultural interests south of the border were not always satisfied with the accord, however, as they decried the loss of Mexico's greatest resource: labor.

By the time José began his campaign to win Conchita's heart and hand in marriage in the early 1960s, the "Mexican Miracle" of rapid economic development and growth as well as rising agricultural productivity in Mexico was at its peak. Yet for José and the Mexican men like him who enrolled in the bracero program, the miracle was a mirage. For José, the immediate future remained in el norte, where he had recently obtained a "green card," a symbol of coveted permanent residency, allowing him to work without fear of detention and deportation. José, however, was fulfilled neither economically nor personally and emotionally, as he communicated in his letters. Rather, he worked to live and was lonely and likely tired of living among men only—since the bracero program excluded women, for fear that braceros would bring their families with them and attempt to settle permanently in the United States. While living near the U.S.-Mexico border allowed him to escape on weekends to a familiar cultural and social space, and while socializing with male expatriates helped pass the evenings after long days, José was looking for the emotional, sexual, and domestic comforts a heterosexual woman and family could bring him.[3] Conchita, in contrast, was an eighteen-year-old young woman on the verge of graduating from *secundaria* or secondary school, which, at the time, was a relatively uncommon feat for young women living in Mexico's rural areas. She had plans for a future education and career and had no interest in marriage—although the attention of the courtship intrigued her and allowed José to continue to write to her as a "friend." He had other aims. He told her repeatedly and elaborately of his desire to make her his wife.

As I completed my research and analysis about how to situate my parents' personal letters and experiences in a broader historical, social, and economic context—primarily that of migration north and south across the U.S.-Mexico border at midcentury—my uncle Paco mentioned that he, too, had some missives from his earlier days and was willing to share them. As I found out, he had sent and received most of those letters when he first immigrated to the United States in the early 1960s, following in the footsteps of his older brothers, including my father, José, with whom he lived briefly while my father courted my mother through the letter writing. After several searches in the basement, my uncle found the trunk—really, the treasure chest—containing the remaining 230 or so notes that would make up the family archive of more than 300 pieces of correspondence. (A few extra notes contained in my family archive belong to Paco's youngest sister, Maura Chávez Esparza, who is based in Mexico and holds onto her original letters.) I set out to organize them and quickly realized that, miraculously—I have no other word for it—my uncle's letters and my parents' were written during the same time, in the 1960s, and to many of the same people across the borderlands. I soon discovered, too, that they contained the missing pieces allowing me to situate my parents' epistolary relationship (as well as that of many family members and friends, whose names appear among the letters) in a web of intimate cross-border relations and social networks. Equally significant, as I learned in the research and writing process, the letters demonstrate rural Mexican migrants' personal and emotional wherewithal—their audacity and agency as historical actors—in taking charge of their future where little or no hope for their future existed. By toggling between the micro and macro as we read them, as Alice Echols suggests we do in writing family histories, the letters allow us to see, too, how the individual stories embedded in the lines of the paper reflect and intersect with broader historical and, in this case, migratory, experiences.[4]

I realized then, as I do so even more today, that the letters provide a once-in-a-lifetime opportunity for a glimpse into the emotional and social lives of ordinary men and women, specifically rural Mexicans whom we know little about, from their personal, immediate firsthand accounts. While I must preserve scholarly distance from the letters and contemplate my own subjectivity, as we do with any source material and our relationship to it, I have spent and continue to spend time thinking about the intimacy of the missives and what they reveal about individual lives as well as those of the larger migrant community in and outside the United States and Mexico. That is, what do the letters tell us about migrants' dreams and desires as well as the challenges they faced? What do they tell us about the strategies used and the successes and disappointments encountered by those who traveled north as immigrants and south as return migrants? What do they reveal about gender, intimacy, courtship, marriage, and identity in a cross-border context? How did migration in the 1950s and 1960s shape transnational relations and social and cultural networks across the border? And, more broadly, what do the letters indicate about Mexico's plan for industrialization and modernization in the World War II and postwar era that gave rise to urbanization on a massive scale and to migration on a smaller, though no less significant, magnitude to el norte?

As this study argues, the correspondence attests to migrants' desire to improve not only their personal, family, and economic lives in the face of increasing impoverishment in rural Mexico but also to cultivate and nurture cross-border intimate, emotional, and household relations that could sustain them in their new environment. Indeed, the missives provide a wealth of insight on migratory processes, social networks, and individual relationships in alleviating migrant longing for bridging aqui and allá and demonstrate the power of remaking identities in adjusting to a new space.[5]

The "Mexican Miracle" and Migrant Exodus of the World War II and Postwar Eras

To understand what drove Mexican men such as my father, uncle, older brothers, and their father before them, in the 1940s, 1950s, and 1960s to take their chances in el norte, this study begins in late 1930s Mexico, a period that witnessed the beginning of a watershed in the political trajectory and economic development of the nation that eventually impacted hundreds of thousands and, eventually, millions of Mexicans. Until then, Mexico, largely a rural and regional society, had focused on fulfilling the 1910 Mexican Revolution's goals of land reform, access to education and health care, and relief from poverty, among other ideals. Three decades later, those aims had yet to be realized fully, despite the sacrifice and loss of thousands of lives (nearly one in eight Mexicans died) in the civil war over the concentration of power, wealth, and land in President Porfirio Díaz's government, which lasted from 1876 to 1910, with its tight relationship to the Mexican elite and foreign investors. Yet, beginning in the late 1930s and more emphatically in the early 1940s and 1950s, political leaders largely abandoned revolutionary principles and sought to modernize and industrialize Mexico akin to its northern neighbor. They did so by regaining the central authority that had fissured in the postrevolutionary era, eliminating independent political parties, and reaching out to foreign investors.[6]

To rebuild central power and carry out its modernizing project, the federal government initiated programs providing education, health, and basic services, including roads, potable water, sewage systems, communication, and electricity, to rural Mexicans. As Stephen R. Niblo has found, those expenditures increased significantly, from 631.5 million pesos in 1942 to 3.46 billion in 1950. While government leaders invested in projects allowing for the growth of commerce in the rural and urban zones, they turned away from radical, Leftist, land-based revolutionary aims in the name of economic development and, eventually, integration at the global scale. Rather than strengthening rural *ejidos* (collective landholding ventures), agriculture, and the production of basic foodstuffs, goals of the revolution, the government invested in building and strengthening commercial agriculture at the expense of *ejidatarios* (ejido shareholders), whose numbers dwindled over time and whose land was expropriated steadily, especially after President Miguel Alémmán (1946–52) proposed changes to Article 27 of the 1917 Mexican Constitution, which upheld land reform. At the same time, investments in social services fell in favor of economic projects, leading farm laborers and workers to sink deeper into poverty. Indeed, real wages plummeted beginning in 1938 and did not recover until 1971. Over time, allocations to social programs decreased under the presidential administrations of Lázaro Cárdenas (1934–40), Manuel Avila Camacho (1940–46), and especially Miguel Alemán, falling from 18.3 to 16.5 to 13.3 percent, respectively, while allocations to economic projects increased from 37.6 to 39.2 to 51.9 percent, respectively.[7] As support moved away from campesinos and the countryside to foreign investors and the city, a new business elite composed of powerful politicians and private industrial leaders emerged. "It represented a new vision of industrial modernity, linking national and international capital," Niblo observes.[8]

Equally devastating to the goals of the Mexican Revolution and support for rapid industrialization was the emergence of World War II and backing for Mexico's Import Substitution Initiative (ISI). The initiative was designed to wean the country from its dependence on exporting raw materials and importing finished goods in favor of locally produced goods. President Avila Camacho supported the ISI's protection of weak Mexican factories from foreign competition by establishing protective tariffs and import quotas as well as providing subsidies and tax breaks, among other benefits, to encourage private investment. According to Gilbert M. Joseph and Timothy J. Henderson, initially the ISI seemed to work "spectacularly." "The Mexican economy grew at an impressive average annual rate of 6.5 percent between 1940 and 1970," they note, with little inflation. "Mexico was transformed from a predominantly agricultural country to one where industry accounted for more than a third of total production," leading to the emergence of the Mexican Miracle.[9] At the same time, the ISI encouraged uncompetitive, inefficient, and capital-intensive (not labor-intensive) industries, resulting in chronic unemployment and underemployment, which would eventually come to dominate the Mexican economy in the 1960s, 1970s, and 1980s. The onset of the war, in turn, allowed Avila Camacho to shift to more conservative policies as well as an aggressive program of industrial modernization and further move away from revolutionary goals as well as the artisanal and campesino economies, which were so important at the local level. Indeed, these industries, based out of small workshops linked to households, not only provided jobs to individuals and sustained families but also supported local communities.[10]

Industrialization efforts proceeded at an unprecedented clip, especially under President Miguel Alemán, whose goal was to modernize Mexico no matter the cost. Among the many strategies he carried out to realize his plan was appealing to foreign investors for financing of industrial projects. To do so, Alemán turned to support from personal contacts and business partners. Soon, U.S. investors responded with financing. To boost Mexico's agricultural commercial sector, for instance, Mexico received 1.7 billion pesos to assist with the building of dams to irrigate new farmland and bring it under cultivation. Mexico then matched that sum with 1.5 billion pesos. The costs of these projects eventually grew astronomically, along with the financing of the loans, which stood at about 4 percent annual interest. In the end, the payments benefited the private sector at the expense of the agrarian class, and Mexico fell deep into debt. Like his predecessors, Alemán continued to welcome foreign investors and their companies, especially U.S. businesses, including Westinghouse, Anaconda Copper, Republic Steel, and Monsanto Chemical Company, and used the growing centers of tourism and entertainment, such as the beachside resort of Acapulco, to sell the splendors of Mexico.[11] To achieve his goals, Alemán engaged in corruption, including the looting of public coffers, abusing authority, accepting kickbacks, and carrying out hidden deals.[12] To stem opposition, Alemán authorized attacks on organized labor, using state violence when he deemed it necessary, as well as on "political opponents, working-class organs of expression, and the individual's right to criticize the government."[13]

Alemán, like his predecessors Avila Camacho and Cárdenas, utilized the media, particularly the increasingly wildly popular cinema, to move the country away ideologically from radical nationalism to revolutionary nationalism, which evoked nostalgia for the rural past while moving firmly toward an urban future. Realizing the widespread popularity of films and their ability to transmit propaganda among captive audiences, the Alemánista Mexican establishment—big business and government—used cinema to communicate cultural nationalist political messages of *lo mexicano*, of what it meant to be a Mexican, as it was initially conceived in the 1920s. The government also used films to discourage immigration to the United States and to steer attention away from Mexico's increasing international economic agenda.[14] To do so, the government tapped into federal coffers and borrowed heavily from its northern neighbor—especially during World War II, when the United States was most interested in promoting a pro-Allied stance in the Western Hemisphere—to finance film production, technology, and distribution in Mexico. Those films and their pro-war political messages, in turn, were distributed throughout Latin America. Knowing that not all *mexicanos* could afford to attend movie theaters, the government subsidized theaters as early as the 1930s, bringing ticket prices in line with campesino and working-class wages and strengthening the industry's infrastructure. "As the film industry became more popular," Niblo writes, "the movie houses became larger and more ornate, which contributed to the attraction of attending the theater."[15]

To obscure the Mexican government's increasing internationalism, politicos worked with a handful of movie studios in promoting a golden rural past and the heroic figure of the *charro* (Mexican cowboy) on a national scale. Among the most popular charros were Jorge Negrete and Pedro Infante, who, along with María Felix and Dolores del Rio, leading actresses in Mexico, not only interpreted the mythic life on the rancho on the big screen but also were central to the rise and popularity of the *comedia ranchera*, which depoliticized life on the rancho. Soon, dozens and even hundreds of movies appeared in the same genre in the 1940s, 1950s, and early 1960s, depicting the charros far removed from revolutionary figures such as Emiliano Zapata, who fought in the revolutionary war of 1910 for land reform and campesinos' basic human rights. Rather, the charro represented a romanticized interpretation of the past and "the traditional and Catholic values in defiance of the leftist, modernizing tendencies emanating from the cities."[16] Comedias rancheras were most popular in the countryside and had less of a following in the urban areas, particularly Mexico City, where the focus was on modernization.

The Mexican government also welcomed the presence of Cantinflas, an influential comedic, popular underclass, lumpen proletariat figure. Cantinflas's *pelado* or "street bum" character of the 1950s and 1960s was anything but radical in his politics.[17] Though Cantinflas, né Mario Moreno, challenged the pomposity of social hierarchy as well as the middle class and the elite, he did not criticize the governing class or espouse a new or alternative political establishment.[18] Cantinflas, as well as other popular actors and actresses, was not inclined to critique, much less oppose, Mexico's ruling party, for the actors' trade union was in close alliance with the government. In contrast, oppositional films that criticized the move away from revolutionary goals toward rapid industrialization, urbanization, and modernization, such as *Los Olvidados*, a gritty tale of urban poverty and decay directed by Luis Buñuel in 1950, were often censored.[19]

The control of the film industry, however, came at the cost of creativity, leading many moviegoers to attend imported U.S. films, which were more popular than Mexican films, especially among young people, including most of my family members and their friends, who watched them in Mexico and the United States. To contain the popularity of U.S.-made movies in the 1940s, 1950s, and 1960s, the Mexican government—at the insistence of the Mexican film actors' union—forbade the dubbing of foreign films into Spanish, limiting many viewers in less developed rural zones from enjoying the full scope of the films, as illiteracy remained at about 50 percent or higher nationally.[20] That did not stop unlettered Mexicans from watching English-language films and being influenced by U.S. popular culture, however, which was also communicated through other forms of media, including magazines, advertisements, radio, and, soon, television. As Arthur Schmidt argues, "Mexico forged a strong national identity [not only] through public education, [and] new government cultural institutions [but also] modern mass media of magazine, radio, cinema, advertising, and television."[21]

By the early 1950s, many of the goals of the revolution—particularly land reform and the social and economic elevation of the campesino in the countryside—were but a faint memory, even while the government purported to "institutionalize the revolution." To do so, it renamed the ruling party, the Partido de la Revolución Mexicana (PRM, or Mexican Revolutionary Party) the Partido Revolucionario Institucional (PRI), the Institutionalized Revolutionary Party, in 1946, on the eve of Miguel Alemán's election. The reality was that "the strategy of development was based upon a massive transfer of resources from the poor to the rich and from the country to the city."[22] In time, the top 10 percent of the population, which enjoyed 49 percent of the national income in 1950, would accrue an even larger slice of the pie, while the bottom 20 percent would lose even more of the 6.1 percent it held that same decade.[23] During this same period of intensive private capital accumulation, Eric Zolov observes, Mexico was promoted "domestically and internationally as a modern, cosmopolitan nation, one that offered both comfort and a healthy return on foreign investment." The marketing of Mexico as a place with "a friendly, exotic, folkloric charm not found at home," Zolov continues, "coincided with a sustained period of relative political stability, an unprecedented expansion of its middle classes, and a harmonious relationship with the United States."[24] This golden age of Mexico's political, economic, cultural, and social life, while favorable to the middle class and the elite, proved anything but golden particularly for the rural masses.

Indeed, rapid industrialization and modernization as well as unlimited private capital accumulation from the late 1930s to the early 1970s came at the expense of disinvestment in the countryside for the benefit of urban zones, particularly Mexico City, which grew at an exponential rate and was aided by a postwar population boom. In contrast, villages and pueblos in rural zones, which still dominated the Mexican landscape, as the nation remained primarily rural until the 1960s, were largely untouched by modernization, and many campesinos were unable to access land and basic agricultural supplements to feed their families. Even with the new opportunities provided by educational programs in postrevolutionary Mexico, which brought teachers to the ranchos—including to my paternal grandparents' village, Las Tinajas, a hamlet of adobes a few kilometers outside of Calvillo, Aguascalientes—villagers had few options to sustain their families. Like most rural people who depended on the land to feed their families, those who cultivated the fields of Las Tinajas relied on seasonal rain to irrigate crops. When the showers failed to materialize, families had no choice but to migrate to larger pueblos such as Calvillo, or to cities such as Aguascalientes, where means of survival were more readily available than in ranchos. Artisanal textile production, including the wool textile industry—a trade at which my paternal great-grandfather and grandfather had labored at the turn of the twentieth century and later—was abandoned in favor of cheaply produced and manufactured fabrics.[25]

While villagers could see the influence of the United States on the shelves of the local *tienditas* (tiny stores) and in the newly installed *hieleras* (iceboxes), which kept Coca-Colas and Pepsi Colas cold during the hot summer months, and felt the influence of modernization with the appearance of electricity, asphalt roads, buses, and tourists, the misery and isolation remained.[26] The dearth of local, regional, and national highways kept most villages disconnected from urban areas and nearby rural areas. While Mexico

City was linked to core cities such as Guadalajara and Monterrey, it was cut off from the north until about 1950, when a road was built between the capital city and Ciudad Juárez, "el paso al norte," Chihuahua. The railroads, while available, were beyond the reach of most campesinos, for that form of transportation was costly as well as slow and difficult. Without much communication with the outside world and limited access to newspapers, books, the radio, television, and the cinema as well as conveniences such as household appliances, clocks, and calendars, campesinos lived in a world seen as backward, uncultured, and uncivilized.[27]

Health care too remained out of reach for campesinos. Access to antibiotics, for instance, was difficult, and many children died from poor nutrition, infections, and common childhood diseases. Relief came in 1938 when the Secretaria de Salubridad y Asistencia (SSA, or Department of Health and Welfare) was established and carried out a national sanitation and inoculation campaign to fight infectious diseases. The SSA also supported the development of a national network of hospitals and required doctors to carry out an internship in the countryside, leading to the improvement of health in many villages throughout the country. Indeed, in the 1940s, deaths from gastroenteritis, which claimed the lives of many children—including three of my father's younger brothers, Celso, Carlos, and Pedro—were drastically reduced, from 487 to 280 per 100,000 during the 1940s.[28] Those changes, however, were slow in coming to villages further away from Mexico City and were not implemented in outlying areas until a decade or more later. Equally important to the overall health of the family were the real wages and purchasing power of rural dwellers, which fell drastically in the 1940s to levels not seen since the 1920s and earlier.[29]

The shrinking opportunities in the countryside, fueled by the mechanization of commercial agriculture and the lure of the metropolitan cities with their growing demand for industrial workers in commerce, transportation, and communication, among other sectors, sent thousands and soon millions of villagers to Mexico City and other growing industrial zones, including Guadalajara, Jalisco, and León, Guanajuato. Between 1950 and 1970, approximately 4.5 million people migrated from rural to urban areas. From 1940 to 1960, Mexico City's population nearly tripled, from 1.6 million to 4.7 million. Much of that growth came as a result of migration to the city by the growing class of landless agricultural workers, whose numbers continued to increase in the 1960s and 1970s.[30] The result was an increasingly urban society that was largely unprepared to handle the full brunt of rapid urbanization and the concomitant rising demand for jobs, housing, and public services. The growth was not confined to Mexico City. Nationally, the population, especially in the urban areas, surged between 1940 and 1970. In 1940, Mexico's population stood at 20 million, with nearly 65 percent living in rural areas (defined as villages with 15,000 or fewer inhabitants). Ten years later, in 1950, that figure had jumped significantly, to 25.7 million, with a lower proportion—57 percent—residing in the countryside. By 1970, the nation's population had exploded, nearly doubling to 51 million, putting extreme pressures on the burgeoning urban sectors.[31]

In the cities, the fortunate found work in the newly established domestic and foreign-owned industries, including automotive work at companies such as General Motors and Ford. Those laborers, former campesinos and mostly males, earned more income than they ever had or would in the rural areas. The steady pay meant that they and their families had access to the new shopping centers, department stores, theaters, and restaurants as well as the latest automobiles and television sets, all symbols of modernity associated with the United States and coveted by the small yet growing middle class. As Eric Zolov argues, in Mexico City in the 1960s, "appropriating 'Americanized' cultural forms was viewed as an indicator of class and worldliness."[32] Most of the latest consumer goods and services as well as new housing (*colonias*), however, remained beyond the reach of the working classes and the poor, and were affordable only to those in the emerging middle classes and the elite, leading to residential zones some scholars have called "improvised and dehumanizing slums" reserved primarily for the poor.[33]

While most displaced villagers and ejidatarios headed to Mexico City and other urban areas to find a means of survival, usually as industrial workers or entrepreneurs in the informal economy, many headed north to Mexico's northern border states or directly to *el oltro lado* (the other side) for work in the United States. The primary lure for the 2 million or so Mexican men who emigrated in the 1940s and 1950s as part of the bracero program was the steady wages of that accord. Equally important, the program proved a crucial safety valve in Mexico for providing economic opportunities for unemployed, unskilled, or semiskilled males, allowing them to earn enough money to purchase a small plot of land back home, as was my father's and countless other migrants' dream.[34] From 1942 to 1964, nearly 4.6 million contracts were issued to some 2 million workers, demonstrating that many took on multiple stints, as did my father and his older brothers.[35] For Mexican officials, as Deborah Cohen finds, the program was significant for those same laborers who, transformed as transnational citizens, would eventually return to Mexico with their new skills and work ethic and, in turn, help modernize agricultural production as well as the larger society.[36] Mexico was indeed invested in their return. As Kelly Lytle Hernández argues, Mexico needed a cheap and flexible labor supply given the new emphasis on "land privatization, mechanization, and export orientation of agricultural production." Yet, combined with population increase and food shortages, as a result of the focus on the export economy, many campesinos were forced "to seek economic survival through migration."[37] Though braceros made up only about 4 percent of the economically active population in Mexico, they left an indelible mark on postwar labor and migration regimes as well as social and political life in the United States well into the twenty-first century. Despite Mexico's insistence that braceros return, the majority did not. By some estimates only four out of ten returned home.[38]

The bracero program was not the only labor-based project that drew mexicanos to the densely populated border region in the World War II and postwar period. The 1965 Border Industrialization Program (BIP) did so as well. Migration and population increase along *la frontera* (the border) was not, however, initially stirred by the BIP. Rather, urbanization occurred in response to the relative economic prosperity enjoyed along U.S. border "twin cities" and the dollars generated by American tourists in Mexican border towns. By some estimates, the number of border dwellers on the Mexican side rose some 300 percent in the 1960s, largely as a result of recently unemployed braceros looking for work, as well as through natural increase. The region provided few employment opportunities, however, other than taking advantage of decades-old tourism and vice-related industries. The BIP, Mexican politicos believed, was the solution to those problems because it would stimulate foreign investment and local manufacturing and provide jobs to unemployed *hombres mexicanos*.[39]

In contrast to the government's effort to promote internal market development through ISI, the BIP embraced international trade and the emerging global market of the 1960s to lift Mexico and Mexicans out of poverty. To do so, the BIP invited foreign-owned manufacturing and assembly companies, also known as maquiladoras or maquilas, to invest in Mexico by setting up shops, primarily in the cities of Tijuana, Baja California, and Ciudad Juárez, Chihuahua, to take advantage of Mexico's greatest resource: cheap, flexible labor. At a small fraction of the cost of U.S. labor and with a forty-eight-hour work week as well as the region's close proximity to el norte, the border was an ideal location to set up foreign-owned shops. Resources lacking in Mexico, such as capital, machinery, supplies, and technical know-how, came from abroad and were used to establish and run the maquilas. Besides proximity, the lure for U.S. companies was the 1965 U.S. tariff law, which assessed tariffs only on the value added to the final product assembled in whole or in part outside of the United States. Under Mexico's terms, however, finished goods had to be exported and sold abroad so as not to compete with domestic products.

Despite the attempt to provide former braceros employment and develop the border economy, few men took positions in BIP industries. Doubtless the low-paying, repetitive, labor-intensive, and unsafe industrial-based tasks involved in the early maquiladora industries discouraged them from applying. Instead, ex-braceros tried their luck in el norte, working without "papers" (permanent residency) in rural agricultural zones and urban manufacturing and, increasingly, in service areas. The lack of male employees in the maquilas did not, however, disrupt the foreign employers' plans for productive workers. From their vantage point, the most desirable laborers were young, single, undereducated, motherless women whom they could employ for low wages and long hours. Employers believed such females were docile, compliant, easily controllable workers who could and would endure harsh working conditions with few complaints or little involvement with private, non-governmental labor unions. Foreign investors as well as their managers and staff also perpetuated the myth that the female anatomy—that is, women's small hands—made them ideal workers in assembly plants and hired them in numbers disproportionate to men. The result was the feminization of the maquiladora workforce and exclusion of male workers, including my father and his brothers and almost all their male friends.

Indeed, few Mexican migrant males in general labored in the export processing zone in the 1960s and 1970s. The vast majority, from 80 to 90 percent, were females. Not until the expansion of the maquilas and the advent of sophisticated and vertically integrated companies in the 1980s were more men hired, especially in low-level managerial positions, though women continued to predominate until the early 1990s. The effects of the "peso crisis"—the collapse of Mexico's currency in the early 1980s—as a result of falling petroleum prices, rising international debt, and a turn to neoliberal policies and austerity measures did not stymie the industry. Rather, it brought increased profits. Mexico's decision to halt the decades-old tradition of artificially inflating the currency led to massive depreciation and inflation in the national economy; but for foreign investors the news was welcome, as it cut labor costs nearly in half, allowing the industry to continue to flourish even while other sectors of the Mexican economy lagged or collapsed altogether. The passage of the North American Free Trade Agreement (NAFTA) in 1995 further expanded the maquiladora industry, for the liberalization of trade and commerce did away with most restrictions, including taxes on imported products, enabling expansion throughout Mexico's northern region and into the core southern areas of the country. The result was the proliferation of maquilas and increased investment, technical sophistication, and employment of women and men, the latter of whom took on positions in male-designated areas of the labor force. While in 1980 the industry employed 120,000 workers, mostly women, by 1998 that figure had ballooned to 700,000, with men making up nearly 40 percent of the workforce. In the new millennium, those numbers continued to rise, to over 1 million in 2005 and to nearly 2 million by 2012. Male and female workers, however, continued to receive little pay despite the long hours, hazardous working conditions, and health and environmental degradation caused by the unregulated industry. And while employees in the border zone earned more than their laboring peers in central Mexico, the high cost of living made it (and continues to make it) difficult for individuals and families to survive in the desolate and remote *colonias* where they are forced to live, leading many men and women to abandon the maquilas to try their luck as *mojados* (wetbacks) at worst or as residents at best across the border in the United States.[40]

Yet, even years before the passage of NAFTA, Mexico's integration into the global economy had continued steadily. Begun decades earlier, in the 1940s, 1950s, and 1960s, it left little room for displaced campesinos who lost their land and government support for agricultural production for themselves, their families, and larger communities. With no other options, most migrated to the bustling urban centers of Mexico City, Guadalajara, and Monterrey to find employment in the rapidly industrializing zones, while braceros and former braceros, such as my father and his brothers, kept their sights on the United States. There, in el norte, they hoped to take advantage of the incessant demand for cheap labor in agricultural zones and in the growing service sector, spurred by the expanding technology and information industries brought about by restructuring of the global economy of the 1960s and 1970s.

Indeed, in the early 1960s, the United States began to witness a gradual shift from a high-paid manufacturing and industrial workforce to a low-paid, unskilled service base of workers. The transition from a blue-collar sector with highly paid union jobs, such as those in the steel and auto industries, to a growing white-collar sector with highly educated and well-paid technicians, consultants, and information specialists brought the need for armies of low-paid workers to assemble parts and carry out other routine jobs. The new economy also led to the increasing economic polarization of the workforce, with those at the top demanding more personal services, such as those provided by car washers, cooks, janitors, domestics, and nannies, and those at the bottom finding only jobs that provided little mobility, training, or opportunity. To migrant workers from Mexico, other parts of Latin America, and Asia, and women in particular, who needed *dolares* to survive and to send home to impoverished family members, the lure proved highly attractive. In Mexico, economic opportunities had deteriorated significantly as a result of the recession of the 1980s, which had led to drastic cuts in government services and subsidies to the countryside as well as soaring unemployment. While many continued to migrate to Mexico's urban and northern border sectors with their promises of employment, many headed, too, to urban areas in el norte looking for jobs in restaurants, hotels, and construction. At the same time, migration became more permanent and less seasonal, especially as Mexican families reunited and established permanent roots in el otro lado. Estimates show that between 1965 and 1986, a net immigration of 5.7 million Mexicans made their way north, 80 percent of them undocumented, largely as a result of the tightening policies for Mexican migrants as reflected in the Immigration Act of 1965. As the risks of unlawful migration increased, migrants in the post-1965 era were more likely to stay longer than those in the past, leading to larger, permanent communities throughout the United States. Those populations, in turn, proved crucial in providing the remittances that were the lifelines for family and community members left behind. The result was Mexico's increased dependency on exporting surplus labor and importing remesas, a feature that continues to this day.

As the letters indicate, however, Mexican migrants who traveled north, such as my father, did not leave everything behind. Rather, as migrants they brought with them cultural and political influences of the government's ideology of revolutionary nationalism as communicated through dominant modes of media and popular culture, as well as their own interpretations of those same messages and meaning in their everyday lives. Often, these ideas were in conflict with dominant modes. My father, for instance, read "alternative" political magazines that poked fun at Mexican politicos and middle-class ideals, whereas his youngest brother, Paco, preferred Spanish translations of U.S.-produced writings, suggesting that migrants varied in their political interests and leanings. Because they were literate Mexicans, the correspondence at the core of this study provides an opportunity to examine and analyze how "common people"—members of my family— mediated Mexico-based ideologies and practices along with those that they confronted in the United States.[41] And though migrants had learned much about U.S. culture and society through imported popular American films as well as advertising, magazines, consumer goods, and other products, they had yet to experience life in the north. My family archive of letters allows for an exploration of how family members—migrants—negotiated not only gender, culture, and society but also the economy, polity, and the law. Equally important, the *cartas* (letters) give us an unusual, almost voyeuristic, vantage point from which to observe and interpret the personal, emotional, and intimate impact of that migration on the emigrants as well as on those who stayed at home.

Migration, Gender, Intimacy, and Identity in the U.S.-Mexico Borderlands

To date, few histories on twentieth-century Mexico have examined and analyzed closely the firsthand personal experiences of migrants—both as emigrants and immigrants—who left home as braceros or as unauthorized laborers (the latter popularly known as *espaldas mojadas* and *alambristas*— wetbacks and wire crossers—in the 1950s) who crossed the U.S.-Mexico border without inspection.[42] The preference of scholars of Mexico has been to focus on the social, political, economic, and cultural histories in central Mexico in the World War II and postwar eras. This has left us with an incomplete understanding of the social and personal impact of rapid industrialization and urbanization as well as private capital accumulation and foreign investment on ordinary Mexicans abroad and at home. As Arthur Schmidt has argued, "The failure to see the intimate linkage between the global and forms of daily life in Mexico will have to change if the period since 1940 is to be comprehended fully."[43] Arguably, the small percentage of Mexican males who joined the bracero program has more than likely dissuaded researchers in Mexico from focusing on the histories of braceros who left their homes and eventually settled in the United States.

Among the few historians who *do* recognize the significance of the bracero program and how it institutionalized labor migration from Mexico to the United States in the contemporary era is Deborah Cohen. Trained as a Latin American historian, and relying on hundreds of oral histories,

Cohen has probed the experiences of former braceros deeply and widely in two communities in Durango, Mexico. Rather than focus on their experiences either in a Mexican or U.S. context, she situates men's roles and relations in a broader transnational context shaped by cross-border influences. Cohen's *Braceros: Migrant Citizens and Transnational Subjects in the Postwar United States and Mexico* then, provides a rich understanding of the transformative experience of living and working across the border and the ways in which former braceros formulated their identities as gendered transnational citizens.

Other than Cohen, few scholars have studied braceros or other migrants as emigrants who left Mexico for work and adventure and later returned home, or as immigrants who eventually settled in the United States. The braceros' crossing of the northern border has led most Mexicanists to turn them over as historical subjects to the purview of U.S. historians, the majority of them borderlands, western, and Chicana and Chicano specialists. Fortunately, these scholars have contributed a vast body of literature, but primarily in a U.S. context. This narrative seeks to go beyond what we already know about braceros and former braceros. By linking national and international trends in the United States and Mexico with local and personal experiences, this study demonstrates how Mexico's integration into the global economy impacted Mexican migrants economically as well as emotionally in the most familiar and intimate of spaces, namely, courtship, marriage, the family, home, and the pueblo. By exploring how economic trends such as the increased expansion and modernization of urban areas impacted campesinos in the countryside, this work also shows how shifting political economies influenced personal decision making around migration, identity, and long-term settlement.

By framing braceros not only as immigrants (migrants who cut ties with the homeland) or transnational subjects (migrants who live between two worlds on equal terms) but also as emigrants who carried with them ideologies and customs as well as cultural beliefs and practices rooted in rural Mexico, this study embraces the works of Roger Waldinger, Jesse Hoffnung-Garskof, and Robert Smith, scholars who call for studies that complicate our understanding of migration as more than permanent settlement. Waldinger, in particular, argues that migrants are marked by a duality that identifies them as both foreigners and nationals as well as aliens and citizens, who link here and there, resulting in the creation of a "zone of inter-social convergence." In that zone, they rely on cross-border social networks to stay connected to family and home and, in the process, they pull households, communities, and regions together. While migrants do not turn their backs on their homeland, over time, Waldinger maintains, physical distance, miscommunication, relocation of family from here to there, cultural absorption, and "territorial capture"—immobility as a result of harsh immigration policies and practices—transform emigrants into immigrants and the zone of convergence into one of divergence. As a result, motivations to maintain ties are weakened. Emigration and immigration, he observes, are always in tension, creating challenges for cross-border ties and for migrants such as my father, who longed to be here *and* there and to enjoy the best of both worlds, including economic, cultural, personal, emotional, and sexual fulfillment.[44]

While Waldinger's, Hoffnung-Garskof's, and Smith's studies force us to rethink the nature of migration as a cross-border phenomenon that impacts the sending and receiving country and the identity of migrants as both emigrants and immigrants, historical narratives on the emotional and personal impact of migration on gender, courtship, marriage, and the family provide the foundation for understanding the nature of intimate cross-border relationships that are at the heart of this study. Until recently, much of that literature has examined the contingencies shaping the movement of migrants north and south across the U.S.-Mexico border. While some scholars have explored the personal decisions involved in migrating as well as the impact on gender and identity across space, place, and time, most have probed the policies and practices that provided both opportunities for and limitations on cross-border movement. Ana Elizabeth Rosas's research is an exception. Using oral histories primarily and photographs and personal letters secondarily, Rosas explores the immediate and long-term impact of separation and loss, specifically on women, children, and the elderly left behind in Mexico. She demonstrates that, despite the emotional anguish and estrangement among family members, sometimes for years at a time, women and their children adapted resourcefully to their changing situation by forming new relationships, identities, and strategies, enabling them to thrive amid evolving contexts. This work goes beyond Rosas's by using sources that speak to the immediacy of relationships as they were built as well as destroyed and allow for the rendering of details often forgotten, distorted, or overlooked in the re-creation of memories through the process of oral histories. As such, personal letters—sources infrequently used in Chicana/o, Mexican, and Latin American history given the limited literacy of those who wrote them, as well as the tendency of such sources to remain in family archives rather than being preserved in public repositories—provide a vivid and immediate account of the processes of migration and their impact on members of the family and community who stayed at home.[45]

This work also builds on the rich literature in sociology, anthropology, feminist studies, and Latina/o studies focusing on migration, labor, love, home, and identity in Mexico and the United States. It does so to show that migrants were not simply cogs in the increasingly global, capitalist, and postindustrial machine of the 1950s, 1960s, and 1970s. Rather, when faced with the loneliness and isolation that came with leaving family and friends behind, migrants worked to replicate the family structure familiar to them— patriarchal, heterosexual, and sanctified by the Catholic Church—even when it took on a new cultural meaning and operated imperfectly in the border- lands. Many also worked hard to maintain ties across the vast divide and did so by writing letters, returning home for visits when they could do so, and calling home when they could afford to do so. As the letters attest, migrants sacrificed to build their homes, even if it meant leaving behind everything they knew and forming new identities to satisfy their needs and cultivate a future for themselves and their families.

This study also mines the literature on the transformation of masculine and feminine identities through the process of migration. Today, most scholars agree that migration is a gendered process. Indeed, why and how migrants leave their homes for new homes across international divides is shaped by social and cultural meanings assigned to men and women in and outside the family, community, and state structures. As Ramona Pérez, Cris- tina Rosas, and, M. Bianet Castellanos have found, for Mexican men and boys, migrating across the U.S.-Mexico border forms a rite of passage in proving oneself a "man" who has the ability to support his family. Those unable to cross, as a result of being detained, denied, or obstructed by the state or other men, as happened to one of the men at the center of this study, must deal with that immediate fracaso as well as the long-term implications for their identity as men.[46]

The act of migrating to a new social, cultural, and political context also leads to the renegotiation and reshaping of understandings of gender and sexuality, specifically masculinity and femininity. As Leisy Abrego has shown, Salvadoran migrant women, who in the 1970s and 1980s had no other choice but to leave their children behind in El Salvador in hopes of finding a means of survival in the United States, faced a much heavier social and cul- tural burden than men who did the same. While women ("good mothers") were expected to continue to provide remittances to their children, men ("good fathers") were not and were excused from their paternal obligations of supporting their children.[47]

The power of gender and, specifically, patriarchy and its ability to reach across vast divides largely unscathed is also not lost on scholars. Deborah Boehm, for instance, demonstrates the ways in which migrants—specifically, male heads of households—employ *chisme* (gossip) and family members to police their wives' social and gender relations in an attempt to contain departures from female obligations as dutiful wives and mothers. While husbands or *novios* (boyfriends) sometimes turn to cross-border social networks to watch closely their wives' and *novias'* (girlfriends') social activities, the letters in this study indicate that women did so as well, employing family members and friends to ensure the integrity of their husbands' and boyfriends' communications. In the surveillance of males, females challenged patriarchal privilege and power. This study builds on Boehm's scholarship as well as that of Abrego, Rosas, Cohen, Pérez, and Castellanos to show that, while deeply entrenched notions of patriarchy, masculinity, and femininity resulted in the monitoring of women left behind, those same women resisted those ideas by remaking their gender identities and using them to establish relations that worked to provide them with the emotional, personal, and economic comforts they desired.[48]

A central concern of this study is mapping the meaning and nature of intimacy, that is, how it was understood and practiced among migrants in the U.S.-Mexico borderlands. Defining and locating intimacy is not easily accomplished, however, as the literature on intimacy, transnational migration, and globalization suggests. Laurent Berlant and Viviana A. Zelizer argue that intimacy is about sharing personal experiences and insights—that is, secrets, private languages, terms of endearment, interpersonal rituals, vulnerabilities, and shameful moments—between two people who have a close bond or affection. They also remind us that intimacy depends on mutual trust and willingness to exchange such knowledge and attention despite the risks. Intimacy is not confined exclusively to couples, Berlant and Zelizer note; it is also cultivated among parents, grandparents, children, siblings, and friends, who tell each other stories, listen, connect, and respond.[49] In a transnational context, Rhacel Parrenas argues, physical proximity, contact, and presence are keys to preserving intimacy and the emotional stability and security between parents and children who are separated for months and sometimes years at a time as a result of economic pressures from globalization. The use of the phone, remittances, and other forms of communication, including social media, works to create a "semblance of intimate family life across borders," but these means do not, she finds, substitute for the presence of loved ones.[50]

Deirdre McKay and Anne Stoler, in separate studies, challenge those ideas and, in the process, expand the meaning of intimacy. McKay argues that we must not impose a Western standard of intimacy, which usually involves "long periods of face-to-face contact, shared expressions of affective states, and the mutual disclosure of a person's emotional self-understandings, desires, dreams and individual life story."[51] These notions, argues McKay, are based on "relatively recent (post-Victorian era) western norms for heteronormative, middle-class romantic and nuclear-family household relationships." McKay reminds us that "emotions and intimacies have never been either static or universal and scholars are documenting other, newer, versions of intimacy that do not require face-to-face interaction as a necessary precondition."[52] The letters written among family members and friends across the U.S.-Mexico borderlands indicate that the meaning of intimacy was (and remains) contested. While some migrants rarely demonstrated dominant notions of love, as expressed through a physical embrace or a kiss, others boldly engaged in sexual relations outside of marriage and did so as an expression of the passion and deep bond they held and sought to maintain when migration and potentially long-term separation were imminent. As Anne Stoler reminds us, we need to call into question our cherished assumptions about intimacy: that "the intimate is located primarily in the family, that the family is a ready model for, and microcosm of, the state, and that affective ties are inherently tender ones."[53] Indeed, the letters demonstrate that intimacy existed within and without the confines of the family and, at times, was used as a weapon to wound deeply those who cared for them most.

Letter Writing across the U.S.-Mexico Borderlands

Narratives of the hopes and dreams as well as love and loss found in letters written by and exchanged among Mexicans, Mexican Americans, and other ethnically and racially diverse peoples living in the borderlands remain sparse. Today, we have only a handful of histories of Mexican-origin peoples as re-created exclusively through their epistolary practices. Scholars have, of course, used the correspondence of nineteenth-century Californios as well as Spanish-speaking labor organizers and activists in the early and late twentieth century to enhance our understanding of the personal and emotional toll of their struggles and rewards with the social, political, economic, legal, and cultural forces of their day. Few, however, have had the opportunity to delve into a significant set of richly textured and nuanced writings among a wide variety of family and community members divided across a vast region, as I have in my family archive.[54]

Fortunately, scholars working in the fields of U.S. and European history have had access to extensive archives of correspondence belonging to migrants and those who stayed behind. Among those are David A. Gerber and Sonia Cancian, who provide useful tools and techniques for understanding letter writing as a craft of narrating the self or self-making as well as re-creating self-identity. As Gerber remind us, "Migration is a profound challenge to the self-defining narrative of identity," involving alienation from the self.[55] Corresponding with loved ones left behind helps repair, rebuild, and, if so desired, redefine identities disrupted by migration. In analyzing the letters, Gerber argues convincingly, we must focus not only on their content but also on their purpose, for the missives "are deceptively complex and laden with meaning."[56] While they serve as "purveyors of social intelligence as well as education in modernity," they also represent the authors' "authentic representations of themselves."[57] Indeed, the attempt to take ownership of personal identities is revealed through the creativity in the writing as well as the care and concern with attempts to improve it and make it interesting and legible.

While Gerber studies the correspondence of British immigrants in the United States, focusing on the literary techniques for insights on the strategies of coping with estrangement, Cancian pays close attention to the impact of migration on the "hearts and minds" of Italian immigrants who settled in Canada. Cancian's "micro-level study" of immigrants bound by extensive kinship and social networks allows her to delve deeply into the social, cultural, and emotional responses to migration. "[L]etters in the context of migration," Cancian argues, provide "access to the immigrant's attitudes, values, aspirations, and fears as no other source has the potential to do."[58] They also provide insight on the wide range of coping mechanisms, including the use of the imagination, she states, to interpret the thoughts and actions of family members located thousands of miles away.

Though Cancian's and Gerber's works are instructive and insightful, this book goes beyond those approaches to the study of epistolary practices among migrants. Specifically, it challenges Gerber's finding that "[i]mmigrant personal correspondence did not exist for the purpose of analyzing the . . . social order" or for "evaluating the merits and flaws of the peoples the immigrants encountered . . . [It] was concerned more with personal identities and private relationships."[59] The letter writers in this study were also vested in their personal and emotional relationships but took time as well to discuss at length, or at least reference in passing, the larger issues of the day, including agricultural work routines and employer-employee hierarchies in Imperial Valley, patriarchal household dynamics and gendered expectations in their families and communities, as well as changing U.S. immigration laws easing migratory policies and practices. Moreover, although Gerber found little evidence of conflict or ambiguity in the immigrants' correspondence he studied, my family's archives contain varied layers of tensions, including open confrontations over rumored affairs as well cryptic, speculative messages, leading to ambiguous communications. Indeed, contradictory messages about the authors' feelings of loneliness, despondency, and uncertainty bounced back and forth across the border and did so because, most simply, the letters writers, too, could not make sense of their emotions. Finally, unlike the correspondence Gerber studied, which contained no love letters, my collection has over 100 letters (or a third of the over 300 pieces of correspondence in the collection) that were expressly *cartas de amor* (love letters), demonstrating that love and confessional letters *are* representative of the immigrant letter, at least in the twentieth-century U.S.-Mexico context.[60]

The Tools and Techniques of Interpreting Family Archives

Using personal letters to interpret and write a slice in the life of a family history situated in a broader context of social, political, economic, cultural, and migration history is a challenging yet inviting task. To recoup the intended and unintended gaps and silences in the collection of letters as well as in the memory of my father and mother and other family members who have died, this study mines a family archive of over 300 pieces of correspondence as well as oral histories, photographs, music, radio programming, film, memorabilia, newspapers, magazines, censuses, and government reports. Interviews with my parents' siblings, extended relatives, and close friends, as well as with community leaders in their hometown of Calvillo, are particularly rich in recovering little-known intimate aspects of my parents' childhood and young adulthood as well as the social life in and outside the pueblo where they spent much of their early years. Though filtered by re-created memories, personal pain and collective trauma, and the respect due to the living and the dead, the interviews help, too, in charting my parents' trajectory and the decision-making process that came to redefine their identities as part of a larger cohort of migrant men and women who decided to take a chance on improving their lives by immigrating to the United States and altering their sense of who they were as individuals, family members, and community members of Calvillo and the larger nation-state of Mexico.[61] Indeed, my parents were not alone in this journey. Family members and friends soon joined them as well, taking on the challenges and rewards of migration in the 1960s, a period undergoing rapid changes in migratory policies and practices that would leave an indelible mark on the future of migration patterns across the borderlands.

To gain an understanding of the significance of the correspondence among all letter writers, the narrative breathes life into the letters by situating them in the cross-border social, political, economic, and cultural context in which the authors crafted and exchanged the missives. By toggling between the micro and macro, that is, between the letter writers' experiences, on the one hand, and immigration policies and practices, systems of communication, and popular media, on the other, *Migrant Longing* reveals how migrants' lives intersected with national and transnational trends. This study also makes sense of the letters by reading them as literary texts, as do Gerber and Cancian, among others. Interpreted as tools of courtship and social surveillance (with all their manipulations and intentions) and read closely as emotionally restorative confessions of the heart (with all their sincerity and vulnerability), the letters nurtured and, in many instances, constituted the relationship.[62] The correspondence not only allowed migrants as well as the stay-at-homes the opportunity to communicate the challenges and rewards of the migratory process and their changing social and cultural environment but also provided them with an outlet for disclosing their innermost dreams and desires. In the process, they crafted idealized gendered identities—akin to what Gerber calls "plural subject positioning"—as hardworking, sophisticated, and successful migrant males as well as dutiful daughters, respectful women, and hard-working females.[63]

Writing in the shared spaces of their bedrooms, kitchens, and patios, as well as in their places of employment, letter writers in my family rarely enjoyed the luxury and privilege of privacy, which those in the United States often imagine accompanies the epistolary practice. Simply put, poverty and lack of personal space prevented most from keeping their letter writing a secret or at least shielding their correspondence from prying eyes. The exception was among those who successfully hid their correspondence from family members who opposed the relationship fostered by the practice. In those rare instances, the letters were designed to be read only by the intended audience. The act of hiding courtship notes under the mattress, as my mother's older sister sometimes did to keep them from her family's knowledge, however, did not prevent inquisitive sisters from finding and reading the private correspondence. Indeed, more frequently than not, the notes and their contents circulated as a form of social consumption among friends and family members and functioned as communal letters when they included a secondary note—usually written on the bottom or back of the page—by another to the same person.

Equally important to the public-private nature of the letters is the authorship, especially in a place and time in which literacy was uncommon in rural Mexico. Though literacy was limited in the early to mid-twentieth century, especially among campesinos, many mexicanos did use the letter as a form of communication. Manuel Gamio's interviews with Mexican immigrants in the U.S. Southwest in 1926 and 1927 indicate that many migrants regularly wrote home to family members and friends with news about their travels in el norte. That form of exchange, as well as word of mouth, was central to motivating scores of mexicanos in the early twentieth century to try their luck in el norte. Like some of Gamio's informants, the majority of the letter writers in my family were literate and had either enjoyed some formal education at school—no more than *primaria* (primary school)—or informal instruction at home. A close analysis of the handwriting style confirms the consistency of composition of the correspondence and indicates convincingly that nearly all authors were the original letter writers. With the exception of my paternal grandmother, whose handful of letters were written by her daughter and an unknown member of the community acting as a scribe, all authors penned or typed their own correspondence.[64] Scribes, or *escribanos*, were regularly used in Mexico. My paternal grandfather, José Chávez Torres, for instance, who learned to write in the early 1900s, an uncommon occurrence among the working classes and poor, worked as a scribe, making a few extra pesos on his time off from work at the Civil Registry for the municipality of Calvillo. Though it is unclear if he worked as a scribe for fellow braceros—as he too lived and worked among them—it is known that literate braceros took on the job of writing letters on behalf of their compatriots while they were in el norte.[65]

Writing notes on paper that was commonly available for a few cents at a local stationery shop as well as mailing that correspondence (and receiving it) was equally feasible throughout the twentieth century until the near-collapse of the Mexican postal service in the 1980s. In Calvillo—as in most towns in Mexico in the early decades of the 1900s, when the government made the postal service widespread through the modernization of the countryside and expansion of the railroads—the local post office was located on the main plaza in the heart of the town, usually no more than a ten- to fifteen-minute walk from the outskirts of the pueblo. In the 1960s, with forty cents in hand, most could mail their notes to or receive their money orders (*giros postales*) from loved ones across the U.S.-Mexico border. Though the price for international mailing doubled to eighty cents in that decade, as a result of air service, and *papelerias* (stationery stores) sometimes closed early or correspondence paper was difficult to find, the effort to send a letter was priceless, for the letter represented, as Gerber has written, "an intimate, if long-distance, conversation with another."[66] Other options included the telegraph, which was developed in the late nineteenth century and used primarily for urgent business purposes, and the telephone, which was often less readily available and cost prohibitive for ordinary people, especially in early twentieth-century pueblos such as Calvillo. Indeed, it would take decades, until the 1970s, for telephones to become common in households. Until then, the postal service met the communication needs of most rural and urban Mexicans. Later, in the 1980s, with the near-collapse of the Mexican economy, the postal service would suffer a severe blow to its efficiency and reliability, leading most people, at least those who could afford it, to rely increasingly on the telephone and private postal services.[67]

Unlike much of braceros' correspondence to Mexico, which the Mexican and U.S. governments intercepted in an effort to prevent negative publicity about the larger program or its detrimental effects on family life and household relations, the notes in my family archive escaped censorship, allowing for the exchange of personal experiences such as the physical dangers and emotional difficulties of living and working in the United States.[68] Indeed, the letter writers represented in my family archive, that is, my father, mother, uncles and aunts, grandparents, extended family members, and friends, expressed their innermost thoughts of love and desire, fear and doubt, desperation and failure, and shame and self-loathing with relatively little oversight from the state. Collections of personal letters, though, are rarely complete, as Gerber reminds us, as many have been lost or thrown away, leaving only partial sets of correspondence. The use of what Gerber calls "double voice," however, in which authors repeat the statements made in the senders' last message ("In your last letter, you say that . . ."), fills many of the gaps.[69] Through that practice, which many letter writers, especially my grandfather, carried out, we can reconstruct the larger arc of the narrative running through the missives.

The presence of letters does not, of course, mean that they are complete interpretations of a particular moment that we can piece together like a puzzle. Many purposely withheld or filtered information, resisting full disclosure as well as a complete understanding of the evolution of the relationship. Doing so was not always accidental, for it allowed letter writers the ability to escape censure and reprimand from their intended audience, particularly when they made decisions that contradicted family advice. It afforded them the opportunity to avoid sympathy and pity when their migratory plans went awry. Not writing, remaining silent, and failing to reveal the intensity of the pain and loneliness they experienced as a consequence of their migration and isolation in a new and foreign land also enabled them to protect loved ones who stayed at home. To whom, when, and why they chose to disclose information or withhold it is equally significant and says a lot about how they structured their personal, familial, and social lives across the border. While some attempted to keep their intimate, personal relations in el norte separate from their household and peer relations back home, the tight-knit family and social networks in the pueblo and free exchange of chisme often made that nearly impossible.[70]

Understanding my role in the process of writing my family's history and my relationship to the sources, that is, my subjectivity, has been a constant preoccupation in crafting this study. Admittedly, my desire to recover the lives and legacies of my parents, who died when I was a twelve-year-old girl, was the initial motivation for carrying out this project. I now realize that by holding, reading, and, later, transcribing, translating, and interpreting their words, I had tricked myself into believing that I could bring them back to life, or at least get to know them, in their youth, the way I was never able to do in real life. I now realize that the letter-writing process, which I had come to rely on as a medium or mechanism for rendering and reconnecting with them, is an imperfect séance, as are all source materials, including oral histories, census records, and government reports, which also suffer from manipulations, silences, and distortions. While the notes have mitigated my own longing and desire for a need to know who they were and what they hoped for and desired, they do not make up for the lack of the intimacy of a motherly embrace or a fatherly conversation (my father was not one for physical or emotional expressions). Nevertheless, the correspondence has proved a rich and unparalleled source, a relatively untapped window for mining the experiences of Mexican migrants and the relations they developed, sustained, and experienced in a larger social network and historical context.

As the daughter, niece, and granddaughter of the central characters in this narrative, my perspective and positioning in relation to my subjects are also informed by a desire to preserve their memory as respected, honored, and loved members of multiple families and communities. As a scholar, my purpose is not to glorify or distort who they were as individuals or fathers, mothers, brothers, and sisters. Rather, it is to interpret and craft their multiple identities as they emerged in the sources and to invest them with meaning given what little we know about the personal, local, national, and global histories that shaped and informed them. Yet, I would be fibbing in saying that I did not choose intentionally or unintentionally to disclose one story over another. What I chose to reveal about one family member over another was decided by weighing the available evidence against the larger impact of disclosing that information. Suggestions, for instance, to render my mother's stepfather as a less than savory fellow have to do not only with years of growing up and hearing unflattering stories about him but also with finding a newspaper article confirming his run-in with the law and subsequent imprisonment. These were my approaches in writing this larger history, which is the framework I turn to next.

To explore the ways in which migrants negotiated longing, gender, intimacy, courtship, marriage, and identity across the U.S.-Mexico borderlands in the 1960s and 1970s, chapter 1 opens by examining and analyzing the broader racial, labor, and environmental contexts shaping José's—my father's—experience as a Mexican laborer in Imperial Valley in the 1950s and 1960s. Specifically, it pays attention to working and living conditions in *el valle* and how those contributed to his loneliness, isolation, and ambivalence as a border dweller, despite his status as a green card holder and his ability to engage in return migration. Next, it examines letter writing, as a form of courtship, as detailed in the love letters he crafted and the cultural tools—stylized letter writing, the English language, portraits, songs, movies, and the radio—he drew upon to convince Conchita to accept his marriage proposal. Finally, it shows that while Conchita never formally agreed to the nuptials, she walked down the aisle and married José, an act that set her life on a new course. Indeed, within a few days, she left her hometown and relocated with José to the Mexicali-Calexico border, where they set out to craft a new future for themselves. Within a few years, they traded the rural agricultural zone for an urban environment, where they found increased economic opportunities and social stability.

Chapter 2 turns the historical lens to south of the border—to Calvillo, Aguascalientes, specifically—to probe how and why Conchita, a vibrant, free-spirited young woman, eventually went through with the wedding, even though she had little interest in settling down and forming a family and expressed few emotional and romantic feelings of love toward José. As a *muchacha* (young woman) in a relatively insular pueblo, Conchita lived a life that revolved around schooling and her friends, attending the local movie theater and participating in festivities, and spending time at her cousins' rancho as well as supporting an increasingly impoverished and conflicted household. Yet, after only three face-to-face meetings and three years of an epistolary-based courtship, across hundreds of miles, Conchita married José and migrated to the border region where he lived and worked. In the process, she left behind her youth, her family, her closest confidante, Asunción (Chifis), her older sister, and the only world she had known for eighteen years.

Chapter 3 continues with a focus on gender and family life in Mexico, centering on the shifting power relations in the patriarchal household. Using dozens of letters written by José Chávez Torres to his son Paco, who was living and working in the U.S.-Mexico borderlands, the chapter examines the personal, emotional, and economic toll of migration on family members who stayed at home. It demonstrates the profound ways in which the migration of family members and loved ones affected their social roles and identities, that is, the real and perceived understanding of who they were in relation to their changing circumstances in their family and community in Mexico and the United States.

Chapter 4 reveals that maintaining relationships between parents and children, though challenging, paled in comparison to the work needed to keep alive passionate romantic relationships between male migrants and the female partners they left behind. This chapter focuses on the on again, off again relationship between José's younger brother, Paco, and Conchita's older sister, Chifis or Chonita. It demonstrates that the rudimentary systems of communication, distance, rampant chisme, and shifting interests and personal goals proved too burdensome for them to maintain a long-term, long-distance courtship. Though the *noviasgo* (courtship) did not result in marriage, it allowed them to express their greatest hopes and dreams as well as their everyday social and cultural experiences across the vast divide. While letters often worked to maintain and build relations, this chapter shows how and why they sometimes worked to destroy them as well.

To understand migrants' longing for opportunity and adventure, the final chapter traces the experience of Paco's friend Rogelio Martínez Serna—and that of his male peers—across the U.S.-Mexico borderlands and his attempts to achieve his hopes and dreams for an economically, physically, and emotionally stable family life. To do so, the chapter opens by examining Rogelio's effort to migrate lawfully across the U.S.-Mexico border. It shows that his motivation for migration was stoked by Paco's recent successful journey to and settlement in California. Like his peers back home, Rogelio imagined Paco, who was already living in the United States, earning pockets full of dollars, attracting women with his convertible car, and enjoying new adventures. Life was much more difficult for Rogelio, who resided in Ciudad Juárez. Inspired by his friend Paco, and not easily defeated, Rogelio developed ingenious plans to achieve his purpose and, even when faced with roadblocks, as he was repeatedly, he pressed on with his larger aim in mind: migrating to California to save enough money for an economically secure life as a "man" who could support a household in Mexico. As he soon learned, however, life as an undocumented worker in the Golden State proved too difficult. Indeed, the harsh labor, measly pay, and the constant threat of *la migra* (the border patrol) led him to retreat to Ciudad Juárez. Rogelio never lost sight of his aims, however, especially with peers providing practical, emotional, and economic support for how to lead the life of a successful male Mexican migrant with his masculinity and manhood intact. As Rogelio's experiences and those of his peers make clear, migrants relied on each other and on the broader social networks to achieve lawful migration, employment, housing, and transportation as well as entertainment and companionship, facilitating their temporary or permanent settlement in and transition to the new environment.

The letters provide a unique and once-in-a-lifetime opportunity to probe deeply and broadly the shifting meanings of migration as well as gender, intimacy, courtship, marriage, and the family among migrants living between here and there and among those who stayed at home in Mexico. They provide a window onto their intimate and personal decision making as well as the broader social, political, and economic circumstances beyond their control in shaping those choices. Neither beasts of burdens nor automatons in the capitalist, postindustrial machine of the late twentieth century, migrants sought to a carve a better life for themselves and their families with the means at their disposal.

CHAPTER ONE

Oye Shelly
Migrant Longing, Courtship, and Gendered Identity

In December 1963, a week after returning to Imperial Valley following a brief visit home to Mexico for the holidays, José Chávez Esparza, a farmworker, sat down to write a letter to María Concepcíon "Conchita" Alvarado, a young woman he met during his trip. Thirty years old, single, and longing for a female companion, José wasted little time in boldly initiating a letter-writing campaign to win her heart and, eventually, her hand in marriage. He forced himself to wait a few days before crafting the message, but he could not wait any longer, he told her, as he had "returned enchanted with your personality and all your ways."[1] He feared, too, that she might forget him and his intentions if he waited too long. José reminded her that they had agreed to correspond not only to build a friendship but also to establish a relationship in which "she was committed to him (*me corresponda*)" and he, in turn, "was committed to her," a theme he raised repeatedly. "I see no point in a courtship (*noviasgo*) as you said 'from afar' ('*de lejos*') without the principal objective . . . of marriage." "I am not asking you to agree to my proposal immediately but rather when you are able to feel love for me." "I can assure you," he said confidently of his talents, "that I will grow to love you the way no other has loved you."[2]

José's optimism for the possibility of a long-term relationship, even a long-distance, cross-border one, transformed his outlook overnight. "Life seems different now everything seems better than before," he wrote in that same letter. His hope seemed to buoy his confidence to take the next step. "I would like to ask you in a special way if I can continue to write to you even though you are not my declared girlfriend but in the future ahead when I describe to you my qualities and what I like or how I am in real life, you will reciprocate." He ended his beautifully composed letter with feigned humility, as he thought that perhaps his sixth grade schooling (*primaria*), as opposed to her ninth grade education (*secundaria*)—both admirable achievements for rural Mexicans at the time—as well as their differences in upbringing (she came from a once-propertied family and he from poverty), might lead her to disparage his letter or him as a letter writer. "A thousand apologies for my writing for there are times that even I don't understand it."[3]

The first letter of courtship José Chávez Esparza sent María Concepción Alvarado ("Conchita") in late December 1963. Florid in his praise of Conchita's virtues and serious in his marital proposal, José would go on to write at least another forty-four missives in his attempt to conquer her heart and hand in marriage across the U.S.-Mexico borderlands.

Digital copy of letter in author's personal collection.

The carefully crafted and eloquent communication seemed to have little effect on Conchita, for she did not reply. Nearly a month later, dismayed at her silence and what it might mean for any future relationship, José broke with the convention of waiting for a response and dashed off a second letter, knowing he risked annoying her.[4] "Conchita," he wrote, "please forgive me for boring or bothering you but three weeks ago I wrote you a letter and I am not certain if you received it or not for I have not received any kind of response nor has the letter been returned." "I beg you," he pleaded, "to please respond even . . . if it's true that you prefer not to have at least a friendship with me."[5] He then entertained possible motives for her reticence, including the likelihood that they had violated generational and gender norms about female and family honor or that rumors or gossip (*chisme*) about his character had prejudiced her against him. "If for some reason you were scolded in your home for [my] having written to you at your address you can give me another," he suggested as a ruse, as many star-crossed paramours did to hide their epistolary relationship. "Or another thing," he continued, "if they have told you something about me you can tell me with confidence as I have nothing to be ashamed [of]."[6]

Two weeks later, José's flagging optimism was revived when he received Conchita's much-anticipated, though lukewarm, missive. She apologized for the delay and explained that her silence was a consequence of her loss for words. Since then, however, she had gathered her thoughts. "I am going to be sincere with you the way I think you were with me, look I don't feel I love you in a way that would take us beyond a friendship," Conchita said bluntly. The reason for her thoughts, she said, was "because of the little time we have known each other you can almost say that we barely met."[7] "Nevertheless," she conceded, "I do feel an immense affection and a profound gratitude," but not romantic love or the kind of passionate and emotive love she witnessed on the movie screens at the theaters she frequented in the pueblo. "Look keep writing to me I like you for a good friend and as you say God will decide (*Dios dirá*)."[8]

Though Conchita was reserved in her enthusiasm for the relationship, José was overjoyed, putting himself in what David A. Gerber calls an emotional state, or a heightened state of emotional intimacy often associated with receiving and sending correspondence.[9] "Conchita, I wish I could find the most beautiful words to express the joy I feel as I imagined you would not respond," he said. "True," he explained in response to her concerns about their brief courtship, "that we barely got to know each other physically but we can know each more intimately writing and speaking the truth then you can say what your heart dictates."[10] José's ability to craft his identify as an attentive yet lonely and vulnerable suitor apparently worked, for she agreed to accept the correspondence and courtship.

José's letters of courtship, while often confessions about his desire for female companionship, love, and marriage, reveal the personal isolation and longing that he experienced as a single, heterosexual Mexican male migrant farm laborer living and working in Imperial Valley in the 1950s and 1960s. For more than ten years, José inhabited a homosocial male world roughly 1,500 miles north of his hometown of Calvillo, Aguascalientes, then a small, insulated, and largely agricultural- and rural-based community. While he wrote home frequently and established meaningful male bonds of friendship with fellow laborers and farmworkers' families, particularly those from Calvillo, and had the opportunity to venture south of the border relatively quickly, he went without the sustained intimacy of a female. Whether he ever had a girlfriend or paid for the services of a prostitute, as did many men working for the bracero program, is unknown, for he never mentions or suggests having had either experience in or around Imperial Valley or in Mexicali, Baja California, about an hour's drive from his home in Brawley, California.[11] Over time, though, the social networks he developed were not enough to assuage his lonesome working and living conditions. The urgency and, perhaps, anxiousness in finding a sexual and domestic partner and in establishing a patriarchal (read: male-dominated) household spoke not only to his need in finding an intimacy that fulfilled his emotional, physical, and material needs but also to the realization that as a slightly older, single man, he needed (or was expected by the social and cultural norms of gender of the day) to settle down with a wife and family. Indeed, as scholars of Mexico have found, between 1960 and 1980 the average age of marriage among couples in towns of fewer than 20,000 inhabitants was nineteen years of age for women and twenty-four for men.[12] Doubtless, José felt the pressure to tie the knot, especially given the limited numbers of eligible marital partners in Imperial Valley. As a migrant torn between here and there (*aqui y allá*), he longed to reconcile his home and future as a patriarch and a married man.

José's correspondence not only reveals a deep longing for heterosexual companionship, love, and marriage but also evokes a desire for the emotional, sexual, domestic, and economic comforts of a home situated in a cross-border environment. Like most contemporary male migrants, such as his older brothers, uncles, and father before him, he migrated to the United

States in search of employment and financial stability for himself and his family in Mexico. He remained ambivalent, however, about leaving everything behind for the United States, a place he scarcely recognized as home. Though unhappy in Imperial Valley, he was equally dissatisfied residing in Mexico, where he knew his future was dim. As a young man, he had hoped to study agricultural engineering, but the reality of his impoverished family life obligated him to find employment soon after graduating from the sixth grade at the age of sixteen.[13] Within a few years, he had moved to Aguascalientes, the state capital, where he worked as an apprentice in his uncle's tailor shop and, later, as a driver for Pepsi Cola, delivering *refrescos* throughout the city. Yet, even then, he and his father—who told him as much during one of his visits home—knew that his immediate future was in el norte with the higher wages and opportunities it provided Mexican male migrants like himself. He remained undecisive, however, about how long he planned to stay *en el otro lado*.[14]

What follows is an account of the personal, emotional, and creative world of a single male migrant farmworker in Imperial Valley. Relying on eighty letters exchanged between José and Conchita, forty-five from him and thirty-five from her, written between 1963 and 1971, this chapter explores migrant longing, courtship, and gendered identity in the U.S.-Mexico borderlands. It begins by exploring the broader racial, labor, and environmental contexts shaping José's experience as a Mexican laborer in Imperial Valley in the 1950s and 1960s. Specifically, it pays attention to working and living conditions in *el valle* and how those contributed to his loneliness, isolation, and ambivalence as a border dweller, despite his status as a green card holder and his ability to engage in return migration. Next, it pays attention to rituals of courtship as expressed in the letters he composed as well as his use of carefully crafted letter writing, English-language word games, pictures, Spanish- and English-language music and films, and the radio to draw Conchita closer and to forge an intimate relationship where none existed. As the letters reveal, José reinvented his gendered identity as a poor, rural, and solitary migrant male laborer to one of a sensitive, sophisticated, and urbane man to persuade Conchita to accept his marriage proposal. Finally, it demonstrates that while Conchita never formally said yes, she eventually married José and relocated with him to the agricultural valley. In time, with assistance from family and social networks, they migrated to northern California's growing urban environment, where they found increased opportunities and stability for themselves and their extended families in Mexico.

Race, Labor, and Mexican Male Migrants in Imperial Valley

When José arrived in Imperial Valley in the early 1950s, demand for male agricultural workers was strong, even though the end World War II and the return of U.S. service men and women from abroad had eased the so-called labor shortages on the home front. As Don Mitchell and other scholars have argued, agricultural employers exaggerated the shortage of laborers during the war to gain support for a labor importation program and the captive workers it provided.[15] José, like most emigrant Mexican men of his generation, came to the United States seeking employment in agricultural work in response to the continual demand for cheap male laborers and flagging economic opportunities in the Mexican countryside. Despite Mexico's program of rapid industrialization, modernization, and integration into the U.S. economy in the 1940s and 1950s, the "Mexican Miracle" of that era proved illusory for campesinos and rural folk, such as my father and his family, living on ranchos and pueblos throughout Mexico. José originally migrated to el norte as part of the Emergency Farm Labor Supply Program or, as it is commonly known, the bracero program, a binational labor agreement between the United States and Mexico that lasted nearly uninterrupted for twenty-two years, from 1942 to 1964. After the war, sustained demand by agricultural employers for low-cost, dispensable, and manageable workers as well as professed labor shortages due to the onset of the Korean War in 1950 convinced U.S. State Department officials to extend the program repeatedly, despite heated protests from organized labor, nativists, and Mexican officials, among others.[16]

The incessant demand for captive laborers and the practice of hiring workers outside of the official parameters of the bracero program convinced many other unemployed, rural Mexican men, in turn, to head north to try their luck as laborers and, if needed, as undocumented workers, as they knew employers hired first and asked questions later. The result of the unexpected surge was the migration of hundreds of thousands of potential male workers—given the misnomer "wetbacks" or *espaldas mojadas*—seeking agricultural labor from U.S. employers who knowingly and willingly hired them regardless of their legal status. While most farm owners preferred to hire laborers under contract, giving them the ability to control the workforce, many hired them as "illegals"—a term that would later come to supplant the racialized "wetback" designation for undocumented workers—or "legalized them on the spot," as Kitty Calavita has noted was commonly done. Within a few years, the hiring of undocumented workers as well as the institutionalization of the labor importation program led to the mass migration and, eventually, permanent settlement of Mexican men and, later, their families.[17]

Not willing to risk crossing the border as undocumented migrants, in the mid-1950s José and two male cousins traveled north by train from Calvillo to the closest recruiting station on the West Coast, Empalme, Sonora, hoping to land a contract.[18] In Sonora, José had to compete with hundreds or potentially thousands of would-be braceros for a spot as a contract laborer. None of those competitors, however, were females, as the program excluded women's direct participation for fear that their presence would lead to the migration and, eventually, the permanent settlement of increasing numbers of Mexican families in the United States.[19] As a young, strong, single male, José was a desired laborer and, after likely going through what has been described by former braceros as humiliating physical exams, inspection, and delousing, he was hired promptly, signing on to the first of many contracts, lasting roughly three to six months, and having little understanding of the daily working and living conditions in Imperial Valley.[20] Even though his father, José Chávez Torres, and two older brothers, Jesús and Juan, had experience working on farms throughout California and other parts of the United States, including Illinois, Wisconsin, and Texas, they infrequently exchanged insight on the practice.

Soon after arriving in Brawley, in the heart of Imperial Valley and less than thirty miles from the Mexican border, José quickly realized that, unlike the cool, balmy, and temperate seasons of Calvillo that he enjoyed as a young man, the region was (and is) dry and extremely hot. A desolate zone, the valley is known for intense to extreme heat- and sun-filled late spring and summer seasons with temperatures reaching 120 degrees.[21] Situated approximately 100 feet below sea level and bordered by mountains to the west, the valley receives little Pacific moisture, making for extremely dry conditions, and is considered to be among the most arid regions in the United States. Yet, the relatively warm weather and fertile soil make it a highly coveted region for nearly year-round agricultural development, a process that began as long ago as the late nineteenth century with the expansion of the southwestern agricultural economy that eventually made California the leading producer of fruits and vegetables in the country. To profit handsomely, as investors had in other parts of the Southwest, Euro-American capitalist developers—led by the California Land Development Company, founded in 1896—negotiated with the U.S. Congress to divert portions of the Colorado River through an elaborate and extensive network of canals, known today as Imperial Canal, to Imperial Valley. By the early

1920s, the much-needed water quenched the parched landscape and brought into cultivation more than 300,000 acres of land. Within thirty to forty years, by the time José was living and working in the region, agricultural capitalists farmed some 400,000 acres. Agricultural production slowed a bit thereafter, as increasing attention was paid to the diversification of the local economy, but farming continued to drive production. By the early 2000s, farmers cultivated nearly 545,000 acres year round, making it the sixth most productive region in the state.[22]

The tremendous economic growth of Imperial Valley in the early twentieth century relied on the importation and control of significant numbers of cheap, dispensable, ethnic and racialized laborers, namely, Mexicans, Chinese, Japanese, Punjabis, and poor white male workers, as the area's harsh environment had repelled settlers for hundreds of years.[23] No one understood this better than eighteenth- and nineteenth-century Spanish colonists, who, along with mestizo-mulatto (racially mixed) settlers, crossed the area heading north in search of more hospitable environs to establish their settlements for the conquest, colonization, and defense of the territory. With little water, wild game, or vegetation available for grazing animals, most colonizers who managed to survive the voyage and the resistance encountered from Native peoples stayed briefly, preferring to move along to the milder western and northern coasts of Alta California.[24] By 1910, few people—no more than 13,500—among them white workers lured from across the United States by Imperial Land Company with promises of land and water, called the area home.[25] Ten years later, in 1920, with the expansion of the agricultural economy and the use of Mexican migrants, who were desired for their perceived docility, biological suitability for harsh labor, and status as temporary laborers, or what employers called "birds of passage," Imperial County's population surged significantly, to 43,453, with Euro-Americans representing 67 percent, Mexicans nearly 15 percent, and others nearly 18 percent of the local populace.[26]

With the hostile and legal exclusion of Chinese and Japanese laborers that emerged in the late nineteenth and early twentieth centuries, the proportion of male Mexican workers climbed in the next decade.[27] By 1930, Mexicans made up 35.5 percent of the valley's 60,903 inhabitants, with Euro-Americans accounting for 54.4 percent of the population and others 10 percent. Yet, by 1940, the overall population, including Mexicans, dipped to 59,740, a reflection of the severe economic downturn of the Great Depression and the repatriation of hundreds of thousands of people of Mexican descent, including U.S. citizens, throughout California and the

José Chávez Esparza, 1956, as a young man migrating
to the United States as a bracero, an agricultural worker
in California under contract with a U.S. employer. By the
end of 1958, his boss, J. C. Reeves, based in Brawley,
California, had sponsored his permanent residency,
enabling him to obtain the coveted green card and secure
his legal status.
Photograph in author's personal collection.

larger United States. Not until the establishment of the bracero program,
during the years José and his cousins arrived on the scene, did the region
bounce back slowly, as the population figures increased slightly, from
nearly 60,000 in 1940 to 62,975 in 1950 and 72,105 in 1960. The presence of
braceros was particularly strong among the workforce, as they made up 80
percent of the laboring class.[28] By 1960, too, the overall proportion of Mexicans began to swell in relation to Euro-Americans, a trend that would continue well into the future. By 1970, Mexicans accounted for 30.5 percent of
the populace, whereas Euro-Americans made up less than 62 percent, despite

the end of the program in December 1964, indicating that many laborers, such as José, stayed in the United States rather than return to Mexico. And, indeed, many did remain or were sent home and returned promptly. By some estimates more than half of braceros settled either as documented or undocumented workers. The former were able to do so as a consequence of employers' active sponsorship of their employees' legalization. Eventually, under the provisions of the Immigration Act of 1965, which encouraged family reunification, those same workers brought their wives and children in the late 1960s and 1970s.[29] Despite the increased numbers of newcomers, Imperial Valley remained relatively sparsely populated until the mid-1970s, when it climbed closer to 90,000, still a far cry from the larger and growing urban enclaves nearby, including San Diego to the west, Los Angeles to the north, and Mexicali to the south.[30]

Agricultural workers in Imperial Valley, like José, not only found themselves living in a relatively isolated rural region and working on large farms in the intense heat but also residing in poor housing with little access to adequate health care and familiar food and dealing with exploitative labor practices. In the 1950s and 1960s, local activists and sympathetic local newspapers such as the *Imperial Valley Press* and the *Brawley News* brought attention to the run-down shacks employers forced braceros to endure as well as the shoddy nature of health care and astronomical food and supply prices. Rather than allow them to purchase such goods from local stores with competitive prices, bosses often obligated the workers to shop at company-owned stores or to select retailers with higher prices, forcing them to part with much of their earnings.[31]

José escaped many of these exploitative working conditions when he obtained the coveted green card—literally printed green like the colors of the border patrol—sometime in the late 1950s or early 1960s. José's employer, J. C. Reeves, owner of J. C. Reeves Ranches, a commercial farm in Brawley, California, dedicated to growing sugar beets, alfalfa, and wheat for market, made it possible for him to do so by sponsoring his application for U.S. residency. Thus, Reeves essentially agreed to maintain José economically if he lost his job or in other ways fell on hard times. Apparently, Reeves agreed to sponsor José after a few years of the latter's loyalty and friendship, even though he knew he risked losing him as a worker to another employer. Indeed, in subsequent correspondence, José referred to "*el patrón*" (the boss) as a "*buen amigo*" (good friend). Reeves's son, Steve Reeves, recalled years later that the two had established a strong bond, with José occasionally visiting the

Reeves family home.[32] No doubt José's green card brought him peace of mind, for it not only enabled him to leave the precarious life of a contract or undocumented laborer for other types of employment but also made it possible for him to leave his post at a moment's notice when work slowed or when emergencies developed at home in Calvillo. In the meantime, the green card elevated his status on the farm, for it meant that he could drive a tractor or operate machinery, which braceros were not allowed to do. It gave him, in short, what he called *"preferencia"* (preference) at the work-site. As he later told Conchita in 1964 with a measure of shame, "I have (even though it is wrong to say it) preference that is I have the lightest and simplest work."[33]

His green card status provided him with the opportunity not only to es-cape back-breaking stoop labor—not unlike that experienced by black share-croppers in the U.S. South—but also to earn more income than most of his peers.[34] A surviving income tax return from 1962 indicates that José earned more than twice as much as an average single male farm resident living at the poverty line in the United States. That year, he made $4,500, while the U.S. poverty line for single males living on farms was $1,370.[35] He was, of course, by no means wealthy, as he was dependent on the availability of work on a day-to-day basis to meet his basic financial obligations, such as housing, feeding, and clothing himself and sending money to his parents in Calvillo. Plus, life was more expensive in California than in other parts of the United States the government used to determine the poverty line.

More significantly, José's green card altered his gendered identity from a temporary to a permanent male migrant farmworker in the United States, providing him with the opportunity to settle in the United States indef-initely if he so wished and to eventually obtain U.S. citizenship. Indeed, as Douglas Massey has found, the legal documentation of migrants from Gua-dalajara, a region bordering that of Aguascalientes, facilitated the transition from rural, temporary labor to urban, permanent, and long-term settle-ment in the United States.[36] José's legal status also afforded him a measure of security from any possible deportation campaigns, which the Border Patrol and the Immigration and Naturalization Service (INS) carried out throughout the twentieth century. Most recently, and perhaps known to José, was Operation Wetback in 1954. As Kelly Lytle Hernández has argued, that campaign began years earlier, in the 1940s and early 1950s, in response to the swelling numbers of undocumented Mexican immigrants on farms throughout the Southwest and the public uproar over the appearance of an "uncontrolled" border. The massive military-style campaign to apprehend and deport 1 million undocumented workers resulted in the deportation of hundreds of thousands of Mexican nationals throughout the United States.[37]

José's identity as a green card holder, however, seemed to do little to diminish his responsibilities at work or lessen his sense of isolation. Rather, his new status apparently increased his duties at the worksite, including operating the newest machinery and working year round with the exception of two weeks of unpaid leave during the holiday season. The rest of the year, the crops and paltry but consistent pay kept him tied to Imperial Valley, for his work afforded him the most basic of necessities and allowed him to send remittances intermittently. José's responsibilities at work also made it difficult for him to spend much time in Calvillo, reuniting with his family or socializing with friends and meeting potential female mates, making for an isolating existence that, combined with a harsh environment and living conditions, chewed at his personal and emotional core.

Indeed, alone in the California–Baja California borderlands, José lacked the female companionship and intimacy he desired as well as much social contact. Occasionally, one of his three brothers visited or stayed a few months to earn wages in the fields, but when they did so they rarely spoke about intimate personal matters, including relationships with women. When Conchita, for instance, asked José to intercede in her older sister's relationship with his younger brother, he refused. "Among us," the brothers, José explained to Conchita, "we have dealt with these matters on very few occasions."[38] Indeed, the male siblings communicated so infrequently that José did not know the name of Conchita's older sister even though his younger brother had dated her for several years in Calvillo.[39] While distance and lack of communication likely contributed to José's ignorance of the relationship, notions of masculinity as well as the brothers' estrangement—as Paco Chávez, José's younger brother, recalled years later, due to the differences in age and not having grown up together—meant that the men in his family did not speak to each other about intimate affairs.[40]

Besides his interactions with his brothers, José had little time for socializing with locals, especially in the summertime, when his six-day workweek and eight-to-ten-hour shifts left him exhausted at the end of the day. He did, however, develop trustworthy friendships (*de confianza*) with male coworkers, most of them from Calvillo. Among his closest friends was Juan "Juancho" Ramírez, originally from La Chona, a hamlet in Calvillo's municipality, with whom he spent many mornings and afternoons eating meals prepared and sold by Juancho's wife, Beatríz, and mother-in-law, María del

Refugio, or "Rufus." As Paco recalled, the women provided breakfasts and lunches in a barracks formerly used by braceros working for the Orita Land & Cattle Company. There, at the makeshift restaurant, Mexican, white, and black workers who either lacked facilities to cook in their living quarters or could not muster the energy to do so after a long workday came to enjoy the Mexican fare. While José often ate at the barracks, he knew how to cook and frequently made meals on the gas stove in the home provided at no cost by J. C. Reeves.[41]

As with the homosocial relationships Deborah Cohen identified among laborers in the bracero program, which the men forged through living, working, eating, and drinking side by side, José spent much time with Juancho at work and play.[42] On Sundays they went to church together, conceivably with Juancho's wife as well, and on occasional days off, they traveled across the border to Mexicali to visit friends of the family or to take care of personal needs, such as obtaining haircuts or eating Chinese food in the city's Chinese district. On special occasions, they sometimes headed for cooler pastures. For Juancho's birthday, which landed on a Sunday in 1964, the day off from work, they organized a "pee nick" (picnic), as José called it, near the Pacific coast. "It was fine," he later wrote to Conchita; "we had fun in the cool weather because here in the valley it is somewhat warm but in the mountains, about 75 kilometers from here, it is somewhat cold. The place," he explained, "is along the road traveling to San Diego."[43] On the Fourth of July holiday, they journeyed, too, to Ensenada, Baja California, and took pictures of their leisurely excursion. José's bond with Juancho and his family was so strong that Juancho would lend his car to José when he needed it for emergency trips to Calvillo.[44]

José's relationship with Juancho, while significant to his social and cultural life and in mitigating his loneliness in Imperial Valley, did not replace his ties with those left behind in Mexico or make it unnecessary to pursue the intimate and emotional bonds he hoped to develop with young women. Rather, José, like most migrants who had the opportunity and willingness to return home, engaged in return migration, making trips to visit family members and take care of household affairs as well as to meet young women who could potentially become his mate. José's excursions were infrequent and relatively brief, however, lasting no more than a week or two, and were carried out during religious holidays or when slowdowns at work gave him the opportunity to leave with little fear of losing his position to a fellow Mexican laborer who was eager to take his job. Unwilling to risk his position or economic livelihood and future in el norte, José never lost sight of his roles and responsibilities—his gendered identity as a responsible male farmworker—and he returned as soon as was feasible. Yet it was precisely on one of those brief trips in December 1963 that he met Conchita and, as he explained in his letters, became enamored by her charms and took up a writing campaign to win her heart and hand in marriage.

Confessions of Longing, Loneliness, and Desire

Nearly five weeks after José began his letter-writing campaign, he seemed no closer to winning Conchita's heart and hand in marriage. While she eventually responded to his early correspondence, she was too preoccupied or, more likely, reluctant to continue the epistolary relationship. After waiting twelve days for her to respond to his latest letter, his third, José hurriedly sent an "extra" letter, his fourth, at the end of January 1964, once again interrupting the one-to-one regulative writing Gerber found among European immigrant letter writers. The delay, though, was unbearable for José. As Gerber reminds us, "[W]riting is a time-consuming, strenuous activity that may be accompanied by a good deal of anxiety for those who do not commonly use literacy for work and recreation and who do physical work that leaves them exhausted at the end of the day."[45] José wrote that letter, he explained to Conchita, not because he had become disillusioned with her silence, which spoke volumes, but rather to reveal his true feelings. "I am not sad I have faith that I will soon receive your letter and with that [hope] I have enough to be happy in addition I have faith that you will be my partner hopefully it will be soon."[46]

Though he remained confident, José was not completely blind to Conchita's lukewarm attitude, for he attempted to ease her doubts with reassuring words. He had not spoken to her, he explained, because he lacked the nerve, especially because she was "*muy bonita*" (very beautiful). "[R]emember the day that you told me it was not you that I had spoken to but your cousin? Well I still don't believe it, true I had a few drinks but I was not drunk I had merely lessened my fear of speaking to you and declaring my intentions since I saw you for the first time I had the desire to speak to you but I'm not that type who has the ability of speaking easily to the girl[s.]" "And, do you know why?" he asked. "It is because I think . . . I am not attractive (*soy feo*)," he said, using self-denigrating language to position himself strategically as a vulnerable man needing rescuing. "I want you to know," he reiterated, undeterred, "that I will not defraud you if you declare yourself to be my girlfriend. I offer you all my love, which is bountiful and very sincere."[47]

To convince her of the fateful nature of the relationship, José explained a coincidence (*algo curioso*) that occurred the day he received her first letter. That day, he said, he had nearly given up hope that she would write. He had become so disappointed, he continued, that he had erased her name—"Shelly," which he had translated literally from "Conchita"—from where he had written it inside of the cab of the machine on which he worked. He likely used her name, which he recited every day, to keep alive his memory of her and his hope for marriage. Moreover, by translating her name into English and, essentially, Americanizing it, he went a step further in demonstrating his expectation that she would not only join him as his wife in the United States but also adapt culturally, as he had, to the new environment, and potentially on a permanent basis. The day her letter finally arrived, he continued, "I said today I must receive a letter from 'Shelly' (that's how it was written I translated it to English . . .) and if I don't receive it I will not write it until S[h]elly writes to me and on that day I received your letter."[48] While José believed it was more than a fluke that her correspondence arrived on the day he had given up hope, Conchita was not convinced that that was the case.

Nearly two weeks later, Conchita finally responded, though her letter was brief and less enthusiastic than José had desired. "Believe it or not I don't have a lot of free time as I am studying and have additional housework that I have to do that time escapes me," she explained curtly. As the two eldest daughters living at home, she and her older sister, Asunción (or Chifis), were responsible for many of the daily domestic chores, including washing, ironing, and cleaning for a family of twelve. (The eldest sibling, Sanjuana, who had been responsible for much of the housework, had recently married and moved out to live with her spouse and his family.) The household's increasing impoverishment, as a result of the stepfather's poor financial planning and misappropriation of the family estate left behind by Conchita's biological father, who was killed by an unknown assailant when she was a child, also meant that her labor was crucial to the unit. Moreover, when she did not tend to domestic chores, Conchita focused on her studies, as she was nearing the completion of la secundaria, which took up any spare time she might otherwise have been able to dedicate to corresponding. Yet, Conchita had not completely closed her mind to the idea of the courtship and the attention and flattery that came with it, as her sister Asunción recalled years later. Conchita said encouragingly, "But if you have more time which I don't think is the case, and if it is, you do it that I, as soon as I can, will respond to them."[49]

Aware of the growing disinterest signaled by Conchita's correspondence, despite his aggressive epistolary campaign, José made an unplanned trip to Calvillo to rescue the fledgling relationship. The visit, though brief and unannounced, was significant, for it meant risking his employment and his relationship with his boss. At the same time, the trip motivated him to continue to pursue the courtship, and he hoped it would do the same for her. However, the day he arrived in Calvillo and throughout the entire weeklong stay, he neglected to tell her the depth of his longing and loneliness, likely because he lacked the practice—not the vocabulary—to do so, as he and his siblings seldom demonstrated affect, such as expressing *palabras de amor* (terms of endearment) or enacting an intimate physical gesture like an embrace.[50] As Paco mentioned years later, all the siblings rarely received what we in the United States today consider overt signs of affection between loving parents and children. Paco explained, though, that lacking a hug or kiss from their mother or father did not mean that their parents did not love or care for them. Instead, their parents expressed their affection in other ways: by supporting and maintaining them and providing for all their basic needs and wants, despite dire poverty and lack of economic opportunity.[51]

Rather than express his emotions in person, José saved his most sincere and familiar form of intimate communication—the letter—for when he returned to Imperial Valley, a distance safe from potential personal, face-to-face rejection. José did not write immediately after he returned, however, hoping she might express an interest and do so before he wrote and thereby ease his doubts of her commitment to the relationship. The wait, however, was unbearable. When he wrote ten days later, he admitted that it "felt like 10 years." Despite her lack of correspondence, José remained devoted. "I am writing to you to tell you that I have not forgotten you and . . . I wish that you too would think of me, if you only knew how much I wish that you would grow to love me for that is what I long for (*hanhelo*) most."[52]

José's somber mood turned even more glum as he recounted his dreary living and working conditions in Imperial Valley. "Today was Sunday and I had to work the day," he explained, "the day was terrible (*feo*) it was windy and I spent the day remembering you." Such momentary melancholic thoughts, though woeful, also seemed to lift his spirits, even if temporarily. "I felt happy," he said, "because it was as if I saw you and since I expected to receive a letter from you soon that is what made me happy." "I told myself that it didn't matter how much I waited for you as long as you didn't forget me." As he had confided in the past and would reiterate periodically, she had helped settle the uncertainty in his life and the arrival of her letters put him in an emotional state. "Look now that I have met you I feel happy (*feliz*) I don't know how to explain it to you but it's that before I lived without faith or hope I didn't know what to do I wanted to return to Calvillo and never return here again. Sometimes I said this to my father and he advised me to stay that later I would want to return." More than likely his father, a former migrant, understood the lure of the economic security of the north. "Believe me," José concluded his letter in a tone of desperation, "that I will not defraud your love (*no defraudaré tu cariño*) . . . In my life I have dreamed of marrying the young woman who reciprocates (*me corresponde*) my affection (*cariño*) and dedicate my life to her . . . and I want that *muchacha* to be you, you have everything that I value and desire."[53]

José's confessions seemed to work, for a few days later Conchita responded to his pleas but did so with brutal honesty. "Look I love you (*quiero*) with a cariño very different from love (*amor*), well (let's see if you understand) I wish I could reciprocate your feelings, but as you know you cannot obligate the heart." For Conchita, love was not only an emotional expression but also a physical feeling, such as having a corporal passion for another, as she had likely witnessed on screen in the movies she attended religiously in town. "I too have never fallen in love I think it is because the right moment has not arrived or because I have a very bad concept of men perhaps not all are the same except for some," she said, suggesting trouble with males in her recent past. For José, though, Conchita made an exception. "You are one of those few men in reality that we can call men and not only because they wear pants, at least I have that concept of you." Assuming he would become upset at her response, she said, "The letter you can tear it up or read it if you want but don't return it to me." She ended with an apology for her candor but also reminded him that he had asked for it.[54]

Conchita's forthright response did not lead José to despair further. Instead, this letter's arrival and detailed nature—in his view, evidence of the developing relationship—and the ones that followed in the months to come made him optimistic about their future. When José failed to receive correspondence, however, he felt empty, a void, indicating that the letters constituted the relationship. "After I got home every day and I didn't find a letter from you I felt rejected (*sentia feo*)," he told her nearly two years into the relationship. "That day . . . it was as if I knew I was going to receive a letter from you," he said. "I'm a bit of a fortune teller (*adivino*)," he joked, making light of the situation.[55]

José understood the symbolic and strategic role of the letters in holding her interest in the relationship, and he used them repeatedly to draw her into what he described as a lonely and isolated, homosocial, gendered world that needed sustained female companionship, which could come only through marriage and not brief relationships or sexual encounters. Days of significant celebration, including *el 10 de mayo*, Mother's Day in Mexico, led him to feel particularly melancholic, he told her. "Tell me about the celebration they carried out for the mothers on this day since today is the 10th," he said. "You know I spent the whole day remembering everything about over there (*allá*), about my mother, about you about the festivity well about everything." "You know here I am sad (*triste*) because I don't [know] why but I don't like the environment here." More than likely the culture lacked reminders of home. "Today on the 5th (cinco de mayo) some clubs celebrated parties but I didn't go because the weather was bad and I had to work." In reality, he confessed, "I want to be over there."[56]

José's desire and longing, whether honest or embellished, continued to have little effect in stirring Conchita's heart. After a month of corresponding regularly, a second unannounced visit to Calvillo, and pleasant dreams about her, her home, and life with her, José had yet to hear words of commitment. He then decided to use gentle but firm pressure. "Shelly I have the need to ask you about something," he said in June 1964, six months after initiating the letter-writing campaign, "that I don't want you to misinterpret or that you dislike." "Is there any hope that you will love me[?]" he asked. "You know I can't lie to you . . . I feel I love you I don't know how much but I know I can love you even more," he declared. "I want to tell you something since I met you, you seemed (like I told you before) amazing (*Marabillosa*) for you are beautiful and intelligent and sincere." "Well," he said, "I cannot ask for more and perhaps I don't deserve so much but if you end up to love me I can assure you I will not defraud you."[57]

José's latest communication failed once again to elicit a response, as Conchita was preoccupied with her graduation as well as her thoughts of a future career. She was not interested in marriage and family life. Rather than insist with his request for an answer, José praised her immediate accomplishments, graduating from la secundaria, the 9th grade, the first graduating class in Calvillo. "I was going to telephone you today . . . to congratulate you," but because he guessed correctly that they did not have a phone, which were rare throughout Calvillo and most rural areas of Mexico, he decided to write. "Even though you might not believe it I feel happy in the superlative sense." "Since you took a while to respond . . . imagine how happy I was to receive your letter and your invitation." "Today all day I thought about you I imagined you or I thought of you in my mind as very happy." "Congratulationes once again," he wrote in rudimentary English, "on your graduation S[h]elley."[58]

José's emotional state, however, seemed to unravel just as quickly as it had emerged when he learned about her enthusiasm for pursuing a career, a move that could potentially take her away from Calvillo and the prospects of marriage. "I wanted to ask your opinion about studying," Conchita asked innocently. "What do you think? Would it be worth my while to continue studying? If you think so, please tell me what you would like for me to study." Though she seemed to give José extensive liberty in deciding her future, even though they had yet to make any long-term commitment, she likely asked for his opinion out of respect for the gendered expectations of the day in which women (daughters and wives) asked men (fathers and husbands) for permission to carry out decisions about their immediate and future lives. Likely, too, in her view, his worldly experience as a migrant to the United States made him a wise choice for advice. "I think you have more experience," she wrote, "and know more about life you will be able to offer me better insight, I leave it up to your criteria."[59] She wanted to study nursing or teaching, she told him, but neither seemed feasible, particularly because of the demands in her household.

José replied encouragingly and honestly, though he did so with measured enthusiasm, for he feared what such a move to an urban setting might mean for a young, impressionable rural girl. "Shelly, I am happy that you ask me about your studies and I want to tell you that whatever . . . career you like, if you can pursue it do so, even though in my egoism I feel confused but I understand that I can imagine if you continue studying." Attempting to cover his tracks about his mixed messages, José explained: "Don't pay any attention to my last comment or much less to what people will say (*lo que diga la gente*) what I do wish with all my heart is that you don't leave town but alas as the saying goes let it be God's will."[60] Doubtless, José worried that if she moved to an urban area, likely Aguascalientes, twenty-six miles from Calvillo, she might be exposed to negative influences that might taint or corrupt her sexual virtue, honor, and reputation and, by extension, his as well as that of their families. This belief was not uncommon in Calvillo, as many men and women in the community believed that sending young females to the university in urban areas corrupted them morally. Moreover, the belief in the trope of the "peasant in the city" and the personal corruption that followed was a powerful one that José and many of his fellow Calvillenses believed. As Gerber has noted, scholars have identified such beliefs among rural folk reaching back hundreds of years. Indeed, for José, the thought of her move to the city provoked anxiety. "I hope I can go there quickly," he told her nervously, "so that we can talk about this." "You know I have the urge to be over there for a few months since every time I go I stay for very little time . . . but . . . next time I am going to stay at least three months hopefully . . . they will be more."[61]

José's promises about visiting home, while perhaps uplifting to Conchita's ears, were disingenuous and likely made to buy himself time. He knew he could not leave work in the summer months because of the demands imposed by the capitalist agricultural system of Imperial Valley. "Shelly I really do want to go but right now I can't because I have a lot of work and I don't want to leave it because they would put someone else in my place." "Right now in this month we are preparing to plant *remolacha* (sugar beets) and I think my plans for the trip are sound," he concluded, asking for patience.[62]

Bridging the Geographic, Physical, and Emotional Divide

To bridge the divide between Conchita and himself, José employed a repertoire of cultural tools to draw her closer and build a deeper connection than he had been able to do with the correspondence and its content alone. Among those tools was his beautifully crafted, highly stylized writing. Conscious of their differences in schooling, José doubtless worked hard to pen nearly perfect, lengthy, longhand letters, sometimes on unlined sheets of paper, hoping to convince her of his refinement, even with his limited formal education, common among rural and poor Mexicans such as José. Indeed, in the 1950s and 1960s, education in Mexico remained limited, especially among the rural population, despite the enactment of compulsory primary education laws in the 1920s and 1930s and the gains in midcentury among urban dwellers. According to Mexican researchers, in 1940, at about the time José attended school, only 44 percent of children (six to fourteen years of age) were enrolled in primary schooling. Doubtless, even fewer completed their studies, particularly in rural areas. Indeed, José's sixth grade education was the highest achieved among his five siblings. Conchita's ninth grade education was perhaps even more unusual for a young woman from a largely rural upbringing. According to Mexican government statistics, in 1960, when Conchita attended secundaria, about 700,000 children in Mexico attended middle school, the majority of them in urban centers. In the early 1970s in Aguascalientes fewer than half the children eligible for secundaria attended school.[63]

Comparing correspondence between José and Conchita with that between José and his younger brother, Paco, written at the same time, reveals that José took extra time as well as care in composing letters to Conchita, for the penmanship was neater and more consistent in his letters to his potential mate. José's punctuation was, however, inconsistent, but not any less so than that of Conchita or that in letters between José and Paco. According to Gerber, the use of inconsistent punctuation is quite common among nineteenth-century European immigrant correspondents and, according to Larry Siems, among late twentieth-century Mexican and Central American immigrant letter writers as well.[64]

From the start, José's deliberate letter-writing tactic appeared to work. Conchita was so dazzled with his skill, she confessed, that she attempted to emulate it, with little success. "It might seem strange to you that I write to you on paper without lines but you know I was becoming envious seeing that you do it and you keep your handwriting quite straight but regardless of how hard I try," she said a few months into the courtship. "You can see that I don't manage to keep a straight line, some lines go towards the heavens and others probably hell and in the end everything is a disaster," she joked, revealing a lighter side of her personality that would become apparent.[65] Her words seemed to encourage him, for he continued to write cleanly through the three-year courtship, while her writing remained less clear and, at times, illegible.

José not only used his penmanship to win her over but also his English-language skills. His earlier correspondence had hinted at, or rather overstated, his English-speaking abilities, particularly when he called her "Shelly" or used other English-language words sporadically in his attempt to convince her of his adaptation to the dominant language and, by extension, culture. José, however, had far from mastered English, as his subsequent writings revealed, particularly after Conchita initiated a friendly language competition early in the courtship. "I want to ask you some questions let's see how well you are doing with English don't get upset, if you have the time, you'll respond and if you don't it's not an obligation." In a list, she wrote: "honey, honeymoon, sweetheart, Christmas Eve, handbag, bear, monkey, bird, short sighted, chicken." "Every word is worth one point respond to me in Spanish and . . . I will send you your grade." Conchita then asked him to do the same, sending her a list of words. "Ah! And you send me another," she said, hoping to continue the exchange, "easy like the way I have done for you, alright?"[66] Demonstrating interest, José replied to the quiz, answering most of the words correctly, except for "eve" and "short sighted." "Well, you grade them the way you have studied them," he explained, "but here the English language is modified when spoken," suggesting he might not need to know formal English, since the colloquial version was more commonly used, particularly among farmworkers and their employers.[67]

While José dismissed the need to know formal English, Conchita's quizzes compelled him to consider his rudimentary language skills, given that he had resided in the United States for more than five years and knew little English. He had spent much of that time among Spanish-speaking laborers who had limited formal education as well as English skills. "You know classes have started here in the barrio . . . but I haven't gone more than one day," he said. "I didn't like it much but perhaps I'll keep going," he said, hoping to impress her. José admitted, though, that his English was poor. "I don't think it is written correctly for what I know is based on what I have learned by ear I only read two lessons of 'La National Schools' [a popular correspondence school originating in Los Angeles in the early 1900s and used throughout Latin America for learning English and technical trades] before I came here," he explained. "If it wasn't for that, I wouldn't even know how to say 'yes,'" he said sheepishly.[68]

Despite José's apprehension with English, he continued with the language lesson and used it as an opportunity to reinforce his proposal. But because of his spelling errors, she had been unable to understand what he meant. He then stepped in quickly to clarify the meaning. "I'm going to tell you the ones you didn't know so Attention! First: I really=*yo realmente*. Wish=*deseo* y Marriagge is matrimony that is why I think I have a good grade," he joked, even though he admitted he had erred.[69] To demonstrate his interest in improving his skills, he repeated his intent. "You know once the class starts in the next session I am going to go to see if I can learn something and then I will send you questionnaires alright!"[70] Despite José's plan, he never enrolled in the class, and they ended much of their communication in English.

While the word games kept Conchita's interest in corresponding with José, the exchange of personal photographs proved even more significant, for they brought their physical likeness into sharp relief and provided tangible evidence of the relationship, until then, constituted primarily through the correspondence. Early on in the courtship, they had agreed to exchange photographs, but José's fear that she might respond negatively to his portrait delayed him from sending a snapshot that satisfied him, for he was unsure of his looks. José had a prominent and relatively fresh scar on his right cheek as a consequence of a serious car accident he had suffered a few years earlier on a brief trip home to Calvillo from Imperial Valley. And, in all likelihood, he worried that the scar as well as others he had developed from years of adult acne would repel her. Unaware of his fears, Conchita was most concerned about the wait. When she finally received the image, she was relieved. "You really had me intrigued with the tardiness of your reply I even began to think that you had been offended with something I said or I didn't know what to think." The wait for the photograph, though, "was worth it for I loved the photo (*me encantó*)."[71]

For José, the exchange of pictures, though unnerving, occupied a central role in the long-distance courtship, for the photos worked to render them closer physically and emotionally than they had been in the past, diminishing his longing. Photos can also cause anguish, as Sonia Cancian reminds us, in recalling the absence of a loved one, but to what extent José experienced personal pain in viewing Conchita's image is unknown, for he never expressed such feelings.[72] What is known is that the images brought him solace. "Something that may seem simple to you," he said about his epistolary practice, "is that I write a few sentences and then I turn to see your photograph the large one the one that sits in front of me and it seems to me that I am speaking to you." The idea was not impossible to fathom, he explained, "as the mind and the soul can overcome the distance so when you read this imagine that we are together."[73] To bring her likeness and their relationship into his daily life, he kept her portraits out in the open, among his most prized possessions. José's attempt to animate her presence with the photographs was not (and is not) an uncommon practice. According to Gerber, British immigrants in the nineteenth century frequently used that approach.[74] "Your photographs I have them in front of the radio," José explained. "Look in one of them you and Chifis are seated in front of the kitchen of my house and in the other you are with your hands close together and smiling I don't know what you were saying but I see you very happy. Do you recall what you said when they snapped your picture?"[75]

The seemingly simple act of exchanging photographs was not an easy matter, especially for relatively impoverished Mexicans, for neither José nor Conchita owned a personal camera. Nor did they have the resources to pay for studio-quality photographs even though they desired them. More frequently, they relied on Paco for the occasional photo, as he frequently borrowed cameras and snapped shots of quotidian life in Calvillo. For José, however, living alone in Imperial Valley, carving out time from work and other responsibilities to have his picture taken in Mexicali, where he tended to most of his personal services, was no trivial matter. Conchita, too, had to find the means to travel to Aguascalientes to have her picture taken there, as she disliked the quality of photography in Calvillo. "I am not sending my caricature," she explained, "because I have not been able to go to Aguas[calientes]." "Here," in Calvillo, the images "come out uglier than the person hopefully I can go soon if you have some send them to me, yes?"[76] Despite her protests, José reassured her about her likeness yet remained unsure of his own. "I really liked your photograph, I don't know why you didn't," he said. My image, he said, "looks like a caricature and not yours it's not the photographer's fault," he explained, disparaging his image, "it's just that I am that ugly if not worse."[77]

Though José expressed dissatisfaction with the image and others he sent, he prized them and asked for their return when she tired of them, knowing they were difficult to procure. As José explained to Conchita, in reference to a picture in which he posed with dark sunglasses, looking *"bastante sangrón* (very conceited)," in front of a prized possession, an automobile, "if you don't like them I do and a lot for that reason don't fail to return them to me."[78]

While photographs provided a vivid reminder of each other's likeness across the vast divide, Spanish-language songs encouraged a deep, thoughtful connection, as they touched an emotional core, strengthening the epistolary-based relationship. Like many Mexican farmworkers of his day, including braceros, José enjoyed listening to Spanish-language music, for it brought reminders of home, family, and culture.[79] As he told Conchita, he listened to tunes in the car, on his way to and from work, at home on a transistor radio, and, later, on a phonograph (*tocadiscos*) that he purchased specifically to hear records he shared with her. For José, the lyrics of the music served as a primary form of intimate expression and personal communication with Conchita, assisting him with the language, tone, and mood he needed to conquer her heart. "You know," he told her, "I wanted to tell you about a song that is new and when I hear it I think a lot about you it is called 'I give myself to you' (*Me regalo contigo*) the 'Impala' sing it if you haven't heard it hopefully when you hear it you will like it."[80]

Dressed in his Sunday best and posing for the photographer in front
of a symbol of social mobility, an automobile, José Chávez Esparza displayed his
playful nature, despite the hardships of life as a farmworker in Imperial Valley
in 1965. Though he referred to his image as *"bastante sangrón,"* José prized the
photograph and asked his girlfriend, María Concepción Alvarado ("Conchita"),
to whom he sent the image, to return it if she disliked it.
Photograph in author's personal collection.

Conchita, however, was not easily swayed to the music, as she was not
partial to Los Impala, a bolero-singing trio from Mexico. She preferred
young musical artists, belting out the latest Spanish-language "roc and rol"
mexicano, though she was willing to try to appreciate the tunes of Los Impala.[81] "I do like the song, but not much but now that I know that you like
it I will try and make myself like it even more." "I like 'Laverinto' by Sonia
López and 'the Mailman,'" she explained, mentioning popular ballads by a
well-known Mexican singer-actress.[82] Armed with the knowledge that

Conchita had a fondness for López, José went out and purchased her latest song, "Javersito," seizing the opportunity to strengthen his connection with her. "It's beautiful," he said weeks later. "I bought it about a month ago." He listened to it often, usually in the evenings after work, he informed her.[83]

While José and Conchita used the songs of artists such as Sonia López and Los Impala to communicate, the Spanish-language tunes of Connie Francis, an Italian American singer popular among Spanish-language listening audiences in Latin America and the United States, were among the most frequent topics of conversation, as José was particularly enamored with her music and used it in the courtship. "You know," he said in June 1964, a few months after they began writing consistently, "I'm going to ask if I can send some records in order to purchase them and if they allow me I'm going to send you those of Cony Francis."[84] This time, José's recommendation of a musical artist proved successful, for Conchita warmed quickly to her singing. "By the way I'm listening to a song that some time ago I had wanted to ask you if you liked it is called 'Invierno Triste' (Blue Winter) with Conie I don't know how to spell it but you understand who it's about given that she is your favorite."[85] "Invierno Triste" seemed to take a particularly significant role in the courtship, for the 45 rpm record is the only one that remains among the courtship letters they saved over the years. Given its worn state, they likely played that tune dozens, perhaps hundreds, of times over the years of their noviasgo and, later, their marriage.[86]

As much as José enjoyed Spanish-language music, he could not always keep up with the latest releases from Mexico. As a farmworker in Imperial Valley, he lacked the opportunity to hear the newest and broadest range of Spanish-language releases, for he resided on the edge of Mexico's northern region, far removed from the epicenter of cultural influences emanating from Mexico City. "I have not yet listened to the songs that you indicate," he explained to Conchita. "Here," in the United States, "they arrive a bit behind the songs that are in style in the interior." "Regularly the musical 'hits' are played during the day and I don't have the time to listen to the radio until the evening," after work.[87] Apparently, he preferred to listen to radio stations based in Mexico rather than in the United States, even though by 1966 there were nearly 200 Spanish-language radio stations in the Southwest, playing tunes and *novelas* (soap operas) primarily from Mexico.[88] "Perhaps that is why I have not heard them. Hopefully soon I will hear them and I will let you know if I like them or not." But, he reassured her, the songs "have a rather suggestive title and for that reason I think I will like them. Plus, 'Conny Francis' sings very beautifully, she has a beautiful voice."[89] Even if he could not listen to them on the radio, he would go to the *discoteca* (record store) and purchase them.

While José dedicated most of his listening time to Spanish-language music, he also heard and enjoyed English-language tunes, even though he could not always decipher the lyrics. And though it is unclear where he heard the songs—on a radio station based north or south of the border—he adopted them as a part of his repertoire. "Here I have heard one that I don't understand what it says as I've heard it only a few times," he told Conchita. "And I liked it I'm going to pay more attention to the title and what it says and then I'll let you know the only thing I've learned from it is 'on the mis[s]ing moon light' I can't translate it, but I think they are going to translate it" into Spanish, he inferred. "That is what has happened to a lot of songs that I have liked even the new songs."[90]

José's enjoyment of English-language music did not, however, eclipse the role of Spanish-language tunes in his life, for it transported him to faraway yet familiar places, spaces, and moments occupied by family, friends, and loved ones, especially Conchita, providing him with the emotional relief he needed to cope with living between here and there. After his holiday visit to Calvillo in December 1964, José returned especially lonely, thinking about the brief yet tender moments he and Conchita had spent together, and used music to bring him comfort. In January 1965, after his brief visit home, he told her: "Look one detail that helps me feel like I am there (*allá*) I put the radio on the XEW from Mexico as it is the only radio station from over there that reaches all the way over here (*acá*)."[91] Following a subsequent visit later that year, in August 1965, he elaborated on the emotional gratification of the music in its ability to bridge the distance. "Right now I am listening to that record of Conny F[rancis], do you remember? It is 'Quiereme mucho' (Love me deeply) it is one of the songs I like best," he confessed. "I often recall that day when we were at the rancho listening to the record . . . do you recall? It is one of the most beautiful days that I have lived and it brings me much pleasure to recall it."[92]

José used not only Spanish-language music to bridge the physical and emotional divide but also Spanish-language programming on radio stations across the borderlands and as far south as Mexico City. Among the most popular programming was music, including the "top hits," soap operas (novelas), and news (*noticias*), respectively. Some of those stations also made time for call-in dedications, enabling listeners to tune in for messages from their sweethearts.[93] In the evenings, after work, José enjoyed listening to XED, a border blaster from Mexicali, whose "hits and forecasts" (*exitos y pronosticos*) reached northern Mexico and the southwestern United States. The program, however, aired in the evening, during the time he bathed, he told Conchita. Despite the limited airtime, the programming brought him much comfort, easing his evening reveries of home. "Well, you know at night I listen only to the [Mexican] diffusers from here since they have some very beautiful programs."[94]

The variety in radio programming, particularly the call-in dedication shows, provided José with the perfect opportunity to profess his love on the air for Conchita and listeners across the borderlands and into the Mexican heartland. He instructed her to tune into XELO's *Seranata Internaciónal*, an hourlong radio program in Ciudad Juárez playing tunes solicited by sweethearts. "Tell me if you can hear it so I can dedicate something to you that way we listen to it at the same time."[95] When Conchita had access to a radio, she promised José to tune in.[96] Content with the news, José responded, "On Tuesdays a disc jockey (*locutor*) goes on the air . . . and to him I want to send a request to dedicate some songs to you."[97] José's plans were foiled, however, when he learned that the disc jockey went on vacation. "Fine," he conceded, "later we will attempt that."[98]

While José and Conchita spent a significant amount of time bonding over musical interests, they also turned to popular American and Mexican films to cement their relationship. In Imperial Valley, a relatively poor agricultural and rural region, movie theaters as well as the latest English- and Spanish-language films were less available than they were in urban areas. When José wanted to see a movie he went to the small downtown district of Brawley or attended an outdoor drive-in style venue. In the summertime, when days ran longer than in the winter and when work responsibilities mounted, he had less opportunity to watch the films that came through the area.[99] "Let me know what movies you have seen here I have seen *55 dias en Pequin* . . . I also saw *La Noche de la Iguana*, which they filmed in Puerto Vallarta," he said with some authority.[100] Located on the Pacific Coast, Puerto Vallarta was an emerging tourist destination, though it had less glitz than Acapulco, further south along the coast and well known as a playground for the rich and famous in Mexico and the United States. Nevertheless, José's knowledge of the significance of Puerto Vallarta indicated to Conchita that he, as a worldly male, knew about the latest hot spots in Mexico.

In Mexico, attending the movie theater was a mainstay in rural as well as urban areas, among young and old alike, even though the golden age of Mexican film had declined by the 1960s. Despite the scarcity of theaters in pueblos such as Calvillo, especially in the 1940s and 1950s, moviegoers enjoyed watching Spanish- and English-language films religiously, according to longtime resident Eligio Hernández, and did so on outdoor screens provided by traveling film companies. Those same companies, in turn, eventually sold their rights to local businessmen, Hernández among them. Within a few years, by the late 1950s, one main theater, Cine Azteca, emerged on one of the two main thoroughfares in town. That location, in turn, helped bring in a sizable clientele, though doubtless the crowd-pleasing nature of the American and Mexican film industries contributed to the regularly packed movie house.[101]

Conchita was among those who regularly filled the movie theater on nearly a daily basis hoping to catch a glimpse of well-known Mexican stars including Pedro Infante, María Felix, and Mario Moreno (known as Cantinflas) as well as foreign-born actors, including Miroslava (Stern), a Czechoslovakian immigrant, among others, who dominated the Spanish-language silver screen. She had, as a consequence, seen more films than José. Her ability to attend frequently was facilitated by her close childhood friendship with Dolores "Lola" Salazar Rodríguez, whose family co-owned Cine Azteca, giving Conchita the opportunity to attend at little to no cost. There, at the theater, she and her friends watched classic Mexican films, many of them 1940s and 1950s *comedias ranchera* with heroic *charros* (rural male peasants) set in a golden past, as well contemporary movies with views of urban life in the modern metropolis of Mexico City. As Paco recalled years later, those images of modernity influenced audiences in Calvillo, for townsfolk had rarely, if ever, seen the latest consumer goods and household conveniences, such as refrigerators and televisions, as well as the newest modes of transportation, such as state-of-the-art automobiles. (At that time, no more than a dozen cars filled the streets of the pueblo, and televisions were useless, for the signal could not reach the town, which is situated in a valley.)[102] Subsidized by the government with backing from the United States, the moving images represented state-sponsored cultural nationalism by promoting nostalgia for *lo mexicano* even while the Mexican government firmly promoted and invested in a modern, urban-oriented future. Mexican films Conchita saw included *Las novias de mis hijos* (1964) and *En la vieja California* (1962).[103]

Conchita also rarely missed the popular Hollywood, English-language films that came through town. Subtitled in Spanish, and consisting of a mix of classic and recent movies, they remained the most favored of all those shown in Mexico particularly and Latin America more generally. As the film scholar Gaiska S. de Usabel has found, "Hollywood stars and stories dominated Latin American screens."[104] Those images often portrayed idealized splendors of el norte, including views of the U.S. South, as portrayed in *Gone with the Wind* (*Lo que el viento se llevó*, 1940), which alone ran for three years in Mexico City. It played in Calvillo as well, for Paco recalled years later watching the film in Mexico. When not observing religious days, Conchita could be found in the theater seeing American films such as *El ladron de Bagdad* (*The Thief of Bagdad*, 1960), *El Americano feo* (*The Ugly American*, 1963), and many more, she explained to José.[105] Though burdened by housework, schoolwork, religious observances, and, later, a brief stint of employment in municipal government, Conchita had the flexibility to see the latest movies and took advantage of the opportunity to escape the burdens of her household. She could not, therefore, discuss many of the same films with José, though she did convey her passion for the industry.

Saying "I Do" and Struggling to Forge Ahead

After more than two years of working to win her heart and hand in marriage, José moved ahead in planning the ceremony, though Conchita had yet to say yes to his proposal. Neither the correspondence nor the oral histories indicate that she ever agreed verbally prior to the ceremony. The only evidence of her growing acceptance of his proposal is in one of José's letters, which he sent in April 1966 shortly after he returned to Imperial Valley from Calvillo. "Conchita if you saw how happy I returned this time it wasn't like the other when I came home very sad," he confessed. "I wish the days would turn to seconds so that I could go [to Calvillo] and no longer separate ourselves," he continued, "there are so many thing[s] I wish I could tell you but I can't because I wish to tell you them all at once and I think that only one word can suffice and that word is 'I love you.'"[106]

Despite José's joy over the impending ceremony, Conchita remained ambivalent about the marriage and likely went along with the marital plans thinking she might be able to change her mind later, as they had not set a definitive date and would not do so for months. Conchita's uncertainty toward the marriage was no secret, particularly to José, who, in May 1966, begged for answers to her emotional and romantic investment in the relationship. "My biggest fears have been that you do not grow to love me and that you end up terminating our relationship but today everything seems different and I give thanks to the heavens for having such a hope a beautiful love and that hope and love is you." He continued, "You have no idea how happy I feel and even more when I start to think that soon my dream will come true . . . however it may be we need to marry quickly."[107]

Despite Conchita's hesitancy, José proceeded with the wedding plans and instructed Conchita to inquire at the consulate in Guadalajara about the documentation she would need to obtain her visa or permanent residency. Though they had not yet set a date for the ceremony, José had hoped to speed the migratory process and thereby lessen the time they would have to wait for her to migrate once they had reached *la frontera*. With the reality of the marriage and the move to el norte impending, Conchita expressed uncertainty. "You should see how scared I get when you tell me those things I know it is necessary but I don't know what is wrong with me I wish that everything would happen like a dream so that I wouldn't have to go through that, I don't know if you go through the same thing but in only thinking about such difficulties (*lio*) I get nervous."[108] Sensing her apprehension, José instructed her to disregard the business with the consulate, saying he would handle it later.[109]

Despite his urgency over the migratory process, José was unsure when they would marry, for he had work and family matters to resolve. His heaviest responsibilities involved his agricultural work during the summer months as well as his father's medical concerns, which up to that point had kept him from focusing on the ceremony. His father's recent travel to the United States in an attempt to find a cure for a mysterious ailment also prevented José from returning to Calvillo.[110] Within a month, by August 1966, after receiving the tragic news his father would not recover from what turned out to be Parkinson's disease, José gathered his strength and plowed ahead with the wedding plans, informing a handful people about his upcoming nuptials. Two weeks later, he left work and traveled to Calvillo to make arrangements for a relatively quick and simple wedding, as he told his youngest brother, Paco.[111] By early September of that year, José and Conchita had married and three days later were on their way to Mexicali, from where they would prepare for her migration to the United States. Those plans stalled, however, when they faced a number of financial and health crises at the border that sent José reeling, at a loss to find a way out of his difficulties and onto a stable path.

At the crux of his problems in the months ahead were mounting financial troubles as well as Conchita's pregnancy and medical difficulties. As José explained to Paco, who, by December 1966, was living with Jesús—the oldest brother—in San José, California, José's treasured car and only form of transportation to and from work and across the international border had broken down. To repair it, José would have to shell out $100, a sum he could not afford but agreed was worth the trouble. In the meantime, he had borrowed the car of the compadre who had given him and Conchita temporary lodging in Mexicali. He felt shame (*pena*), he told Paco in his letter, over his inability to provide for his family. Conchita's health and delicate pregnancy concerned José as well, for when he took her to a clinic for medical care she experienced an adverse reaction to an injection, which nearly killed her. José had to leave her overnight at the facility to recover. José's inability to borrow money from friends in town because of the holidays had left him unable to pay for the auto repair or to purchase any gifts at Christmas. "Well, I cannot find my way out," he confessed.[112] What José needed most was a bit of money, twenty dollars, from either Paco or Jesús. Feeling low, José hoped his brothers would come through not only financially but also personally by visiting him in Mexicali, as he longed for their emotional support.

Two weeks later, José's situation had grown dire, as he learned Conchita's migratory process would take at least a year or more rather than the three months he had anticipated, forcing them to find an alternative residence with the little means at their disposal. "Now I will have to rent a house for it is not possible to live *de arrimado* (as a freeloader) you know it is difficult and I had not attempted to find a house."[113] They needed a home, José explained, as Conchita was nearly two months pregnant and in a delicate state, as she was prone to miscarry. Given her health, José had spent many days taking her to a doctor in a local clinic in Mexicali. For these reasons, José explained to Paco, he needed to borrow more money—in addition to the much welcomed twenty dollars Paco had already sent during Christmas—to furnish the dwelling.

For the next several months, José and Conchita managed to scrape by with what little they had with the support of family and friends. To cover the costs of Conchita's pregnancy, they continued to attend the local free clinic, where she gave birth to healthy baby boy Juan Gualberto in July 1967. Conchita suffered terribly after the cesarean surgery, however, as a result of a poorly stitched incision. Chifis, who lived with them in Mexicali during Conchita's pregnancy, recalled years later that Conchita's wound had become infected and that she suffered days with fever and chills. Treatment at an alternative clinic eventually brought relief.[114]

With their new son in tow and José back at work in Imperial Valley, their living situation stabilized, and they never lost hope for a better future. As José told Paco earlier that year, in February 1967, as soon as Conchita gained her residency, they would consider moving to San José, the emerging center of Silicon Valley, where jobs in light industry and the service sector were more plentiful, better paid, and less strenuous than in agriculture in Imperial Valley. Finally, a year later, after the birth of daughter Miroslava in November 1968, Conchita and the children obtained their residency, enabling the family to move across the border to Imperial Valley, where they resided for a few years until their final move to the south Bay Area.

By 1972, José and Conchita, like many contemporary migrants, made plans to leave behind agricultural work in a rural area for industrial, service work in an urban zone. With the support of his brother Paco, who had found José a job in a paint-making factory, they moved to San José, joining the thousands of migrants from Mexico heading to the cities in the 1960s and 1970s looking for work in the rapidly expanding service and construction economies, spurred by the growing needs of educated, middle-class workers in the technological sectors of the economy. There, José and his family would establish roots and work to build an economically stable life.

THE EPISTOLARY PRACTICES of José Chávez Esparza, a Mexican male migrant residing in the U.S.-Mexico borderlands in the 1950s and 1960s, reveal the deep longing and loneliness he experienced living and working in a harsh and isolated region he scarcely called home. Yet, those same practices revealed that he was neither ambitious nor content about returning to Calvillo, Aguascalientes, his hometown, where his economic prospects for establishing and maintaining a family, a defining feature of Mexican masculinity, were dim. Instead, José's letters demonstrate that he desired to establish and cultivate a life with a female companion who could fulfill his innermost desires for a stable home, a loving family, and a prosperous future. Those goals would not be easily achieved. Rather, he worked diligently to convince his future wife to marry him and migrate, and he did so through the use of a repertoire of cultural tools. They included beautifully crafted, handwritten Spanish-language letters, the English language, photographs, songs, and radio programming as well as films. His efforts eventually bore fruit, as Conchita warmed to his proposal, leading her to entertain the possibility of becoming his wife and moving to the U.S.-Mexico border region and ultimately the United States.

José's letter-writing campaign to win Conchita's heart indicates that he, like the many British immigrant authors Gerber identified in the nineteenth century, used strategic language, including sophisticated, florid words as well as self-deprecating terms, to reinvent the self and craft a new identity.

In José's case, he presented himself as a sophisticated, urbane, and well-mannered man who, at times, needed rescuing from the loneliness that came from leading the life of a migrant away from home and in a foreign land seeking an improved existence. Yet, unlike those same British immigrant authors, José was willing to break with epistolary conventions—such as regulative writing, including waiting for a return letter—in order to secure what he sensed were slipping quickly from his grip: Conchita's attention and her hand in marriage. José's risky behavior of writing letter after letter while receiving none from her in return, a move that might easily have turned her off from corresponding, did not backfire, however, for she eventually fulfilled his desire for marriage and a family, which brought with it a patriarchal, hierarchical, and heterosexual structure.

As the next chapter indicates, Conchita's decision to marry and migrate did not come easily or quickly, as she was a young, spirited woman attempting to define her identity in her family and larger community. As one of the eldest among fourteen brothers and sisters, she understood the growing severity of her family's impoverishment and that she needed to help provide food, clothing, and education for younger members of the family. It was only after she realized that her future and that of her family were severely limited economically and might prosper only by her marriage and emigration to la frontera that she went along with the proposal.

Tu Peor Es Nada
Gender, Courtship, and Marriage

In August 1964, a month after celebrating her graduation from *la secundaria*, middle school, in Calvillo, Aguascalientes, María Concepción "Conchita" Alvarado, an outgoing eighteen-year-old young woman, wrote to José Chávez Esparza, her professed admirer, with devastating news. Her hopes to pursue a career, she informed him, had ended. Though she did not explain the reasons, in all likelihood her household's growing size—two older sisters, ten younger brothers and sisters, and one more on the way—along with the family's increasing impoverishment required her to stay home and help support the family. Much to her dismay, she would not journey to Aguascalientes, the state capital, to study nursing, teaching, or some other field. Until then, her mother, Natalia Loera, had been supportive of her studies, taking pride in her education, while the majority of her siblings ended their education with *la primaria*, elementary school. According to her older sister, Asunción "Chifis" or "Chonita" Alvarado, Conchita had the privilege of studying and hanging out with her school friends. Chifis, in contrast, had to stay home to tend to the burdensome domestic chores, given the sizable family, few household conveniences, and dwindling resources.

"I am very sad," Conchita told José, a farm laborer living and working in Imperial Valley and also from Calvillo, "because I am not going off to study you can't imagine how I feel toward education (*el estudio*) that I think I'm going to go crazy (a bit more than I already am) nothing consoles me and everything seems worse."[1] José, thirteen years older and interested in marriage, was relieved to hear that she would remain in the pueblo, under her family's and, likely, the community's watchful eyes, for he worried about the impact of city life and what her move might mean for their future. José, nevertheless, remained supportive and consoled her. "I'm so sorry that you feel sad for not continuing your studies I too wanted to study when I finished la primaria but I couldn't it was too difficult and costly," he said. "Today I wish I could study something with a quick return ... but I have no idea what."[2]

Conchita's diminishing prospects for a career and the economic independence that came with it made her reevaluate not only her future prospects for economic independence but also José's recent marriage proposal, which until then she had not entertained seriously. Following Conchita's disappointing news, the tone of her correspondence with José took a noticeable shift—from lukewarm to showing considerable interest—in his personal and family life. In contrast to her response to his earlier letters, news of his plans to visit Calvillo, this time at the end of 1964 and the first year of their courtship, made Conchita particularly hopeful. "I am very happy to hear that you have decided to come and stay for a long time," she wrote. "I mean compared to the other times but I want to know more or less when you are coming," as she planned to be away at her cousin's rancho.[3] Though he postponed his trip until late December, the wait did not deflate her mood, for she was anxious to correspond and, likely, to pursue the relationship or at least have it distract her from her troubles at home. "I'm letting you know that I have returned," she said a month later, "and want to write a lot of letters so answer quickly."[4]

By the time José journeyed to Calvillo in December 1964 for his annual holiday visit, Conchita's consciousness of the need to ameliorate the economic want in her family's household as well as his desire for marriage cultivated an environment that would, over the course of time, be ripe for nuptials. Though few details remain about the holiday visit, as neither he nor she wrote many details about what transpired, for Conchita the reunion proved significant, for she expressed a warming acceptance of the relationship. She remained uncertain, however, of the marriage proposal and her feelings of love for José. Indeed, nearly two years would pass and dozens of letters be exchanged before she finally walked down the aisle and said "I do." Prior to that, she never agreed to José's proposal.

Using eighty personal letters exchanged between Conchita and José from 1963 to 1971, this chapter explores how and why Conchita, a vibrant, free-spirited young woman, eventually went through with the marriage, even though she had little interest in forming a family and had yet to express any emotional or romantic feelings of love toward José. Conchita's life as a *muchacha* (young woman) living in an insular pueblo revolved around schooling, socializing with her friends, attending the local movie theater, participating in religious and secular festivities, spending time at her cousin's rancho, and, most importantly, supporting an increasingly impoverished and conflicted household. Yet, after three years of an epistolary-based courtship across 1,500 miles of the U.S.-Mexico borderlands and three relatively brief meetings, Conchita married José and migrated to the Mexicali–Imperial Valley border where he lived and worked. In the process, she left behind her youth, her family, her closest confidante, Chifis, and the only world she had known for eighteen years.

To explore the ways in which Conchita negotiated courtship, love, and marriage and how those negotiations impacted her identity, social relations, and family dynamics, the chapter opens by examining her early life in central Mexico, in the Zacatecas–Aguascalientes Bajío region, in the 1940s and 1950s. It then examines how the tragic death of Conchita's father reshaped her family's future and stability, forcing them to reconstitute the household and to move to Calvillo. Despite the family's increasing impoverishment, Conchita was a resilient young woman who managed to take on extended domestic responsibilities, attend school, and engage in the local youth culture. As the letters between José and Conchita attest, she spent her happiest moments at the rancho, the pueblo's central square or plaza, and the local movie theater. Notwithstanding her vivacious attitude toward life, Conchita communicated gendered insecurities about her appearance, intellect, and letter writing as well as her relationship with José's family. Her disparaging remarks, however, were often performative, for in her attempts to convey an identity as a nervous, silly, and at times shallow young woman, she revealed a fierce personality. Conchita demonstrated her strength, especially when dealing with her stepfather and the family's growing impoverishment, by taking on unconventional jobs. Finally, the chapter shows that, as Conchita's family's economic troubles grew, she found José's proposal for marriage and migration to the U.S. border region increasingly inviting, as it allowed her to alleviate the economic burdens of the household, though her emotional and romantic love for José remained uncertain. Within a few years of marriage, however, Conchita developed affection for José, cementing their marital relationship.

Economy and Society in the Heart of the Bajío

In the early twentieth century, the state of Aguascalientes, like most of Mexico, was largely a rural zone sustained by agricultural and livestock production. With the exception of those in the capital city, Aguascalientes, most residents in the state lived in small towns, or pueblos, and in clusters of adobes (mud-brick homes) situated on *ejidos* (communal landholdings) and ranchos (private landholdings) scattered among two valleys, Aguascalientes and San José de Gracia-Calvillo (the latter Conchita's birthplace). Unlike the valley of Aguascalientes, Calvillo had few haciendas, or large agrarian estates, and was composed primarily of small private property holdings used primarily for farming and grazing cattle.[5] While small *proprietarios*, such as Conchita's father, Juan Alvarado Medina, managed to eke out a comfortable existence grazing cattle and other livestock, the landless—the vast majority—had no other choice than to work as common laborers. The result was a region of extreme inequality, with many Calvillenses, like many rural people living in hamlets across Mexico, suffering from poverty, lack of basic health care, little primary schooling, and inadequate infrastructure, as well as high mortality rates, especially among children, and a shorter life expectancy compared to that in the capital, Aguascalientes, and especially in Mexico City. Indeed, Calvillo's first primary public school was not established until 1957, and the pueblo remained nearly cut off from the capital until roads were built years later. In the 1950s and early 1960s, it took three hours by automobile or bus to reach Aguascalientes, some twenty-six miles from town.[6]

The onset of World War II and the Mexican government's efforts to integrate Mexico into the larger U.S. and global economy brought significant improvements to Aguascalientes, though the rural countryside, including Calvillo, saw fewer changes to everyday life. With increased government support and the expansion of state institutions, Aguascalientes witnessed the remodeling of public administration and commercial buildings, paving of streets and main avenues, and engineering of potable water and sewage systems. Electricity, the telephone, and the telegraph also became widely available, and the state school system was federalized, strengthened, and repaired, providing all children in the capital with basic education up to the sixth grade. The first housing developments and planned neighborhoods were established as well, while stables and corrals—symbols of a rural lifestyle—were outlawed in the city. Consumption of food per person increased, too, as did life expectancy—from 36.6 years to 50.6 years—and per capita income. According to Mexican scholars, these changes—part of the "Mexican Miracle"—were the result of the growth of the middle class and the urbanization of increasing numbers of people from around and beyond the state, including Calvillo, looking for economic opportunity and social stability.[7]

Urbanization did not slow down after the war. Rather, it proceeded at a steady clip, leading to the transformation of Aguascalientes from a rural to an urban state. Whereas the 1940s counted nearly half (42.6 percent) of the population living in the countryside, in places such as Calvillo, by the 1990s, those same areas accounted for a mere 15 percent of the population. The catalyst for urbanization was the rise and expansion of industrialization, especially after the 1980s, during which the rural population remained at a healthy 30 percent. The severe economic recession of the early 1980s, known as the "peso crisis"—resulting from a series of government-initiated liberal economic reforms focused on "the deregulation of markets, privatization of state enterprises, and trade liberalization," as well as increased mechanization in the countryside—forced rural people off the land to urban centers in Mexico and to the United States, a process that had begun as early as the 1950s and 1960s.[8] Later, in the 1990s, the promotion of the region as an ideal location for foreign investment in export processing, or the internal *maquila* industry, attracted investors from across the globe and gave rise to manufacturing and assembly plants, including automotive industries.[9]

Throughout the modernization of Aguascalientes, the valley of Calvillo remained largely a livestock region producing meat and dairy products, while the capital's agricultural region was focused on cultivating specialty fruits, including grapes for wine production and crops for feed and fodder, as well as vegetables such as corn and beans for consumption.[10] Unlike Aguascalientes's climate, Calvillo's semitropical environment allowed for the cultivation of its own specialty fruit, namely, guavas (*guayabas*), a yellow, fleshy, firm, seedy, and fragrant fruit that drew much attention for its appeal, transportability, and lucrative potential. Calvillenses began growing the fruit in significant amounts as early as the 1950s, when they farmed nearly 500 hectares. Within ten years, as demand increased across the region, they expanded the land under cultivation to 2,600 hectares. By the early 1990s, that figure nearly tripled, to 7,500 hectares, generating 90 percent of Mexico's guayaba crop and solidifying the deep-rooted culture of guayaba in Calvillo. Indeed, decades earlier, beginning in the 1950s, Conchita and her peers in town attended many yearly coronations of the Reina de la Guayaba (Queen of the Guava) at the annual two-week festival, held annually in December, touting the significance of the fruit to the local economy. According to María de los Angeles Crummett, the focus on la guayaba, however, led to a decrease in food production, particularly corn and beans. Eventually, overproduction of guavas, increased competition, and policies favoring large growers led to a crisis in the industry, sending prices on a downward spiral, forcing most small producers, including members of Conchita's extended family, to sell their small holdings for a fraction of their value. Livestock production and the dairy industry did manage, though, to keep pace with new fertilizers, insecticides, and other techniques, maintaining a traditional source of support for Calvillenses.[11]

Despite the swings in the local economy and the reliance of households on poorly paid embroidery work carried out by women, Calvillo's population saw steady expansion from the 1950s through the 1980s. In 1950, the population of the town stood at 3,006 and that of the municipality as a whole at 14,202. Ten years later, in 1960, those numbers climbed to 5,735 and 19,758, respectively, and in 1970 to 7,376 and 24,178, respectively. By 1980, by the time Conchita's family migrated to a larger urban area, the population had grown to 12,544 in town and 37,009 in the municipality.[12] Though it is unclear to what extent the growth was a result of internal migration from ranchos to the pueblo, a high birthrate contributed to the expansion. The large size of Conchita's family was not uncommon, as it reflected Mexico's burgeoning population, the growth of which was aided by improvements in health care. By the 1960s, the annual birthrate was 3.4 percent, one of the highest in the world.[13]

Conchita spent her formative years in the rural culture of the bajío. Born in the Bajío del Palo Quemado in Zacatecas, on a rancho in the sierra neighboring Aguascalientes, she lived with her parents, Natalia Loera and Juan Alvarado, two older sisters, Sanjuana and Chifis, and, eventually, two younger brothers, Juan and Enrique, tending to livestock and agriculture. Conchita never met the oldest brother, Abel, for he had died at the age of six months from one of the common childhood ailments that claimed the lives of many children due to the scarcity of basic health care. Conchita's father was well versed in maintaining ranchos, for he had previously owned another property, La Congoja, in the sierra of Aguascalientes but was forced to sell it to unknown persons when he began losing some of the land years earlier, presumably to the revolutionary government of Mexico.[14]

Juan's purchase of the Palo Quemado proved fruitful, as the land was fertile and produced healthy amounts of corn, squash, and beans and supported livestock, enabling him to sustain the household. Years later Asunción recalled that the rancho served as a central place and space for the extended family, composed of the immediate members as well as cousins, aunts and uncles, grandparents, and often *compadres* and *comadres*. Conchita and many of her siblings were born at the rancho, as were many of their cousins. Family gatherings were common at the rancho, with sometimes up to thirty or forty children at the property exploring its outer reaches. Many of those same cousins—the older ones—helped work the land as well. All that ended, however, when Juan's life was cut short following turmoil with neighbors.[15]

The family's trouble began sometime in the late 1940s or early 1950s, when Juan decided to protect his food and feed supply from the neighbors' animals, which often ravaged his property on their way to the main water source. To do so, he fenced the rancho, which was rarely done, as most lands remained open, and in doing so he blocked access to the animals' water supply. Disgruntled neighbors, in turn, took the liberty of tearing down portions of the structure to allow their animals access. In the process, the livestock not only drank the water but also ate the corn and destroyed other crops. To prevent his neighbors from ruining his property, Juan went to town to issue a formal complaint. When he finished his business and headed back to his rancho, an unknown assailant—likely unhappy neighbors, according to Juan, Conchita's younger brother, who recalled the incident years later—shot him in the back and killed him.[16]

After the devastating loss of Conchita's father, the family experienced much turmoil and want. "We were orphaned and suffered a lot," Asunción explained through tears years later. "My poor father," she said, reflecting on his unfortunate death, "he could have done a lot in his life, he didn't deserve what happened to him . . . What injustice." Asunción explained that she was particularly close to him and recalled the personal and emotional impact of that loss. "He used to take me riding on horseback," she remembered. After his death, she said, "I recall that every time it was the afternoon and I didn't see that he arrived at the rancho I felt an intense suffering (*tremendo sufrimiento*), I was very close to him." She was a mere child, she explained. "I didn't know why he didn't return, and I asked every day why he didn't return." Her mother, Natalia, however, apparently preferred to spare her the pain of telling her the truth about her father's sudden and tragic death.

When Juan died, Natalia, his young widow (about fifteen years younger, an age difference that was common in rural areas at the time), was left with five children—the youngest only days old—a sizable rancho, and workers to manage, making for heavy responsibilities.[17] According to Conchita's brother Juan, members of the extended family from near and far flocked to the property in the wake of their father's death. They did so not to assist the widowed Natalia and the children but to take advantage of Juan's passing, removing what they could claim as their own, including livestock. To stabilize her family, Natalia remarried within two years. Soon after, the new husband, José Escalera, likely with Natalia's consent, made the decision to sell portions of the property to maintain the family. Years later, Juan Gallegos Díaz, Sanjuana's husband, confirmed that Escalera had taken the liberty to dispose of their means. He "sold everything, all the cattle he sold it."[18] Paco Chávez, a staff worker in Calvillo's municipal government at the time and Conchita's future brother-in-law, also recalled witnessing Escalera's questionable sales of the family estate. The legality of José's and Natalia's ability to sell the property, much of which belonged to Juan Alvarado's five heirs—Sanjuana, Asunción, Conchita, Juan, and Enrique—remains unresolved. According to Juan, the son, Natalia held only about fifty hectares of property in her name, as a separate property, allowed under Mexican civil law. The rest belonged to the children. "I don't know how they worked it to sell everything," Juan explained decades later. "They sold property that was in our name." Apparently, José and Natalia had informed the local officials that the proceeds of the sales were to benefit the children's education. But few of them, Juan pointed out, studied beyond la primaria with the exception of Conchita.[19] Within five or six years, after the birth of an additional five children, a significant proportion of the rancho property had been sold as well, including livestock, furnishings, and personal belongings, and much of the money spent, forcing the family of twelve to move to Calvillo to make ends meet.

Life in the Pueblo

For Conchita and the older siblings, Sanjuana and Asunción, living in Calvillo with dwindling means as well as seven younger siblings and four or more on the way was onerous. Gender norms prescribed that females carry out many of the tedious and labor-intensive domestic chores. "Childhood was hard for the older ones," all of them females, Juan recalled. For many years, though, Sanjuana, as the eldest female and sibling, held primary responsibility for the care of her younger brothers and sisters, acting like a surrogate mother. She tended to their hygiene, sewed dresses for the girls, cut the boys' and girls' hair as needed, and washed mounds of clothes by hand. And because there was no running water in the house, the older girls had to haul the clothes to and from the banks of a nearby river while keeping watch over some of the younger children who accompanied them to the wash. A few years later, when they had water lines installed in the house, chores eased, but household tasks remained demanding.[20]

When the twenty-year-old Sanjuana married and moved out to live with her spouse and his family sometime in 1961, Conchita and Asunción took on primary responsibility for the household, while their mother tended to the preparation of meals and other duties. Asunción, however, carried much of the burden of washing, hanging, and ironing the clothes, for Conchita was often busy with her studies and friends, as she had enrolled in the inaugural secundaria in 1962, and Natalia gave her time off to pursue her academics. According to Asunción, who recalled the past with bittersweet memories, Conchita was her mother's "*consentida* (favorite child)... what she said was law." "I say this because ... Conchita looked a lot like her," Asunción explained years later. "Everyone would say 'she is your mother.'" As a result, Asunción rationalized, her mother "gave her preference." Among the siblings, Asunción said, their mother "was the most tender (*cariñosa*) with Conchita. She would come home and say 'mother of all mothers, how I love you.'" Asunción, meanwhile, was entrusted with a considerable amount of chores, as she had ended her studies with la primaria, which was common among females in the pueblo. It was much more uncommon for females to continue their education, and in doing so Conchita broke with gender conventions. In fact, she was one of two females out of a total of twelve students in the incoming class. Diana Velázquez Mercado, who attended the same school a few years later, affirmed that young women faced harassment for defying gender norms, specifically femininity. "In those days the people of Calvillo were against [women's] education because they had still had the belief that the woman was to remain in the home, she wasn't to study." Locals taunted harshly Velázquez Mercado and her fellow female classmates. "Here come the *machorras* (dykes or lesbians) of the secundaria," they said to us, she explained, "for it was viewed negatively that we mixed with (*conviviéramos*) young males."[21] Conchita's best friend, Dolores "Lola" Salazar Rodríguez, the other female pupil in her class, recalled years later that classes were held in an old hotel and that the founding teacher, Cuauhtémoc Nieto Gutiérrez, invited teachers from outside of town to lead the classes.[22] According to Asunción, Conchita also had among the best scores (*calificaciónes*). While the accuracy of Asunción's recollections about Conchita's performance in school—or the division of labor in the household, among other topics—is not entirely verifiable, given that Conchita's grade sheet survives, indicating that she earned 7s and 8s (equivalent to Cs and Bs, respectively, in the United States) in la secundaria, Asunción's memories reveal a deep fondness for what she saw as preferential treatment for a smarter, prettier, better-dressed, and more charismatic and outgoing younger sister.[23]

As the eldest children in the household, Chifis and Conchita had to deal not only with the burdens of domestic chores but also with the strained relations with their stepfather, José Escalera, as well as increasing

Recently graduated from *la secundaria* in 1963, María
Concepción Alvarado ("Conchita") expected to continue
with her studies and embark on a career in education or
health. The family's growing economic troubles ended
those plans, however, forcing her to stay home to help
maintain the household.
Photograph in author's personal collection.

impoverishment. According to Asunción, life with Escalera was difficult,
as he generally ran the household with an iron fist. "We thought [our
mother] would benefit" from her marriage, she explained. "Later we all
suffered because he would hit her in front of us, he would mistreat us."
"Our childhood," she explained, "was very, very, very difficult and . . .
everyone suffered." "When we were young," she continued, "we didn't suffer
because we had everything in abundance. The poverty came when we moved
to Calvillo, once everything had been lost, they had sold everything." For
that reason, Asunción stated, Conchita later "worked hard for she did not
want to see our mother suffer very much."[24]

The strained family relations and increased poverty notwithstanding, Conchita and her siblings found ways to live out their childhoods in relative happiness, away from the restraint of their stepfather. For Conchita, nothing marked the innocence and free spirit of her youth more than visiting the rancho belonging to extended family members. It was located in Tayahua, Zacatecas, about forty-five miles from Calvillo. She used any excuse or opportunity to escape to that rancho, *El Uncidero*. Apparently, her mother almost always approved of her spending time there, as long as one of the two older sisters remained at home assisting with the chores, though it is unclear if the stepfather approved. Nearly a daylong ride from Calvillo, the property was located in a nearby sierra known for its lush valleys, green grasslands, and warm rivers in the summertime.

After spending two weeks at the rancho in early September 1964, Conchita felt much joy, as she expressed later in her communication with José. "If you only knew how happy (*feliz*) I spent my time at the rancho it is so beautiful that even you would have liked it, well I suppose you would not like the rancho much given that you have never lived there but I as anyone would agree am more of a country girl (*campecina*)" than a city girl.[25] She continued, "Just imagine every day we went to different parts between the ravines and hills on one occasion we went down a ravine so steep and difficult that I even felt like crying I simply closed my eyes and let the horse decide" which way to go. On the way back, "I was unable to move even a muscle and as you might imagine my cousins started laughing at me, saying weren't you supposed to be a good horserider."[26] Excited but sensing she might bore José, she said, "I want to tell you many things but they are unimportant at least for you as compared to the different diversions that you have around here," in Imperial Valley.[27] Nevertheless, for Conchita, the answer to her troubles was visiting the rancho to pass the time and relax.

While her visits to the rancho provided a carefree environment and the respite she needed from her household troubles, Conchita also fancied going out to eat (*a cenar*) with her closest school friends, Lola, Rebeca Serna Macías, Josefina Romero, and Guillermina Gallegos Díaz, and listening to music, particularly regional music by Pedro Infante as well as the increasingly popular symbol of new youth culture, "*roc and rol*," and to radio shows and on-air radio personalities, including *Doctora Corazón*, a popular Mexican version of "Dear Abby."[28] Conchita also enjoyed attending local events, including secular and religious festivities held in town throughout the year. Among her favorites were the municipal *feria* or fair held in May and the coronation of La Reina de la Guayaba in December. Conchita reveled in attending la feria and did whatever was possible to enjoy the local fair's activities, including the food and entertainment stands, bullfights and cockfights, and fireworks. She also made a point of attending the coronation of the reina. While rain sometimes disrupted the event, Conchita did not let that stop her from enjoying the evening. As she later told José, one year the inclement weather forced the coronation to be moved indoors to the movie theater, which, she said, "was no fun (*no tuvo chiste*)" but afterward, she said, the mood improved, as she and Chifis "went to the plaza (*jardin*) and since it was raining we went to a soda shop (*refresqueria*)" with Paco, José's younger brother and Asuncion's boyfriend, who "invited us," that is, paid for their drinks.[29] Though Conchita's stepfather forbade her and her older sisters to go to many of those events, his admonitions often failed to work, for they often sneaked out of the house and went without bothering to obtain his or their mother's approval, especially when heading to the movie house.

Indeed, throughout most of the year, Conchita frequented Cine Azteca, the local movie house, often going with her sister and school friends or alone on a weekly or sometimes daily basis, without her mother's or stepfather's knowledge or approval. The theater's proximity and her friendly relationship with Lola, whose family co-owned the theater, also allowed her and her friends to have frequent access, often for little or no charge.[30] When she was unable to attend, she lamented giving up one of her favorite pastimes. "Look," she told José, "I am sanctifying myself I am carrying out the [religious] exercises," which meant she had to give up her usual diversions, including the movies. "We have to be very honest and with this heat imagine what sacrifice and we also can't go to the movie theater and with how much I like to go." She admitted, "I go to the movies almost every day or rather used to."[31]

A year later, when they moved to Aguascalientes in early 1965, her love affair with the movie theater was placed on hold because of the distance and her new responsibilities. She wrote to José from Aguascalientes, "Speaking of Lola I really want to see her but more to go to the movies." "Imagine," she continued, "here I have not gone once since the movie theaters are far and I can't go alone let alone go without permission (*a escondidas*) as I used to do over there."[32]

On days and nights when she was not at the movie theater or in school, she could be found at the plaza. In Mexico for much of the nineteenth and twentieth centuries, the central squares were at the heart of the social, political, economic, and cultural life of pueblos as well as larger cities, as they were ringed by government offices, the main church, commercial and communication centers, and, often, soda fountains, restaurants, and produce markets. Calvillo's plaza, like most throughout the republic, also had fountains, a central kiosk, natural greenery for beauty, benches for relaxing and talking, and shade trees for facilitating leisure, courtship, and gossip (*chisme*). Like her peers, Conchita enjoyed the plaza, *dando la vuelta* (strolling around the square), a courtship ritual popular on Sunday evenings, when dozens and sometimes when as many as a hundred young men and women from Calvillo and nearby ranchos came to socialize at the square. Males walked in one direction and females—usually arm in arm—headed in the other, hoping to attract the gaze of a potential mate. While Conchita and José's courtship did not begin from a chance meeting at the plaza, given their differences in age—she would have been far too young and he much older and already in el norte—it served as a central reference point for social and cultural life in the pueblo.

Conchita's exuberance for social pursuits in the pueblo clashed, however, with her lack of confidence in her physical characteristics, namely, her appearance, a theme that surfaced sporadically yet consistently throughout the epistolary relationship. Two months into the courtship, for instance, in early 1964, José wrote to Conchita, characterizing her as "*muy bonita* (very beautiful)." Conchita, though, scoffed at his admiration. "I am not beautiful as you say I am considerably ugly (*horrible*), but I concede your reasoning for expressing yourself in the way that you do as you saw me at night, I think that if you saw me during the day you would not say the same thing."[33] In all likelihood, Conchita doubted his views not only because no one else had yet expressed such admiration but also because of Mexican gendered standards of beauty as represented in films with popular actresses such as María Félix and Dolores del Rio, both of whom conformed to European standards of glamour, style, and fashion, though they often portrayed roles of poor indigenous rural women.

Conchita conveyed her belief in those ideals when, a few months later, she critiqued her phenotype, arguing that she was too dark-skinned for acceptable social conventions, especially as several of her younger siblings born to José Escalera, a blue-eyed, light-skinned man, were fair and had blue, green, or hazel eyes. Wearing a white dress for her graduation in June 1964, she said, would make her look like a "*mosca en leche*" (fly in milk). She wrote to José, "It's funny don't you think?"[34] José was not amused. "Shelly, why did you say [you] were going to look like a fly in milk? I don't think you are *prieta* (dark-skinned) to say that." "You are according to my concept a bit modest," he said. Conchita's modesty, however, was offset with a strong and mature personality. He wrote: "In reality Shelly you are of a frightening (*de miedo*) character; I don't know how to say it if it is temperament or much personality something that does not go along with your age."[35] Not easily convinced of her attributes, she shot back: "You attribute a lot of qualities that don't exist within me, if I believed them I would feel wider than a rhinoceros."[36]

Conchita further revealed her self-doubts and need for affirmation about her appearance when she shared photographs with José, a task she did reluctantly. "I took my photograph for my certificate but they didn't do me any favor, I look entirely as I do." "I cannot decide whether to send it to you I really dislike it and plus it is not large like the one I gave you," she explained. "If you want it that way let me know and I will send it to you," she said. Changing the tone of her letter and looking for José's reassurance about her looks, she said playfully, "Imagine (*fíjate*), I'm thinking of taking a large one of 50 [centimeters] by 48 in width. what do you think, that I'm crazy?"[37]

Two weeks later, she wrote again, using humor primarily to disparage her recent photos, in which she and Chifis appeared together, hoping perhaps he might protest her remarks. "Look a few days ago Paco sent Chifis some photos [of us] . . . if you only saw [how] horrible we turned out '*como unas brujas*' (like witches)," she said, "(like Chifis y Concha), do you know them?" Conchita also meant to send him a picture from her youth, she continued, of when she was fourteen years old, but she decided against it because she looked "*muy gorda*," she explained, very fat. "Better yet later I will send you a ton '*para que asustes los ratones*' (so that you can scare the mice) . . . (don't be upset it is a joke)."[38]

Conchita disparaged not only her physical appearance but also her intellect and letter writing and likely did so to go along with the gender conventions of the day, which held that women's intellectual capacity was inferior to that of men's. Her sister Chifis, as well as other female letter writers, also belittled their writing, comments, and actions when they wrote to their boyfriends. While some of Paco's male friends who corresponded with him occasionally resorted to such language, the women, Chifis included, overwhelmingly participated in the practice. Early on in Conchita's epistolary relationship with José, she criticized her correspondence by writing: "Who knows what you think of my letters I don't know how to express myself my penmanship is atrocious," as she compared her writing to his own perfectly crafted handwritten notes. "I'd better not say anything more because I think I'll fill the paper and I won't finish mentioning all the defects."[39] A few months later, she continued to belittle her correspondence and did

A letter written in April 1964 by Conchita to José Chávez
Esparza, in which she attempted to exceed his epistolary
style and technique. Disparaging her letter writing,
she told him she had failed miserably.
Digital copy of letter in author's personal collection.

so more often than she disparaged her looks.[40] "Tell me how many letters
of mine you have kept unless you have burned them because they are so
dumb that is all they deserve."[41] José countered, "There are twelve of them
along with the invitation to your graduation." "I save them all along with a
detail that is going to seem 'simple' the trimmings of the envelope . . . I save
them in the same envelope. You think they deserve to be burned?" he
asked. "I even save the edgings."[42] Some fifty years later, those same trimmings remain tucked in the envelopes.

After she spent nearly two years of denigrating her letter writing, José finally asked her to end the practice, as it pained him to read her words. "Well I wanted to tell you in a special way that I feel bad (*feo*) that you end your letters with Forgive my scratch-marks (*garabatos*). I don't want you to repeat that," he instructed her. "My writing is undecipherable and I hardly ever say that to you therefore no more alright?"[43] José's comments appeared to work, but only temporarily. After a few months of halting the custom, she reverted to the old habit, leading José to ask her to stop on at least three separate occasions.

According to many friends who knew her as a young woman, Conchita's self-doubts were influenced by her early childhood experiences of losing her father suddenly, seeing her mother remarry quickly, and witnessing the family's impoverishment under the rule of a stepfather who was hard on her, her older siblings, and her mother. Rebeca Serna Macías, Conchita's childhood friend, recalled years later that "she had a strong personality, she was a good young woman, but no one could touch the people that she loved, she would get defensive (*se ponia al brinco*). I would tell her, 'Concha don't be so *broncuda* (defensive) ' . . . in primary school she would defend me." In describing Conchita and her older sister Sanjuana, Serna noted their similarities, as both were "quick to anger (*corajudas*)."[44] Pedro "Perico" Sánchez, also a friend and briefly a boyfriend of Conchita's, concurred with Serna's description. Years later, Sánchez remembered that Conchita "had a complex, you can say, no? She felt inferior, she was somewhat aggressive (*pelionera*) for the same, right . . . somebody was walking by and they would laugh and she thought they were laughing at her, right away she would respond to them."[45]

Conchita's self-doubts meant not only that she had a sensitive demeanor in social settings but also that she was a shrewd observer of those around and near to her. Her correspondence with José reveals that she was attuned to his demeanor. "José," she wrote in September or October 1964, "look, your letter disconcerts me at the beginning because it says Concepcion since you always write Conchita I thought that for some reason you had become upset but after I read it I realized it wasn't the case. It's a detail without importance," she tried to convince him, "but as I told you it disconcerted me."[46]

Conchita paid close attention, as well, to his family's interactions with her and their acceptance of her as his *novia* (girlfriend). She grew especially interested in her role in his family after she warmed to his proposal of a serious *noviasgo* (courtship) but felt slighted when they paid little attention to her. In July 1964, Conchita told José that, in response to her attempt to establish a warm, friendly relationship with his family, his younger sister, Maura Chávez Esparza, and his mother, Leovijilda "Jilda" Esparza, had treated her coolly, while they had showered Chifis, whom they knew as Paco's longtime girlfriend, with unwarranted praise. "I think your mother does not like me nor does your sister," Conchita complained, "because when they see me they utter a curt greeting (*adios*) in my direction." She then confessed that his mother was less involved in the personal slights, primarily, she noted, because "I hardly ever see your *mamacita*," she said tenderly. But, she said, "they do praise Chifis more she doesn't even deserve it." "Don't think that I am jealous," she said in a confessional tone, "I only say these things to you to fill the paper."[47]

Amused at Conchita's growing concern for her acceptance by and rightful place in his family, José explained that his sister Maura was likely jealous of their relationship. "When I went" to Calvillo, he said, "she asked me about you and I told her you were my girlfriend and I [am] almost certain she is jealous." As the only female and the youngest sibling, Maura often received special attention from her older brothers and from José in particular. José hoped that Conchita, too, had similar feelings of jealousy, for, in his mind, it signaled her growing interest in the relationship. "Hopefully you are too that makes me feel how do I explain it happy or content because if it is true I know that it is a sign that you can grow to love me as I desire."[48] Whether Conchita's response to the family's cool reception resulted from insecurity about their acceptance of her or was an early sign of love for José is unclear. What is known is that within a few weeks her relations with his family had improved. In early August 1964, she reported to José that she and Chifis had visited his mother, Jilda, at home. "She treated us very well," Conchita said, "and I realized that she calls you her '*lindo*' (beautiful), she calls me Concha and Chifis Chonita but I'm not worried," she commented, indicating she was hurt by his mother's use of an intimate term of endearment for Chifis— "Chonita"—and not the equivalent for Concha—"Conchita"—for her. "But I'm not worried you do call me Conchita," she said, and that sufficed.[49]

While Conchita expressed misgivings about her relations with José's family, she was firm in her conviction about her relationship with her stepfather, whom she "hated" (*odio*) and referred to as "*viejo*," or old man, from time to time, as a sign of disrespect. Over the course of many years, beginning in her childhood when her widowed mother, Natalia, married him, her relations with him had worsened, and she, like her siblings Sanjuana, Chifis, and Juan, held a deep mistrust of his intentions. (Enrique's relationship with his stepfather is unclear, as he died some years ago before an interview was possible.) Conchita went so far as to attribute her mother's ailing health to the stepfather's actions. To restore Natalia's health as well as Conchita's peace of mind, José suggested that Conchita and her siblings make peace with him for the good of the family. Conchita, however, would have none of it.[50] "I wasn't going to say anything to you about José E. because it is a very long story to explain," she said. Nevertheless I appreciate your advice and I feel bad not being able to follow it because I would never (*jamas*) be disposed to do something that I didn't believe, or do you think I could do it if I hate him like no one on this earth for all the ill treatment (*tanto mal*) we have received from him which is the cause of our disgrace and other things that I cannot tell you about I hope you understand for I am sure that if we treated him better he would not change on the contrary he would feel more assured about himself and it would be worse."[51]

According to Conchita's childhood friends, her experience with her stepfather contributed to her insecurity, ill temper, and defiant personality. "Her stepfather was a very bad man," Rebeca Serna Macias recounted. "He mistreated her mother, he came to hit her, that is why she suffered so much. Moreover she would say that Chona, her sister, ... from so much mistreatment from the stepfather was the way that she was. For a while, Chona ... didn't speak with anybody." Serna continued, "When I went to visit Concha, [Chona] would not accept us ... and all that would upset [Concha]." According to Serna, Concha would say, "No, it's that my sister suffered more than I ... with the stepfather. He was a very iron-fisted man, very hard."[52] According to Pedro Sánchez, Escalera was unkind. "It hurts to say it but he was abusive." He beat not only Natalia, his wife, but also the "muchachos. As a result of that situation they felt that way, they had a complex, I don't know perhaps inferiority."[53]

Not losing sight of the gravity of the conflict with the stepfather, as Conchita related, José agreed to drop the conversation until they saw each other in person. Though a delicate matter, it gave José an elevated role in the relationship. "If you want you can tell me your problems don't be ashamed perhaps I can help you even a bit and for me it will give me pleasure in helping you."[54] While they did eventually communicate about her difficulties with her stepfather, it is unclear exactly what she said, as much of it was carried out face to face, when he returned to Calvillo, and they refrained from conversing about it in the correspondence. Nevertheless, Conchita's family continued to suffer from Escalera's mistreatment.

Within a month of communicating with José about the tense family relations, Conchita reported that the increasing impoverishment of the household had forced them to move to Aguascalientes, a decision the step-father had contemplated for some time. Doubtless, he rationalized that if they lived in the city rather than in the pueblo, the older children, Conchita and Asunción in particular, would have a better opportunity to find employment to support the family. Apparently, Conchita's stepfather had no plans to find a job. According to Juan, Conchita's brother, José Escalera never held a job in his life except for a brief stint in a liquor store when he migrated to the United States years later.[55] Plus, as they all knew, Calvillo, with its largely rural agricultural and livestock background and minuscule commercial and industrial base, offered fewer employment opportunities than Aguascalientes, a growing industrial and manufacturing zone.[56] The city also afforded educational opportunities as well as basic services, including indoor plumbing, paved streets, and electricity, and other conveniences that many Calvillenses and nearby ranchos went without.[57]

After months of anticipating the move to Aguascalientes and searching for a home they could afford and that could house a family of fourteen, Conchita's household—with the exception of Juan, who had left the household at the early age of ten because of his disagreements with Escalera—finally departed in April 1965. Initially, Conchita had planned to stay behind, but because of her mother's continual poor health, exacerbated by the stress in the household, she changed her mind. "I wouldn't dare leave her alone," she told José a few months before the move.[58] Conchita knew that, as one of the two eldest siblings, she was needed, especially since her mother's mental and physical health remained on edge. Natalia's frail condition was not a recent development. As Juan recalled years later, when he was a seven-year-old boy, his mother had sent him to fetch the local priest. "I'm going to die," she told him. "I cannot go on."[59]

Despite the anticipated opportunities of the city, the urban environment depressed Conchita. "You should see how sad I am . . . it seems impossible that I will be able to tolerate it," she said. Conchita's difficulties were not with finding work, for she managed to land a job quickly in a *taller* (shop), but she "didn't really like it." Soon enough she left that post behind and found another as an accountant in a clothing store, where she had the opportunity to "make good money" but also did not care for the work. "The owners are all males," she explained, "and . . . some young men are very uppity (*creidos*)." Comparing *hidrocalidos*, Aguascalientes' denizens, to the people she left behind in Calvillo, she noted, "It could be that I want to see people like in Calvillo," humble people, "*gente cencilla.*" "I don't know but what I can tell you is that it's going to be hard for me to work here comfortably sometimes I get the urge to return to Calvillo," she confessed, "but then I also think, what am I going to do there?"[60]

For José, the news of the move was particularly worrisome, as he wondered how it might affect his future plans for marriage and life as a married man with Conchita. And, as he had stressed when Conchita contemplated pursuing a career and potentially leaving Calvillo to do so, José expressed insecurity and fear that she might forget him or, worse, betray him by entertaining another suitor and his sexual advances. "I don't know what to tell you," he wrote in a conflicted tone. "I don't know if I have jealousy or fear of the move . . . I confide in you I know that you are good and sincere I think you will never deceive me plus I have my faith in you and in God let it be God's will." He repeated, "I love you sincerely and with all my heart that is why I confide in you."[61]

Even though Conchita had never given him reason to think she might be unfaithful, the gender ideology of the day held that single women living and working in cities could not be trusted to maintain their sexual virtue, not only because of their moral failings but also because of their physical weaknesses. Unmarried women's bodies needed protection—surveillance—and preferably by men, including fathers, brothers, and other male members of the community. Single men, such as José, living and working in similar environments, however, needed little attention or protection, as gender norms excused males from moral failings such as engaging in sexual relations outside of marriage. As José expressed earlier, he feared that the city, with all of its worldly enticements and moral trappings, would corrupt her morally and, in turn, bring dishonor to him and their families. "I hope you get used to the environment I know it's not the same as in Calvillo," he said, trying to warn her about the city life he knew well from having lived and worked there as a single man in the early 1950s before migrating to the United States. "I lived a year there," working for Pepsi Cola, delivering *refrescos* across town, he explained, "and know how everything is there I even imagine the house you all live in as I know the street only that I forgot the name of the stores that are nearby." "I wish sincerely that you get used to the city that you live happily. Do you know why I say this to you?" he asked point blank. "It is because I have lived very sadly (*he vivido muy triste*) and I know how terrible (feo) it is that is why I don't want you to suffer the way I did."[62]

In the days and weeks to come, thoughts of Conchita's move to Aguascalientes further unsettled José and his plans for the relationship, prompting him to write furtively, expressing his frustrations and urging an answer to the marriage proposal. "*Caray* (wow) Conchita I think this is what I was telling you that I was afraid . . . to come home and leave you over there and have to remember you and for me to be so alone, if it wasn't for the hope that I have to see you soon I don't think I would have an objective to live."[63] José was at a loss.

Despite José's desperate pleas for Conchita's reassurance, the stress of her new responsibilities at work and home in Aguascalientes kept her away from pen and paper and caused her considerable stress, leading her to shed significant weight. In less than two months, from April to the end of May 1965, Conchita reported, she had dropped some sixteen kilos, or thirty-five pounds, a result of dealing with a boss and coworkers who mistreated her and long days on the job. "I start work at 7 in the morning and I only leave work to eat," that is, the midday meal, roughly from 2:00 to 4:00 o'clock in the afternoon, and she went back "again until 7 at night," she explained. "My boss is like a devil (*un chamuco*) all day long she reprimands us in a terrible way," she said. "If you only saw how thin I am . . . something incredible." She was so slender, she continued, that no one recognized her, even friends from Calvillo. After work, Conchita continued, she had to contend with an unbearable amount of housework, as her mother had just had a son, her fourteenth and final child, who was seriously ill from an accident apparently caused by an older sibling, and needed medical attention. "If you only saw the housework I have when I arrive at night I don't know whether to wash since there are mountains of dirty clothes or to prepare my clothes or to sew . . . and so tired I would rather lay down to rest."[64] Plus, she continued, her mother was very ill from her recent delivery, and Chifis, who worked into the afternoon as well, refused to complete chores when she got home, leaving them to Conchita, according to her account.

More threatened about what her weight loss might mean for the courtship and his honor as her suitor than about her troubles at work and home, José made light of her slim figure. "Conchita I am sad to hear that you are not doing well and that you are stressed," he said. "(On the other hand, I wish that you would become unsightly so that no one would pay attention to you) jealousy, right? It is because no one has loved me that I have the impression of being jealous," he explained.[65]

A month later, Conchita's difficulties at home had not abated but rather increased, as the family relocated to another home in Aguascalientes for reasons that remain unclear. The latest change, however, made her feel uprooted. "I hadn't written to you because we were going to move from the house and wanted to send you the new address, it is a tremendous burden roaming from here to there and plus one not being accustomed to doing so but in the end what are we going to do about it?" she said. But, Conchita confessed, "I like it better here where we moved because we are near the temple of la Purisima and a little garden . . . with a fountain . . . near [Infantil Miguel] Hidalgo Park," next to a fashionable zone in the city, she explained. "Let's see how long we last here," she ended on a cautious note.[66]

Conchita's guarded optimism was not without merit, for she found herself transitioning yet again to another place of employment, one that was less respectable than the previous, according to the gender expectations of the day. Sometime between late July and early October 1965, Conchita quit her job in the clothing store in Aguascalientes for an even more stressful and taxing position: working as a traveling sales representative selling beauty creams and medicinal products in northern Mexico. With Chifis at her side, they agreed to work for a local traveling salesman who went frequently to Guadalajara to buy supplies that he would, in turn, sell at a profit to individual households on a door-to-door basis. In an interview years later, Asunción reasoned that the man likely invited them to work for him because he noticed the dire poverty of their family. Natalia, their mother, initially resisted the idea because they were muchachas with little experience outside of the home. "But because of the poverty and not knowing what to do," Natalia finally relented. "We had to work," Asunción explained, "and we weren't used to working because we were among the rich (*los riquillos*) of Calvillo. We had one of the best houses, we had wealth, we had things . . . We were among the best dressed," she explained. "But everything was sold bit by bit."[67]

Acting as sales assistants, Conchita and Asunción accompanied the man and his wife to hawk their wares in the neighboring states of Zacatecas and Durango. To reach their destinations, they traveled by bus and slept and ate in *casas de huéspedes* (hostels). Few people other than their mother, their sister, Sanjuana, and likely their stepfather knew about their movements. Doubtless, traveling as salesgirls under the direction of an older male boss, even with his wife, brought a measure of shame, as it called into question the sisters' sexual virtue and confirmed the family's desperate economic need. Indeed, for many years the sisters' migratory trek outside the home remained a secret, to guard the young women's reputation and, by extension, the family honor. Only years later did the details of the episode emerge. In a 2009 interview, Juan Alvarado, Conchita and Chonita's younger brother, disclosed some of the specifics of their employment but preferred not to include it in the family narrative, not knowing that the girls' experiences were common knowledge, as revealed in the correspondence and prior conversations with other family members.[68] Nevertheless, Juan's instructions and the attempt to exclude the episode from the family history reveal the shame of having subjected the young women to unfamiliar places among unknown people for the sake of the household. Where once they had enjoyed a measure of property and social status in Calvillo and in the larger bajío region they had left behind many years earlier, by the time Conchita had become a young woman she had been forced to give up her studies and reduced to peddling beauty products for the good of the family.

Initially, in her correspondence to José from her travels across the northern region, Conchita obscured the purpose of their trip, indicating that few people knew of their location, including most of her family members who had returned to Calvillo from Aguascalientes. "Look Chifis and I are in Fresnillo nobody knows where we are except my mother and San Juana." "The latest letter you sent [me] my mother sent it to my boss in Ags . . . because my mother too did not know our address and I have only received one" of the missives. But, Conchita told him, her mother had recently received her address, so she could forward any of his notes to her. "It is pointless for you to send them all the way over here because I don't know when we are leaving I think soon," she said hopefully. Rather than explain the purpose of their journey, Conchita described their accommodations, noting that it was a relatively comfortable place, though the food was not agreeable. "It is a boarding house supposedly of first class."[69]

A week later Conchita wrote again but this time explained her extended travel and apologized for keeping silent about her migratory labor. "José I want you to forgive me for not having told you the truth in the other letter but I think you'll understand I am ashamed to tell you not because it is something shameful but because I am not sure how you will take it," she said. Because he was her professed suitor, she likely knew that any taints to her sexual virtue would be seen as staining his male honor as well. "I think you won't judge me badly given that you know more or less the problems that we have in the household," she noted, referring to the growing poverty and strained relations with her stepfather. "You know we couldn't take that man Escalera and Chifis and I left the house of course with our mother's permission and we are working in Fresnillo as *agentes* (salespeople)," in Zacatecas. "Tomorrow," she observed, "God willing we leave for Tepetongo," another town in Zacatecas, "I think for the entire month." Feeling homesick, she confessed, "I really want to see my mother you know how sick the poor woman has been and I think that now el señor takes advantage now that we are not there."[70] Wanting to sound optimistic, Conchita offered some words of encouragement for their future, though the sincerity of her words is unclear, for she remained hesitant to accept his proposal. "Look, let's not be pessimists let's think that our dream is a reality that way we will feel less sad." "Continue writing to me at the house" in Calvillo, she instructed him. "San Juana will send them to me wherever I will be and I will send her a new address."[71]

Though many of the letters they exchanged during Conchita's travels as a salesgirl are no longer extant or remain in fragmentary condition—she indicated that José sent her at least two that she never received—the surviving correspondence details the personal and emotional challenges she had to deal with on a daily basis. "Since some time ago until now I have felt terribly sad," she explained in a torn letter that survives. Before her experience, "I would never cry for anything and now I am so sentimental that only because a dog dies I start to cry, it's not for nothing at least I see it that way," she explained, "with so many things you might more or less imagine," living outside of one's home, she explained, "and working which is the worst for me as I am so 'light' (*liviana*) that I wish I could spend the time lying down." Plus, Conchita told him, she was very unhappy with her boss. While she admitted he had his good moments, she described him as an "ogre."[72]

When José learned about her and her sister's miseries, he was at a loss for words. Rather than raise questions about her travels or her sexual virtue and honor, he said little. Likely he wondered about her experiences and they spoke about them when they saw each other in Calvillo, but it is possible too that they preferred to keep the episode as quiet as possible, away from the ears of local people in the town, though they both knew it was impossible to do so in the pueblo, where chisme, or the exchange of social intelligence, as David A. Gerber refers to it, was rampant. Instead, José communicated a deepening sadness that overcame him. "You know I felt sad for a few days I have been feeling sad." Chalking up his dispirited demeanor to the weather, he explained, "It's as if I'm in line with the weather as these days have been cloudy and it's rained a bit and at the same time it's been cold." "I was a bit sad and wanted to write to you but with my sadness (again) I didn't know what to say to you." Rereading her letter, however, inspired him to write, he said, and he wondered where she was at that moment, whether traveling in other parts of the country or at home in Calvillo, or if she thought about him. "Do you think about me?" he asked. "The days seem so long to me waiting to go soon to see you [I] don't know how I'll do it but I know I need to do it soon."[73]

By the first week of December 1965, when Conchita was nearing her nineteenth birthday, she and Chifis were back home in Calvillo, relieved to see familiar sights and sounds. Conchita, however, knew that the family's economic outlook remained dire and took on needlework to help support them. Generally poorly paid and labor-intensive, the work left her with little time to correspond, as she explained to José. Nevertheless, she was eager to resume their epistolary relationship and hoped he was too.[74]

José was overjoyed to hear her news. "I received your letter," he told her, "with much happiness I was anxious to hear from you if you only knew how much sadness I had and worry at the same time." But "now that I know you are in Calvillo I am relieved (*tranquilo*)."[75] José again refrained from asking many questions about her travels, though she provided a brief summary of the locales they had visited—"Fresnillo, Sombrerete, Durango and many other places," Conchita informed him.[76] Her good news, however, tempered José's disappointing communication: he would not visit during the Christmas holiday season that year, in 1965, despite his repeated intentions to do so. As he explained, the year-round work demands of agricultural production in Imperial Valley, as well as the inclement weather, work slowdowns, and his much-needed skills at the worksite, kept him away.

Conchita's experience as a traveling salesgirl, though relatively brief, reshaped her outlook on life and made her less optimistic about the future in Calvillo. As José was unable to travel to Calvillo for Christmas that year, Conchita spent it in the company of her family but was *muy aburrida* (very bored), she told him. "I didn't spend it here en Calvillo I went to" Aguascalientes, she said. "There was a *pachanga* (party) the *freneticos del ritmo*," a rock and roll band from Guadalajara that took the stage. The party "got really good nevertheless the drunks (*aguafiestas*) started and then we left for home."[77] Apparently, her travels had left her jaded. "You will say that I always tell you that I spend my time bored but . . . even though I go to parties I don't know what's wrong with me in no place do I feel content and nothing makes me happy, and look one thing that I have noticed is that since I've returned from where I was it is as if everything has changed and I don't like to dream the way I used to this time I saw life exactly as it is and to me it has no meaning."[78] What she saw or experienced during her travels remains unknown, but it affected her in profound ways.

Growing Prospects for Romantic Love and Marriage

More than two years into their courtship, in early March 1966, during one of José's brief visits to Calvillo, Conchita finally agreed to go along with the wedding plans, even though she had yet to fall in love emotionally and romantically or to express a firm yes to the marriage proposal. As the correspondence as well as oral interviews years later indicate, Conchita never communicated an "I love you" during the courtship. In the first six months she and José exchanged letters, from late 1963 to summer 1964, Conchita's notes were generally staid, brief, and indifferent and almost always ended with signatures usually reserved for use among acquaintances, such as "your friend" (*tu amiga*), "until next time" (*hasta la proxima*), or "without more" (*sin más*). By October 1964, the tone of her words had begun to change, especially after she realized she would not be able to pursue a career and her family's economic situation continued to worsen. As a sign of her growing interest in the relationship, Conchita started to pay considerable attention to the subtle details in José's use of language, looking for signs of his commitment.

At the same time, Conchita grew more protective of their exchanges. A month later, in November 1964, for example, she neglected to pass along the greetings (*saludos*) Chifis regularly sent to José and, in return, the ones he sent to Chifis, an omission that did not go unnoticed. After a few weeks of hearing no mention of José's respects, which Conchita had conveyed consistently until recently, Chifis grew suspicious and intercepted José's letters while Conchita was away at the rancho. When Chifis opened the correspondence and realized her sister's transgression of not passing along the greeting, she confronted her. Rather than deny the accusation, Conchita admitted it, explaining that the oversight was not intentional but, rather, accidental. Ashamed, Conchita later confessed to José that her egoism had led to such a move, likely wanting to cut her sister from a relationship she wanted for her own.[79]

Conchita's interest in protecting her relationship with José did not, however, indicate that she was ready or willing to declare her love or tie the knot. Rather, Conchita remained conflicted and unsure of her romantic love, as she told him that same month, in November 1964, weeks before his impending holiday visit. "You know I am happy that you are going to come and at the same time I have fear (*susto*) or I don't know what to call it because I think that in seeing you again my sentiments will change ... right now I don't what they are," she explained. "Sometimes I think that I love you but other times the contrary I can't explain it through a letter perhaps when you come and we talk I can do it," she ended.[80]

Apparently, the talk never materialized the way she had envisioned, as Conchita's sentiments toward José remained unresolved even after his visit in December, for she continued to question her emotional and romantic commitment. Conchita was not, however, ready to give up on the relationship and remained attuned to his verbal and nonverbal communication. A few weeks after his visit to Calvillo for the holidays in December 1964, she wrote to him, questioning his recent actions. Why, she asked him, had he failed to bid her farewell in person, and why had he seemed jovial shortly before his impending departure? Both episodes, she said, had made her feel triste and, likely, neglected.[81] In that same letter, she also told him she was angry at the brief nature of his most recent letter, which he sent after returning to Imperial Valley. "You know," she said, "I was very happy to receive your letter but when I saw such a small piece of paper I won't deny it but I felt a bit of anger (*coraje*), I expect the next to be a newspaper."[82] Conchita then ended with a salutation she used for the first time: "quien no te olvida" (the one who doesn't forget you), intimating she kept him constantly in her thoughts, a refrain José often used with her in his correspondence.

Over the course of the next twelve months, Conchita's affection toward José grew deeper, particularly as she looked for emotional comfort during her family's dire economic circumstances, which compelled the move to Aguascalientes and obligated her to work in and outside the city. Finally, in April 1965, shortly before their impending relocation to the capital city, Conchita signed off using the words José longed to hear: "quien te quiere" (the one who loves you).[83] Though she (and he) said little about her closing salutation, she continued to invoke similar expressions in the trying days and weeks that followed living and working in the urban environment. At the end of April, she wrote "en espera de la tuya" (waiting for yours), followed in May with "todo el cariño" (all my love), then in June "tu peor es nada" (your better than nothing), and, by the end of that same month, her last one in Aguascalientes, she scribbled "sin más (without more)."[84] After a few months of little or no communication, partly because of her travels as a salesgirl, she picked up with her subtle hints of affection and signed off in late October 1965 with "quien no te olvida" and in late November with "quien te quiere."[85] Though she wrote an additional letter sometime in early November, it lacked a second and final page, obscuring her closing greeting. Finished with her traveling saleswork and back at home in Calvillo in early December, she wrote in a more relaxed tone than she had done recently and concluded with "quien no te olvida," signaling the forging of an intimate bond.[86]

By early 1966, Conchita's love for José seemed a reality, but she had yet to express it convincingly either in writing or in person, even though she had apparently agreed to go along with the marriage in March of that same year. While she increased the frequency of her use of phrases such as "quien no te olvida," "quien te quiere," "el cariño," and "quien desea verte pronto," she raised long-held doubts about their relationship and did so plainly in April 1966.[87] That month, Conchita told José she worried that her family problems had influenced his decision to propose marriage. "I wish you wouldn't think that I tell you . . . because I want to obligate you to marry me," she said; "sometimes I think you feel committed and since we have never argued you haven't had the opportunity to release yourself from me (*safarte de mi*)." The infrequency of his letter writing in recent weeks as well as the gossip among acquaintances about his marital status also exacerbated the strain. "If you only knew the chisme that you are married and what not don't be offended don't think that I doubt you, but many people have already given me that news." Despite the sordid narratives, Conchita assured him that she confided in him. "The people are just inventing [stories] the only thing that is important is what you tell me." To demonstrate her faith in him, she ended facetiously, "P.S. Send my greetings to your wife."[88]

Conchita's uncertainty about her emotional and romantic feelings toward José and her commitment to their wedding plans were heightened in the coming months with the escalating difficulties in her household. In June 1966, as she explained to José, her stepfather had been imprisoned for stealing cattle from local ranches, and her mother, Natalia, emotionally distraught, blamed her and her siblings for the affair.[89] The family was also dealing with an impending move but this time within the pueblo's limits, for the home was too small to accommodate the family, as Conchita informed José. Years later Asunción recalled that the reason for the move was because their stepfather had sold the home, or, as she said, he "nearly gave away the house and we ended up without a house." When they went to see the new locale, Asunción continued, she thought it was the most "horrible (*horrorosa*) house of Calvillo, the worst! The worst that could be found. We all ended up there," she said angrily.[90] While Conchita knew that marrying José would help alleviate her family's financial burden, she was concerned about the family's future welfare as well as her own happiness and remained ambivalent about love and marriage.

Indeed, despite José's enthusiasm about the engagement, Conchita was not ready or willing to walk down the aisle. Asunción knew of her hesitancy. "I didn't want her to marry because . . . she didn't want to marry," Asunción said in an interview years later. José's letters "were very emotive and very beautiful . . . but . . . you could see that, like, she did not, not yet want to form a family." "Not her," Chifis continued, "her idea was to study . . . hang out with her friends, . . . with Lola from the movie theater . . . and Rebeca Serna [those] were her inseparable friends." Conchita "felt like she was in her moment of wanting to begin . . . to enjoy her youth and enjoy life (*disfrutar*). I never heard her say that she wanted to marry." José, in contrast, "was a person . . . made for marriage, [with] ideas of forming a home . . . and she, no, she did not have that . . . at least she never told me but she was really pleased with the letters. She liked that he wrote to her."[91]

When plans for the wedding unfolded, Conchita was "very opposed (*negada*) to marry[ing]," Asunción stated, "that is the word 'opposed' to marry," for she never, as far as she knew, agreed to marry, at least in the correspondence. "No, no, he only wrote to her and he arrived . . . [and said] I've come so that we can get married . . . and when she saw what was happening . . . . she did not know how to sever the agreement (*deshacerse del compromiso*) how to explain to him . . . that the relationship they had was not as deep as to constitute a marriage." Weeks before the wedding, Chifis continued, "she would cry saying that she did not want to marry . . . And all of us, beginning with . . . Sanjuana," the *madrina* (god-mother or sponsor) of the impending ceremony, insisted that she comply with her obligation. " 'Oh no,' " Sanjuana reportedly said, according to Chifis, " 'you cannot play with the sentiments of a man. You have to marry him, too bad, why were you taking his time? Now you are going to marry.' "[92]

With few alternatives to marriage, Conchita ordered her dress, a handmade white satin beaded and embroidered gown, and helped prepare a simple meal for the reception, while José paid for the event, including the drinks and a local band from Aguascalientes, and made plans for her immigration to the United States. Conchita's sadness, however, was palpable, according to Chifis and Alicia González Rodríguez, José's cousin from Aguascalientes, who also attended the event. "In church, you could see her head lowered, the ceremony was very sad," Chifis said. "If you see the photos from the ceremony," she continued, Conchita "looks pensive and rarely smiling, only José and his relatives are smiling, but not Conchita." Distraught from seeing her sister's sadness and knowing full well she was losing her confidante, Chifis felt a desperation to halt the ceremony. Chifis knew, however, that such a move was impossible. Conchita's somberness finally subsided, Chifis recalled, after she had a drink at the reception.

With the festivities concluded and no time or money for a honeymoon, José and Conchita left the pueblo promptly, as José had to return to work in Imperial Valley within three days of the ceremony. Though José had planned for Conchita's immigration to the United States, believing it would be a relatively simple process "to arrange the crossing (*la pasada*)" given his green card status and the recent passage of the Immigration Act of 1965 (known as the Hart-Celler Act), which gave preference to family members of citizens and residents as well as immigrants with special skills, he was mistaken. Bureaucratic delays and inaction on the implementation of the act meant that they would remain a couple of years in Mexicali waiting for her lawful entry into the United States.[93]

Finally, in December 1968, after more than two years of waiting and living in impoverished conditions as well as seeing the birth of two children despite poor medical care, the family immigrated to Imperial Valley, settling in Brawley and eventually moving to Holtville, about thirty miles distant. Four years later, tired of the physical demands of agricultural work and lured by the prospects of employment in San José and the emerging Silicon Valley, they packed their bags and headed north to city life.[94]

By then Conchita had changed her demeanor and expressed her affection for José, demonstrating that even though she had married him to bring relief to her impoverished family, she had fallen in love emotionally and romantically. In three subsequent letters she wrote in the early 1970s, while she traveled to visit José's younger brother, Paco, and his new family in San José, she displayed deep fondness and intimacy for José by using a variety of pet names, including "*viejillo chulillo*" (beautiful old husband). Years later, contemporary visitors, namely, Asunción and Juan, attested that she had, indeed, developed romantic sentiments toward him. Conchita's family, however, remained impoverished, even though she left the household to relieve some of the economic burden. According to Asunción, after Conchita left the household, the family suffered even more hardships. Unable to afford a stable home, they migrated from locale to locale, including a cave-like dwelling in which scorpions threatened the safety of the children. Apparently, Natalia, their mother, spent nights killing the critters. Later, when they managed to move back to Calvillo, they remained for a short while and made the decision to relocate again but this time to Guadalajara to an urban center with the employment opportunities it afforded rural people like themselves. There, Conchita's family—namely, the younger siblings—managed to eke out an existence in a poor colonia with few basic services. After years of struggle, almost all her siblings as well as her mother and stepfather migrated to el norte with Conchita and José's assistance.

CONCHITA'S DECISION TO MARRY JOSÉ, with whom she had yet to fall in love, demonstrates the negotiated nature of courtship and marriage. She was filled with inner turmoil in having to choose between personal happiness and familial responsibilities. Even though she was unsure of her emotional investment and romantic feelings toward José, a confluence of economic, personal, and familial circumstances compelled her finally to walk down the aisle and say "I do." As a young woman, Conchita had dreamed of pursuing her studies and attaining a fulfilling career, but her family's increasing impoverishment and her mother's growing ailments, as well as the gendered and rural mores of the day, forced her to rethink those options. Though unwilling or perhaps not ready to tie knot, Conchita did so to bring some semblance of financial relief to her household. With one fewer mouth to feed, she hoped to lessen her family's financial burden and set them on an increasingly stable path of economic security.

Conchita's correspondence not only reveals the worsening economic circumstances of her household and her growing acceptance of Jose's proposal but also discloses her self-identity as a passionate and fierce young woman. Like many *mexicanos* of her day, Conchita was devoted to *el cine* (theater), for she attended nearly every day in her attempts to find an emotional respite from the difficulties at home and the daily drudgeries of life in the pueblo. She was committed deeply, as well, to her mother, older sisters, and friends, visiting with them as often as she could. Beneath it all, though, Conchita could not hide her deep disdain for the stepfather and his mistreatment of her mother and siblings as well as his mismanagement of their inheritance, which led, in part, to the household's impoverishment. That transition, in turn, had led her to question her identity and self-worth among her peers in town as well as in her correspondence with José. As the letters reveal, she often disparaged her physical appearance and intellect. Yet, she was not easily defeated, as she found ways to defend her reputation when she believed it was being questioned or ridiculed in the community. In the end, that same bold attitude served her well in making the leap to marry someone she hardly knew and to migrate to the U.S.-Mexico borderlands in hopes of finding stability for herself and the loved ones left behind.

While migration has an immediate impact on those, like Conchita, traveling to el otro lado, it also shapes deeply the lives of those who stay at home. The next chapter focuses on the experiences of family members who stayed behind and the personal, emotional, and economic impact of migration on their lives and that of the broader community. Using the correspondence between José's father, José Chávez Torres, and José's younger brother, Paco Chávez, as well as letters written among members of the family and friends, it explores the ways in which the migration altered José Chávez Torres's understandings of the filial, moral, emotional, and economic support he demanded as the patriarchal figure of authority in the household.

CHAPTER THREE

Contesta Pronto
Migration, Return Migration, and Paternal Authority

In September 1962, fifty-nine-year-old José Chávez Torres, a father of five, wrote anxiously to his youngest son, Paco Chávez, who had recently migrated to the border town of Mexicali, Baja California. José wanted to know when Paco and his older brother, José Chávez Esparza, as well as his elder two sons working in *el norte*, would return home to Calvillo, Aguascalientes. Fond of his father, though waiting to secure his U.S. residency through the assistance of his brother's employer, Paco informed him that he would likely not return to Calvillo until after December once he had obtained his permanent residency or green card.[1] The news consoled the elder José, as he knew that residency meant long-term, stable employment *allá* (there) and the opportunity to have another son contributing *aquí* (here) to the household. Yet, the longer Paco and his older brothers delayed returning home, the more frustrated José became with his sons and their disregard for what he saw as their filial obligation—the economic and moral support of the family as well as respect for paternal authority, a deeply rooted, gendered system of authority.

José's weakening grip over his sons did not begin with Paco but, rather, with the eldest males, Jesús and Juan, both of whom had migrated to el norte in the late 1940s and early 1950s for stints in the bracero program, a bilateral contract labor agreement between Mexico and the United States that lasted from 1942 to 1964. While Jesús stayed away from home for years at a time, sending word less frequently over time to his father, Juan traveled back and forth from *el otro lado* (the other side) to Calvillo with more frequency, as he preferred to work intermittently. Like Jesús, though, when he was in the United States he often sent little notice to his father as to his whereabouts. Young José, the third-eldest son, living and working in Imperial Valley as an agricultural laborer, communicated and visited his father more frequently than his older siblings but did so only during the holidays or when the family needed him urgently. By the early 1960s, the sons would delay months and, later, years, before responding to their father's continual inquiries about their whereabouts and return.[2]

By February 1963, however, after repeated empty promises from his sons that they would soon return and assist with family responsibilities, José had

had enough. Not mincing his words, he declared: "I've been waiting and waiting the return of you all and nothing, that's fine it can't be done too bad, my concern is about Maura," the youngest sibling and the only female, who was in Guadalajara, Jalisco, a five- to six-hour drive (or more) to Calvillo in the 1960s. "I have not been able to go for her and with [the promise] that you are on your way and on your way and like a dummy (*tonto*) waiting, what I have asked you all is to tell me the truth (*desengañen*) if you are coming or not in order to go for the girl or send her money so that she can return to the house."[3] Despite José's stern and direct admonitions as the patriarchal head of the household, few of the sons complied, leaving him questioning his authority in the family.

Contrary to José's belief, Paco was eager to return home to see the family, friends (*cuates*), and sweetheart he left behind. Return migration was, however, difficult economically for Paco as well as for many migrants of the day who longed to see their loved ones and bridge the geographical, physical, and emotional divide. Migrants, particularly those from poor, unskilled or semiskilled, and working-class backgrounds, simply lacked the resources to pay for the expenses for such a trip or the time away from work to do so, as they had no form of compensation on days off and risked losing their jobs. Other migrants, such as Paco's eldest brother, Jesús, formed families and had the responsibility of raising young children and maintaining a household on meager wages, making it even more difficult to depart at a moment's notice.

Using nearly fifty letters written by José Chávez Torres to his son Paco, who was living and working in the U.S.-Mexico borderlands, as well as another fifty penned among Paco and his mother, sister, and older brothers, this chapter examines the personal, emotional, and economic toll of migration on family members who stayed home. It demonstrates the profound ways in which migration of loved ones remade their personal and social roles and identities, that is, the real and perceived understanding of who they were in relation to their family and community in Mexico and the United States. The chapter begins by providing a broader understanding of José Chávez Torres's family's and the Mexican community's history of migration and return migration to el norte in relation to larger patterns across the U.S.-Mexico border in the late nineteenth and early twentieth centuries. Next, it explores José's repeated attempts to rein in migrant sons who failed to comply with the filial, moral, emotional, and economic support he demanded as the patriarchal figure of authority in the household. When they failed to heed his calls, as they did when José asked them to assist with their mother's health, their sister's unexpected courtship, and remittances for much-needed household repairs, José was left reeling. Despite the sons' inconsistency in responding to or obeying their father, José never relented in imparting what Joanna Dreby calls "social remittances," that is, his paternal advice and the ideas and ideologies associated with patriarchy. José consistently expressed care and concern about his children's experiences with employment, familial relations, and travel, and encouraged their independence.[4]

Finally, the chapter shows that José's ultimate decline was linked not only to his sons' growing alienation but also to his increasing physical health problems and his battle with a debilitating disease that would eventually rob him of any remaining power and authority in the family. Only with the full disclosure of José's ailment—Parkinson's, a disease few doctors and scientific researchers in Mexico and the United States knew much about in the 1960s—did his sons come through with the filial, moral, and economic support he had demanded years earlier.

Migration, Return Migration, and Those Who Stayed Home

In the nineteenth century, migration from Mexico to the United States was sporadic, carried out primarily by Sonorans in the 1850s looking to strike it rich after gold was discovered in 1849 in the placer mines of the California Central Valley, and by Chinese migrants in the 1880s and 1890s barred from legal entry to the United States. Migration picked up considerably in the late nineteenth and early twentieth centuries with the expansion of the southwestern agricultural and industrial capitalist economy and the increased demand for cheap laborers as a result of restrictions imposed on migrants from China, Japan, and southern Europe. The onset of the Mexican Revolution in 1910 and the violent chaos, suffering, and want that ensued throughout the country—especially among the poor, who had already experienced land loss, increased impoverishment, and marginalization as a result of President Porfirio Díaz's positivist policies and practices—also spurred the migration of hundreds of thousands of Mexicans in search of political stability and economic survival. By 1930, 1.5 million people, or 10 percent of the Mexican population, had migrated to el norte. That movement, in turn, led to the formation of new and expansion of old Spanish-speaking communities throughout the southwestern and midwestern United States, and aided in the survival of many Mexicans who stayed at home and relied on the economic remittances sent from loved ones living and working abroad.[5]

Some of the migrants who went north returned home immediately after they had finished their stints in contract employment, usually labor on farms or railroads in the Southwest or in steel production in the Midwest, and had family responsibilities and personal business to tend to in Mexico. Given the relative ease of migration and return migration, or circular migration, across the U.S.-Mexico border, as compared to what would be allowed in the following decades, most migrants—men primarily, as women were expected to manage the household—headed to el norte for months at a time and returned home as needed or desired. Though it is difficult to know what proportion of migrants participated in circular migration (and how often they did it), most scholars agree that return migration formed (and continues to form) a significant aspect of the migrant experience. As George J. Sánchez finds, in the 1910s most migrants from the central region of Michoacan who ventured north for seasonal employment eventually returned home after staying in the United States either for a few months or for several years at a time, depending on their personal, familial, and economic circumstances as well as the nature of U.S. immigration policies and practices. Indeed, the U.S. government was and continues to be highly involved in shaping migratory patterns, for throughout the twentieth century it worked hand in glove with employers to recruit and then deport laborers of Mexican descent as needed to satiate the appetite of the U.S. capitalist economy.[6]

For migrants and their families, return migration was often an expected component of family life, though it was not an easy prospect for households— women, children, and the elderly—left at home, especially when migrants stayed away for periods of up to a year or more with no word on when they would return.[7] Though we have little information on how families in early twentieth-century Mexico coped with the long-term absence of family members, other than by sending letters to remain in contact, as Manuel Gamio has found, we do know how similar individuals handled the departure of loved ones at midcentury. According to Ana E. Rosas, among family members of braceros left behind in Mexico, extended periods of delay caused heartache, longing, and anxiety, usually among the wives, children, and elderly, who were excluded from the bracero program and were forced to wait in Mexico for the return of spouses, fathers, and sons. Rosas demonstrates that Mexican women coped emotionally with the absence of family members by exchanging letters, photographs, and music with their loved ones across the border as well as by participating in support groups formed by teachers in their local communities. Life was, nevertheless, extremely burdensome and exhausting for the women and children who stayed home and who were expected to manage the family economy, leading to an exploitative situation especially for young children called on to labor and assist in supporting their households. Abandoned married women, too, faced extreme personal difficulties, for they experienced the shame of single motherhood without the prospect of remarriage.[8]

When José Chávez Torres's eldest sons migrated to el norte to labor in the late 1940s and early 1950s, he was well aware of the unpredictability of the migratory experience, as he and other males in the family had spent decades traveling back and forth across the border in the early twentieth century. José's initial foray to the United States took place when he was a young man in the early 1920s, a few years after his father's return in 1918 from serving many years in President Díaz's army during the Mexican Revolution, as Baudelio Chávez Torres, José's youngest brother, revealed in an oral interview.[9] As the eldest male among four children, one of whom died in infancy, José made his way to California in the early twentieth century to find a means of support and survival for his family and younger siblings, some of them recently born. While it is unclear if he migrated as a contract laborer, it is known that he landed in Lincoln, California, and then soon thereafter the San Francisco Bay area, in what is today Contra Costa County, specifically at Port Chicago.[10] After working there for a few years, José traveled to Oxnard, California, where he found employment in the agricultural fields alongside a younger uncle who traveled with him. When he finished working there, sometime in the mid- to late 1920s, he left for Fargo, Oklahoma, and joined his father, Jesús Chávez Rubio, his mother, Carlota Torres, and his younger siblings—who had migrated to the region to take advantage of the opportunities afforded by the Santa Fe Railroad Company, a major employer of Mexican laborers in the early twentieth century. Fargo was a small town of no more than several hundred residents, but several thousand Mexican *traqueros* (track workers) also lived in the vicinity. Though most migrants came without their families, employers sometimes encouraged the migration of women and family units to stabilize the workforce.[11] According to Baudelio, who spent several years in elementary school in Fargo, his brother José did not care for work or life in Oklahoma, prompting him return to Mexico, while the rest of the family stayed on until forced to move at the end of the decade as a consequence of repatriation during the Great Depression.

Once home, at the family rancho of Las Tinajas, a cluster of humble adobes and barren agricultural fields a few kilometers outside of Calvillo, José married Leovijilda "Jilda" Esparza, a motherless young woman raised as an orphan among five different families. The contemporaneous Cristero Rebellion of the 1920s, a violent conflict between civil authorities and supporters of the Catholic Church, impeded José and Jilda's marriage in the church, forcing them to marry in the hills surrounding Calvillo, which also witnessed the devastating impact of those battles.[12] Soon after their nuptials, José and Jilda had difficulty maintaining their household with the scant opportunities available at the rancho.[13] Though the property had grazing fields, the family plot of land was small as a result of parceling it out among heirs over the years. The unpredictable rain also meant that the rancho yielded little beans, corn, and squash, and people often went hungry. "The people struggled, they couldn't clothe themselves, nor wear shoes," Baudelio recalled. "Look the people didn't wear shoes, sandals only, all farmworkers (*todo el campesino*)."[14] Within a few short years, José and Jilda witnessed the birth of several children but found they could no longer support the family on the artisanal tradition of weaving wool cloth, a family practice dating to the 1800s and carried out by José's father, Jesús Chávez Rubio, prior to his military duty in the federal Mexican army, and by his grandfather Celso Chávez. The expanding industrial centers in Mexico City and more locally in Aguascalientes made it difficult for them to compete with the new cheaply made cloth. With few prospects for support or for educating their children, José and Jilda and the family moved to Calvillo, where he continued to weave wool blankets until the mass production of blankets led to a decrease in price, cutting into his practice and forcing him to find alternative employment.[15]

With few avenues for work or earning a living, life in Calvillo in the 1930s was difficult, leading José to try to take his entire family to el norte—to Laredo, Texas—to make ends meet. Crossing the border proved impossible, however, for it was much more closely regulated than when he had crossed in the early 1920s. At that time, according to Maura, migrants needed only a permit and a few cents to cross the border. The family reached Torreon, Coahuila, in central Mexico, about 340 miles north of Calvillo, but was forced to return when the crossing proved daunting because of the continued violence of the Cristero Rebellion and increasing immigration restrictions and the repatriation of people of Mexican descent. José's parents and siblings in Fargo, though legal residents, returned to Mexico as well, some of them voluntarily, others forcibly, particularly the youngest, Baudelio, who had learned to read, write, and speak fluent English and had taken to the culture. Indeed, Baudelio wanted to remain in el norte among his close friends, but his father refused to leave him behind. Years later Baudelio would return temporarily to el norte to work in the bracero program, but not as an agricultural worker, rather, as staff, assisting U.S. officials in translating and processing paperwork. After José's northern trek ended in failure, he rarely again attempted to cross the border, as migration from Mexico became increasingly restrictive.

After experiencing much want in the years of the economic depression in Mexico, José tried his luck again in the north with the establishment of the bracero program in 1942. The Emergency Farm Labor Supply Program, as it was also known, targeted male workers and witnessed the migration of hundreds of thousands of Mexican men, including José's eldest sons, Jesús, Juan, and José, and José's youngest brother, Baudelio, among many other compatriots from Calvillo and elsewhere. Shortly after enrolling in the program in the early 1940s, the elder José was sent to Elko, Nevada, where he spent several months repairing the train tracks of the Central Pacific Railroad, which carried weapons and supplies for use in World War II. Paco recalls that his father told him that the trains carrying bombs headed for Europe had inscriptions of "Hail Hitler!" meant for the infamous dictator of Nazi Germany. His work finished in Elko, José returned to Calvillo sometime in late 1942 and shortly thereafter, in 1943, received an appointment to the local tribunal as a minor judge (*juez menor*). Apparently that yearlong honorific appointment brought in little remuneration, for the following year he returned to the United States as a laborer—it is unclear if he went under contract—where he worked in Portola, California, and then in Santa Paula, California, picking lemons, oranges, and other citrus fruits. When his employment ended, he returned home sometime in the late 1940s and within a year or so, in 1948, was appointed for a yearlong stint in Calvillo's municipal government as a *síndico* (trustee). In 1951 he was put in charge of the Registro Civil (Civil Registry), carrying out and recording civil marriages as well births and deaths. He remained at that post for at least five years, until 1956.[16]

In all likelihood, José obtained those positions because of his ability to read and write, unusual skills for the time, which he gained as a child in the early 1900s from his maternal uncle Nicolás Torres, who learned to read and write from his mother, Rosario López, years earlier. José's jobs, while requiring specialized skills, were poorly paid (60 pesos a month, less than $5.00 a month, with the exchange rate at nearly 12.50 pesos to $1.00), though he did acquire and maintain a level of respect in the community. Local townspeople, for instance, referred to him as "Don José," an honorific title given to men of respectable economic or political position.[17] Well into his late forties and early fifties by then, José never again migrated to el otro lado for employment and instead remained at his post, from where he attempted to maintain contact with his sons in the United States, while Maura remained at home with Jilda. As the youngest single female living at home with her family, Maura did not experience the same kind of social pressure or gendered expectation to migrate that her brothers did.[18]

For José and his family in Calvillo, surviving and thriving remained difficult economically, especially in the late 1920s and early 1930s, around the birth of the three oldest siblings, Jesús, Juan, and José, and the onset of the Great Depression. "No, there was not much money," Paco related in an interview about home conditions as he heard about them from the family. Jilda, according to Paco, remembered those days as a time during which food, clothes, and shoes were scarce. The family's experience was not uncommon, as misery and want afflicted campesinos throughout rural zones of Mexico, whereas the denizens of urban areas received more support from the central government with its plan to industrialize and modernize the country. According to Jilda, as Paco recalled, when Jesús, Juan, and José were young, they had little nourishment in the house, and even *frijoles* (beans) ran low. To earn a bit of money, Jilda raised chickens and sold the eggs they produced. "No, they wouldn't eat the eggs," Paco explained. "You couldn't afford it," he said in English. "It was preferable to receive the ten, fifteen cents that they paid for the egg . . . there were various individuals who would buy the eggs and send them to Aguascalientes," the capital.[19] Everything was limited, Paco said, including clothing, forcing the children to go without outerwear as well as shoes until they started their primary education, at the age of seven or eight years, where footwear was required.

Medicine was scarce as well, as it was throughout the Mexican countryside, and desperately needed when the children developed stomach infections, as happened with three siblings born between the births of José and Paco, sometime in the mid- to late 1930s and early 1940s. Tragically, but all too common, those three brothers, Celso, Pedro, and Carlos, died in infancy due to lack of medical care.[20] "In that time," recalled Paco, "there were no sulfa-based medicines . . . before penicillin, an antibiotic . . . for wounds, preventing infection, they no longer use it but they used to use it *a lot*." Penicillin did not arrive in town until the late 1940s, he remarked. When it did, it changed the way of life. "It was a miracle, for everything it was 'penicillin,' 'penicillin,' it was the 'top-notch.' "[21] When Paco was born and his father, José, saw that he had survived the perils of early childhood and poverty, he was elated, as he was with the birth of their fifth and final surviving child, Maura.

For José's impoverished household, a decent home was equally difficult to procure. When they moved from the rancho to Calvillo, they lacked the means to purchase their own dwelling, obligating them to move into a house that belonged to José's uncle, Nicolás Torres, his mother's brother, who had lived in that same home in Calvillo in the early 1900s but had fled to Aguascalientes with his family during the Cristero Rebellion. Years later, after living there for more than two decades, sometime in the late 1950s or early 1960s, when Nicolás needed to sell it for income, José was given an ultimatum: either purchase it for 15,000 pesos, the market value, or move. For José and his family the amount was a small fortune, but for Nicolás's descendants, including Alicia González, a surviving daughter, the home was nearly given away (*regalado*), for it was valuable property, as it contained a sizable plot of land.[22]

Despite the want and suffering of the early years of their home life in Calvillo, by the 1950s and early 1960s the scarcities in the household had subsided, largely as a result of the older brothers' remittances. Those funds, related Paco, enabled the family to eat and dress adequately and to live a modest life. "And, well, yes, I did not suffer hungers," Paco commented. "In addition to frijoles and *tortillas*," Paco and Maura ate "*sopa de arroz, sopa de fideo, arroz*, stewed beef, and beef prepared with cabbage, carrots, and garbanzos . . . everything very delicious." "We [that is, Maura and Paco] in reality, when we were children, enjoyed a better life than the older [siblings] . . . I participated in the church. They would take me to offer flowers in the month of June which is dedicated to the Sacred Heart. I had my suit made of velvet (*terciopelo*) . . . I don't know where my mother found the cloth [but] she knew how to make everything . . . . She made me many shirts. Underwear, it goes without saying."[23] From el norte, the older brothers, particularly Jesús and José, also supplemented the younger children's educational needs. Paco recalled that Jesús would send him and Maura school supplies, including backpacks and other items they lacked, while Maura recalled that, on one special occasion, José sent her twenty dollars to purchase a dress for the pueblo's annual celebration in May.[24]

The remittances not only allowed José and his family to clothe and feed themselves regularly but also to open a bank account and save money for future needs and emergencies. Paco recalled that with his brothers in el otro lado, his father entrusted him to manage the family's expenses and savings.

"He told me all about his possessions . . . how much money he had in the bank. This was after Jesús principally sent remittances to my father." Before that, Paco said, they lived day to day. "There was no fortune," he admitted. "We survived (*se logro*) because they sent him [money]."[25] Later, when Paco gained employment in *la presidencia* (municipal government office) collecting rents (*rentas*) or property taxes, making some 150 pesos a month and a bit more when he took on side jobs, he was allowed to keep it for his personal needs, as his father never asked him (or, likely, Maura) to contribute to the household.[26] "My father always provided us with the basic, we ate and everything . . . that was his *obligation* [emphasis in the original]."[27] Rather, Paco went out to dinner, purchased decent clothes, and payed for any extra expenses, such as treating his friends to a refresco. And though his salary was later increased to 300 pesos, Paco realized it was still insufficient for the family's survival and his needs. From his father's and brothers' experiences and the social remittances they brought with them, Paco understood that his chance to achieve economic stability remained in the north. "That was why one leaves to find a better life and I already knew that in this country [the United States] you could gain a bit more. *We didn't come for the American dream* [laughs and speaks in a loud tone], *we came to eat, to live* (emphasis in original), . . . where there were better opportunities. That is what motivated us to migrate. To find a better life. Yeah."[28]

Reinforcing Patriarchal Authority

By the late 1950s and early 1960s, Jesús, Juan, and José's communication with the household became less and less consistent, leading their father to become increasingly frustrated over their disregard of their obligations to the household. Mail service, though slow as compared to the telephone—scarce in Calvillo at that time—remained among the most cost-efficient forms of communication.[29] José's deliberate, consistent, and persistent letter writing—carried out on half-sheets of paper to save on resources and on a personal typewriter his brother-in-law brought him from Chicago for his work at la presidencia—relayed his most significant concerns with household and family affairs, including his sons' growing silence over the past few years. Not one to delay in advising his four sons about their decisions, José responded promptly to any of their letters, usually the same day he received them, and kept them at his side while he pounded out his directives. To ensure he kept his lines of intelligence clear, José kept close track of the letters and the one-for-one reciprocity often practiced among letter writers (as David A. Gerber has found in his research on British immigrant letter writers), noting who sent what and on what day.[30] The relatively quick, weeklong turnaround of mail service as well as José's meticulous organization of incoming and outgoing mail—his regulative process—meant that he kept up with family and community matters throughout his sons' migrant journey across the borderlands. He did so, though, as long as they responded promptly.

Though rarely effusive in his expression of affection, José communicated paternal care and concern when he signed off on his letters, always making sure he sent greetings from the community left behind in Calvillo, including friends and family and sometimes household pets, including the canines Pichirilo, Minuto, and Duque.[31] José was mindful too of the social networks that had facilitated Paco's and his older sons' transition to el norte. Consistently, he reminded Paco to pass on salutations to *compadres* and *comadres* and expatriates from Calvillo living in the Mexicali–Imperial Valley region who had extended economic and cultural resources as well as emotional support to his sons when they migrated to the region. To keep the lines of communication clear, José almost always repeated Paco's words when writing to his son, a process David A. Gerber calls "double voice." José's use of double voice—repeating the news and questions Paco posed in previous letter—is especially helpful in deciphering the full meaning of the correspondence, for Paco's letters to his father are no longer extant. The double voice also allows for an understanding of Paco's concerns about the family, friends, material possessions, cultural artifacts, and life he left behind.

José's correspondence with Paco reveals a caring yet firm and demanding father who worked relentlessly to maintain communication to reinforce his sons' filial, moral, emotional, and economic obligations to the household. Indeed, no sooner had Paco departed for Mexicali, from where he would apply for residency, in September 1962 than José dashed off a letter, reminding him to remain in contact by writing promptly—a reminder José would send in almost all correspondence to his sons—and to find out when he as well as his older brothers, José, Jesús, and Juan, might return to Calvillo—a question he would also pose persistently to the brothers.[32] To José, having his sons tethered to the household—no matter how far they had strayed—was an obligation they owed him as the father and paternal figure of authority. To facilitate their homecoming, José encouraged his sons Paco and José to plan their visit with their sibling Juan, who was in Mexicali and wanted to return in early November of that year. José even suggested they bring the younger José's car so that they might travel together and ease the long haul. Shrewdly, the elder José had already contacted Juan as well, informing him of the opportunity for the brothers to travel together. José understood, however, that it might be hard for all four to coordinate their travel plans and conceded that if they did not come together, they could easily find an alternative way home.[33]

Despite José's repeated requests about his sons' return migration, none of them had any immediate plans to travel home, failing to fulfill what José understood as their filial duty. As noted earlier, Paco was in Mexicali waiting for his residency, while the younger José was in Brawley busy with the fall planting, watering, and harvesting schedule of the agricultural fields. Plus, as José explained to his brother Paco in early September 1962, he needed to save his pennies. "I just finished getting out of my debts (*drogas*) and if your matter takes long I will have to support you here." After saving a bit of money, José hoped he would have the chance (*chansa*) to return to Calvillo in December and stay a month. Before signing off, José told Paco, "Tell my father not to wait for me that I didn't go."[34] Apparently, their father would have to wait even longer for the younger José, as he did not go home in December 1962 or in the months that followed. Jesús, the eldest brother, who was in San José, also failed to return. Much to the patriarch's content, Juan had returned recently to Calvillo from Mexicali, where he spent much of his time when not under contract as a bracero. As José informed Paco, Juan brought with him his infant son, Juan José, as well as the child's mother, for a visit with the extended family in Calvillo.[35]

Unwilling to release his sons from their filial obligations, a month after Paco had left for el norte in 1962 José informed Paco as well as the older brothers that he needed their immediate assistance taking their mother, Jilda, to Guadalajara to see an oncologist, as she was battling "the illness" (*la enfermedad*), which Paco confirmed years later in an interview was uterine cancer. Though it is unclear when she developed the disease, Maura recalled years later that Jilda often complained about a burning pain near her kidneys and abdomen, prompting the elder José to take her to Mexico City for evaluation. Once they were there, the disease was diagnosed and the doctors recommended treatment with Dr. Manuel Riebeling Robles, an oncologist in Guadalajara. Jilda and José then spent several years traveling back and forth to Guadalajara for radiation treatment, though it is unclear who paid the medical expenses. José told Paco that he needed at least one of the sons, preferably with a car, to help take Jilda to see the doctor.[36]

While bus service was readily available, José needed a car to transport Jilda, as she was unable to walk well without crutches and experienced much pain when using them to get around. According to Maura, Jilda's inability to walk pain free stemmed from the radiation treatment, which resulted in brittle bones. Eventually, Jilda fractured a hip. That fracture, in turn, went unattended, leading it to heal improperly, causing her excruciating pain. "Can you imagine what suffering? What pain?" Maura said. To get around, Maura explained, "she would tie a foot with a cloth [and pull on it] to be able to move . . . and she would also use a little chair and she would secure herself with it and she would use it to move around." To walk, Jilda would also take what appeared to be little hops or jumps or, when they were available, she used the crutches.[37] Within a year, by November 1963, her physical condition deteriorated drastically, leaving her unable to walk without crutches.[38]

After several months, José's appeals to his sons for assistance with their mother, another expected obligation, were finally answered. Paco's older brother José managed to take time off from work and return to Calvillo to facilitate the medical treatment in March 1963. Jilda's eyesight was failing, so upon his arrival José took her as well as his father to see an optometrist in Leon, Guanajuato, a little over 100 miles to the southeast, and soon after to Guadalajara for an appointment with Dr. Riebeling for "the other ailment."[39] To fight the cancer, she needed an operation soon, but they had to wait until Paco returned from the United States to take them to Guadalajara.[40] Sixteen months later, José again requested his sons' assistance taking Jilda for a follow-up appointment. Fortunately, José the younger responded to his father's plea and returned to Calvillo to take them to Guadalajara again. The visits, though difficult for everyone, proved successful, for the treatments helped cure Jilda, and she remained cancer-free for the remainder of her life.[41]

While José was satisfied with his sons' assistance with Jilda, he called on them again for their advice and moral support in dealing with Maura's unwelcome suitor. Twenty years old and an attractive young woman, Maura had gained the interest of José Soto, a young man from Las Tinajas. Her father, however, did not approve of the fellow or his relatives. He attempted to end the relationship, going so far as trying to separate the couple on various occasions, particularly in 1963, and needed his sons' support, which he expected as the head of the household. Little did José know, however, that the relationship was not recent but rather had developed as long ago as 1959, as letters of courtship between José Soto and Maura attest. Though they tried to keep their noviasgo a secret—by holding their rendezvous out of sight of her father and the rest of her family and by sending mail to a post office box rather than her home—in the small town where everyone shared information, her father eventually found out about the relationship. Maura recalled years later that once, in the public square, he told her that "he would rather see her dead than marry" her suitor.[42]

In 1963, the affair became public with the disclosure of photographs of Maura and José Soto enjoying themselves at a rancho. They were not alone in the pictures: male and female friends accompanied them in their amusement. "Look I don't know how they found out about the pictures," José Soto told Maura in January 1963 in a letter he mailed to her in Guadalajara, where she had been sent as a ruse to separate her from Soto. But those images had led to "a big controversy (*arguende*) I don't even have to tell you." "Look I want you to do exactly as I tell you," he continued. "Tell them that I sent them to you along with the negatives and that you burned them so that the *lio* (controversy) [over the pictures] will end."[43] While taking snapshots with friends may seem innocuous, at the time doing so as a single young woman or man with your boyfriend or girlfriend was a scandal (*un escandalo*), as it violated gender norms of sexual propriety, particularly for females. As Maura explained, "The biggest fear was having your family and others in town see them." Doubtless, imagery of unregulated and unchaperoned socializing among unmarried young men and women affronted paternal authority and gender norms of sexual propriety, particularly for females, who were viewed as weak and vulnerable to the temptations of males, and brought shame to the family and the head of the household, especially when Maura's father was a well-known public figure.[44] Chaperonage of young daughters was no trivial matter either among Mexican families living in the United States. A few decades earlier, in the 1920s and 1930s in Los Angeles, as Vicki L. Ruiz has found, chaperones—usually older siblings or extended family members—closely regulated young Mexican American women's sexuality in order to prevent shameful behavior, such as engaging in sexual relations outside of marriage, and thereby ensured an honorable household.[45] In Calvillo, decades later, chaperones served a similar purpose, but when they could not serve their purpose, townspeople developed other means of containing their children's sexuality. Indeed, José and the extended family had no other option than to attempt to separate Maura and José Soto for good, for the relationship cast doubt on José's ability to control and contain his daughter.

After weeks in Guadalajara, Maura still remained outside the purview of her father. To bring her home under his watch, José turned to his sons for assistance. Frustratingly, none of them responded to his communications. While he eventually managed to get her to return to Calvillo, José wanted to keep her separated from her paramour, and to do so, it seems, without Maura's knowledge. This time José tried to send Maura in her mother's company to the United States for an extended vacation as *turistas* to visit the brothers. To do so, José needed the sons to obtain a notarized letter of support to help them receive approval of the visa applications. Five months later, however, none of the brothers—Paco, José, Jesús, or Juan— had heeded their father's demands of facilitating the women's migration, for José kept insisting in his letters to his sons that Maura wanted to travel.[46] Maura, though, had little interest in leaving town.

Desperate to maintain control over his daughter's future and to dissolve the courtship, as her suitor was apparently about to propose marriage, José confessed to Paco his plan to separate them. "Look I would like that one of you would find out the way Maura could go join you or with Cuca my cousin, I've heard that they are about to ask for her hand in marriage." By separating the couple, José thought he could prevent the marriage. José continued, "With that son of a gun I would not like it and that is why I had suggested to Jesús to inquire with Cuca if she can help us so that they can take her for a season." Having more confidence in Paco's decisions than in those of his brothers, José told Paco, "Later you can tell me your opinion because you have a different way of thinking than the rest of your brothers, I'm telling you respond the quickest that you can about this matter."[47] Though the sons were unresponsive, José persisted with his plans and in asking for their assistance. "Tell me if you bought the car," he reiterated the next month to Paco, "perhaps Maura can go to that country."[48]

To regain a hold on the family, José turned to his son José for emotional support, but the latter, like his brothers, ignored the plea and privately expressed shame to Paco about doing so. "You know days ago my father wrote to me and it seems he is very hurt (*muy sentido*) with all of us perhaps he is right (*tenga razón*)," the younger José told Paco in November 1963. "I delay in writing him because I don't have anything to send him and also very little to say to him." "You probably already know about Maura well my father has informed me that she has left with José Soto," he told Paco. As Maura recalled years later, she had not only left with Soto but also had married him before a justice of the peace.[49]

Knowing that his son José would likely not return soon, José, the father, became even more upset when he learned that Paco would also delay in coming home—until May 1964—and turned to the force of the letter to move him and his siblings. "It seems to me far out until May, that's how you all have strung me along, I wish it was possible for you to come at the latest in December . . . because I have a matter to discuss with you all, and until then it seems too late for me," he wrote in late September 1963. By then, he feared, Maura would be long gone with Soto, leaving him and his wife alone in the household.[50]

When that plea fell on deaf ears, José used his letter—as constitutive of the self, the father figure—to get them to obey, and particularly Jesús, who had stayed away for nearly three years. He told Paco not only once, but three times, to contact him. "Look I want you to tell Jesús to make the effort (*animo*) to come, you and he, it's been many years that he has not returned and I want to have an interview with you all," he wrote in October 1963. "I'm telling you go see Jesús and you show him this letter so that he knows that I need for him . . . to make the sacrifice and come." José's weakening filial grip over his sons and his urgency for a response were signs of an increasing sense of powerlessness.[51] "I would like you to come because it urgent for me (*me urge*) for us to see each other."[52]

By November of that year, Maura's relations with her suitor were apparent to all, including her father, for she was seven months pregnant. By then, José's anger had been transformed to anguish, leading him to invoke the filial obligation his sons owed the household as well as the shame they carried with them for not tending to their parents' needs. "Look Paco I want you to see Jesús and tell him what has happened to make the effort and pay a visit, as I think we won't be bothering you all, for much time due to our age, and that I want to deal [with] a matter with almost all of you . . . to see what we all think (*opinamos*), because you know . . . a situation has just happened that has been hard on me" as the head of the household, he confessed, referring to Maura. "You will come and you will know what it is that happened but God will decide, therefore if you see Jesús see if it is possible."[53]

Despite José's insistence that Jesús return, only his sons Paco and José returned home in November 1963, after a brief delay caused by the closure of the international border following the assassination of President John F. Kennedy that month. When they arrived in Calvillo, they saw the reason for their father's anger—Maura's pregnancy, a decided source of shame for the head of the household and the family more generally given her unmarried status, gender mores of the pueblo, and Catholic Church teachings about sex and sexuality in and outside of marriage. Unmarried women—single and widowed females—were expected to remain chaste. By then, too, José had lost what little power he had over the situation, for less than two months later Maura married the unwelcome suitor in the Catholic Church prior to the child's birth. "I'm letting you know that Maura has married through the church and we are alone, your mother and I, for heaven's sake what one doesn't expect to happen happens but so it goes it is not much time that we will last you."[54] José and Jilda were never completely alone, however, for Maura ended up living at home for many years. With the help of her parents, she raised her daughter and her subsequent children alone, as Soto spent decades away traveling as a migrant laborer to and from the United States, returning to visit annually. Eventually, he returned to Calvillo, settling permanently.[55]

José's rancor with his sons over their lack of respect for his paternal authority as well as his growing sense of powerlessness sometimes focused on the emotional pain they caused Jilda with their prolonged absences and failures to remember her, particularly on special occasions. In August 1964, a month after complaining about Jesús's extended absences, José reprimanded all the sons for neglecting to communicate not only with him but also with their mother, who had recently celebrated her saint's day (*dia de su santo*), a Catholic tradition of linking every day of the year to a saint. Apparently the sons forgot that San Leovigildo's Day fell on August 20. "Regarding your mother and her saint's day she spent it without worry and without glory, nobody remembered her except your uncle Pablo and Susana," her brother and sister-in-law who lived in Chicago, Illinois. "They sent her some cards and that was it, from her sons none of them remembered her," he informed Paco.[56] Though it is unclear if he used the sons' neglect of Jilda for his own purposes—to invoke filial guilt and get them to obey him as the head of the household, as he did on occasion—José also overlooked Jilda's needs, for he seldom communicated her wants and desires. Instead, Jilda, who could only sign her name, found others—usually her daughter, Maura, or an anonymous scribe—to pen letters in which she voiced her basic necessities.

José complained not only to Paco that the sons disregarded their filial obligations but also to local residents in Calvillo, including close friends of the family. During one of her visits to the family's home to see Jilda, María Concepción "Conchita" Alvarado, the younger José's *novia* (girlfriend), heard the patriarch's complaints about his sons' infrequent communication, which she, in turn, passed along to José. "It's up to you but I think you should write more often," Conchita advised José after visiting his parents at their home.[57] José, however, denied that he wrote them infrequently. "It makes me happy to hear that you went to my house and don't believe that I allow a lot of time to lapse with writing to them. What happens is that I sometimes delay perhaps a week in answering them."[58] While it was true that he often took weeks to reply, José likely stretched the truth to avoid giving Conchita the impression that he shirked his filial duty and was an irresponsible son.

The elder José called on his sons repeatedly not only for emotional, moral, and filial support in household affairs but also for economic sustenance—the much-needed remittances—for the maintenance of the home, which was in disrepair. As the younger José admitted shamefully to Paco in November 1963, nearly a year after the younger brother had departed to el norte, "You know I don't know how to tell you . . . but you know our family has hit rock bottom (*ya está por los suelos*)."[59] Among their father's most pressing financial concerns was paying off 3,000 of the 10,000 to 15,000 pesos he still owed on the home. In response to his father's plea for funds, Paco turned over his severance pay from la presidencia to help cover those expenses as well as much-needed improvements.[60] Three months after Paco contributed his portion, his older sibling José returned to Calvillo and gave his father another sum of money, but it was not enough, leading their father to call on the eldest, Jesús, to cooperate financially. Jesús, though, apparently failed to heed his request, forcing José to borrow money to pay off the balance.[61]

A month later, in April 1963, with the title to the house secured, José did not relent in pressuring his eldest son to contribute and fulfill his duty. He told Paco, "I already told Jesús to help me with something because I am now without a single cent and you all have already helped me with a lot and you cannot continue helping me, and I am waiting for him to respond . . . everything is very expensive material and labor."[62] Despite José's repeated stern commands, Jesús failed to send word or a single dollar, making for a frustrated yet not defeated father who continued to implore his sons to send contributions. While José admitted that, in the past, Jesús and Juan had contributed to the household's maintenance, in recent years they had sent him less and less money. In May 1963, in response to Paco's query whether Jesús had sent any remittances, José responded angrily that he had not and was not willing to keep it a secret. "I'll tell you I don't like to cover for anyone, he has not sent me anything it's been almost two years that he has not sent a single cent Juan did more he just sent me one hundred and fifty dollars."[63] Not one to relent, José insisted that Jesús—who had not helped in three years—and the rest of the sons send cash.[64] By the end of 1963, José had grown frustrated and was out of ideas. "Paco what happened with the money that Jesús was going to send with you, or was going to send, nothing has arrived here." "I've been waiting for that money (*centavos*) that he promised you and nothing."[65]

José asked his sons for money not only to repair the house but also to facilitate their brother Juan's migratory process, as he was the only one of the four males to remain without U.S. residency. Juan's ability to obtain a green card was central in bringing José much emotional and economic relief, as he would no longer have to worry about his son's ability to migrate lawfully and safely and to find steady employment as well as financial independence. Residency, in short, would enable Juan to leave his parents' household. Unlike José and Paco, who had obtained their residency with letters of support from J. C. Reeves, who employed the two brothers, Juan had not done so, even though he too had worked for Reeves prior to José and Paco's employment at the same ranch. In fact, Juan facilitated José's employment with Reeves. According to Paco, Juan preferred to work as a bracero under temporary contract, as he believed the program would continue for years, making it unnecessary for him to obtain his green card. When the opportunity came years earlier to do so, Juan had reportedly scoffed at the idea. Now, with the ending of the program imminent, his father, José, realized it would be necessary for Juan to obtain residency and worked tirelessly to facilitate the process.

José's quest to facilitate Juan's residency began a few weeks after Paco had adjusted his migratory status. "Juan is here in the house, and I want you all to help him fix his entrance that is why I want to go to Guadalajara, to see if I can speak to Lic[enciado] Vergara and if not your uncle Pablo says he will obtain an employment letter (*carta de trabajo*) or whatever is needed to obtain the passport on behalf of the United States." "I only want you to help me with the money," he reiterated, "to see if it is possible to adjust his migratory status (*arreglarle*) because here you know he doesn't work in anything and he needs money." "It is impossible," José admitted, "to give him everything he needs, that is why I ask you all to help me with him."[66] Juan was, indeed, in dire economic straits, for on several occasions he wrote to Paco asking for money to see through his petition, among other things. It is unclear, though, if Paco delivered any funds, given that he had recently crossed the border and started working for Reeves alongside his older brother in Brawley. What is clear is that adjusting Juan's status would be neither quick nor easy.[67]

After a few months, Juan continued without his residency, but José remained optimistic, for he was well aware of the emerging opportunities for Mexican migrants to obtain residency, as he kept himself well informed about changing immigration policies and practices. To do so, José kept in touch with locals—particularly recently returned migrants and their family members—and read Aguascalientes's dailies, *El Heraldo* and *El Sol del Centro*, which made their way to Calvillo in the 1950s and 1960s. An investigation of those papers reveals, however, that they offered little insight on politics at the border as compared to the personal experiences shared through word of mouth.[68] From residents in Calvillo, José learned about individuals such as Emanuel Braude, a lawyer in Los Angeles who specialized in fighting for the rights of Mexican immigrant laborers, namely, braceros and those who might come to replace them. Braude was, indeed, known among farmworkers and their employers. According to the Mexican American journalist and correspondent for the *Los Angeles Times*, Rubén Salazar, in December 1963 Braude had defended 150 Mexican migrant laborers against the federal government's denial of their employment as temporary laborers in California's agricultural fields, even though state officials had allowed it. Under the new rule, the California farm labor associations, four of which Braude represented, had the right to place the temporary migrant laborers in the fields as a desperate measure to deal with the ending of the bracero program. Salazar reported that the U.S. Department of Labor opposed the agreement, as it argued that it hurt domestic farmhands and drove down wages as well as having a negative effect on working conditions. Though Braude lost the case, his knowledge of immigration laws and practices and his defense of Mexican immigrants seemed to give José hope that the attorney might be able to help Juan. With much enthusiasm, he urged Paco to contact Braude's offices in Los Angeles and, if necessary, travel to the city for information and assistance.[69] "Paco don't delay in your request (*gestionar*) the matter with Emanuel Braude, I will send you his address and telephone number."[70]

Though neither Paco nor José made contact with Braude or sought his services in Los Angeles, José remained undeterred in searching for a way to facilitate Juan's migratory status and continued to implore his sons for support. "Referring to the matter of your brother Juan," José said two weeks later in an upbeat tone, "I've learned that it looks like there is now more chanza to adjust his status (*arreglar*), I am asking you after all to see if perhaps he can adjust his migratory status."[71] In all likelihood, José referred to the imminent passage of the Immigration Act of 1965, which would eventually eliminate previous quotas for southern Europeans, Africans, and Asians based on national origin and give preference to family members of citizens and residents as well as immigrants with special skills. A congressional commission appointed to investigate the law, however, took two years to complete its work, delaying the act's implementation.[72] Nevertheless, during that two-year lapse, many immediate family members of former braceros adjusted their status relatively easily, for employer verification forms were not required from family members, usually wives and children. Indeed, all that was needed were letters of support from a reliable U.S. employer willing to sponsor them.[73]

José's optimism about imminent changes to immigration laws was reinforced by a local resident in Calvillo who had recently received news from Braude's offices affirming such news. "I tell you," José said to Paco, "that according to a letter that was written by Braude to an individual (*sugeto*) from here, it looks like they are soon going to get rid of the famous form 320, [Braude] tells the individual (*fulano*) that the person who has in the United States a family member, brother or father or whatever relative, closely related, and is legally in the United States, or rather National, with much ease can adjust the status of the relative who wants a Visa, I personally saw the letter from Braude, hopefully it is true."[74] The new law meant that Juan, like other close family members of residents in the United States, now had the opportunity to gain residency.

Despite José's efforts to gain assistance from his sons to adjust their brother's status, Juan remained working under contract as a bracero, a status he seemed to prefer. At the end of May 1964, two months following his father's latest attempt to assist him in adjusting his status, Juan signed up for a forty-five-day contract harvesting beets in Colorado. José, however, was unhappy with Juan's latest contract, for it was far too short. "After one struggles so much to arreglar, hopefully they will remove that form, which is the one that is so troublesome, as soon as they get rid of it, you have to try and see if it is possible for your brother to adjust his status."[75]

With the migratory process on hold, Juan returned and remained living at home in Calvillo, while José complained bitterly about his son's financial situation. "He does not want to work," he told Paco, "he knows it I cannot force him."[76] Though upset, José was nevertheless willing to assist his son when in need. To help Juan relocate from Mexicali to Calvillo, José sent him 400 pesos.[77] Two weeks later, still angry about Juan's financial dire straits, José confessed to Paco he was unable to resist his son's pleas and provided him with some economic relief. "You know Juan your brother is leaving for Mexicali, it seems he is hell bent on extracting money from me, to the point that I am almost broke, because for everything it is only about money, but I think it is the last that I give him."[78] Though José's rationale for extending a hand to his son is unclear, it is possible that it was either paternal care and concern or simply that he wanted him elsewhere. Normally, José expected his sons to contribute to the household and wasted little time in requesting support when it was needed.

José asked his sons not only for support for Juan's residency but also for his own personal needs and satisfaction, a request that caused him little remorse. Among the most consistent requests he made was for money to play the national lottery or *lotería*, which took place four times a year. According to Paco, José was particularly hopeful of striking it rich, as an extended family member had come into significant winnings in the recent past. For José, engaging in the gambling was particularly easy, too, as an uncle in Aguascalientes sold those tickets. Indeed, within a few months of Paco's migration to el norte, José wrote asking for a contribution to one of his favorite pastimes. "Paco ask José if you all are interested in that we play the lottery for the 5th of May send me to buy a ticket (*cachito*)." Emphasizing his urgency to roll the dice, he signed his name and scribbled "*pero pronto*" (hurry now) below. Less than two weeks later, Paco sent him 100 pesos, enough to buy two tickets worth 50 pesos each, a considerable sum.[79] Despite José's enthusiasm, they did not win any money, leaving little at home for the basic necessities, including the cost of vaccinating the family dogs.[80]

While José expected his children to fulfill their obligations, he also reciprocated in the form of paternal advice, demonstrating affection as well as care and concern. José's letters to Paco—as well as other notes exchanged among family members—demonstrate his interest in seeing his sons succeed in their efforts to find economic stability for themselves and their larger family. Indeed, as soon as Paco had been able to obtain his residency and cross into the United States at the end of December 1962, José was quick to advise him on how to gain economic independence. "You tell me you arranged your crossing, now time to get work and save pennies, because that is the way you accomplish something in life."[81]

Along with their employment, José weighed in on many of his sons' major decisions, thereby reinforcing his role as the patriarch. When Paco bought his first car, a used baby-blue convertible, to ease his travel to and from the agricultural fields in Brawley, California, José approved and offered a quick tip. "Paco you tell me you have a car and that it is used, that is good only be sure that it is in good operational use."[82] When Paco decided to quit his job and leave Imperial Valley after a heated disagreement with Reeves's father over proper watering techniques, Paco ended up migrating to San José, California, to live with his brother. There, in the growing technology and information sector of Silicon Valley, jobs in the service industry were plentiful, as he communicated to his father, who welcomed the news. Soon, Paco found employment working in a restaurant and, later, at a car wash, where he ascended quickly to become lead worker on his shift. That bit of news, in turn, prompted his father to offer more words of wisdom. "You . . . tell me you're working, take care of your job and what you earn take care of it."[83] In response to Paco's news that he had enrolled in school, José encouraged him as well to continue with his studies to establish a trade that would allow him to find stable employment. "Regarding your school attendance, you do well in educating yourself, and if you can study auto mechanic repair, that is good."[84]

In addition to advising his sons about their education, employment, purchases, and even travel, José went out of his way to care for his sons' most valued possessions left behind. For Paco this meant his prized subscription to *Selecciones* (*Reader's Digest* in Spanish), a bicycle, and a cowboy hat. When possible, José sent Paco the magazines, renewed the subscription, and kept track of any stray issues sent from the Mexico City international office. In all likelihood Paco received his father's news with welcome relief, as he enjoyed reading selections of writings from popular magazines across the United States. In addition to collecting the magazine, José also looked after the maintenance of the bike and Paco's hat.[85]

José's fatherly advice also came through when the sons delayed in their communication, particularly when they were known to respond promptly, as was Paco. When Paco delayed in writing, both José and Jilda became concerned. "Paco I was very worried about you because you had not responded to me, we were with concern, but I received your letter and we were consoled." As constitutive of the self, the sending and safe arrival of the correspondence brought a measure of relief for José and Jilda, and they encouraged Paco to remain in contact. "And don't stop responding even if it is only the envelope with that we will know that you are well."[86]

José's epistolary practice reveals not only a caring yet overbearing father figure but also an observant man who used his insights to aid his family. From his desk at the presidencia municipal and from the park bench in the central plaza, José heard the local gossip, or what David A. Gerber aptly terms social intelligence, and communicated it with his sons.[87] In September 1963, for instance, José told Paco that Pedro Jiménez, a local resident likely known to Paco, was on his way to el norte. Jiménez, José reported, "has just sold all his property, I think he will end up going [north]."[88] When the latest telegraph arrived, José quickly informed Paco of the news as well, for the town suffered from limited communication services. Indeed, the late

appearance of the telegraph—which was available decades earlier in less remote areas—indicates that modern means of communication were slow in
coming to the pueblo. "I'm letting you know that we have telegraph service
here in Calvillo . . . we may need it in some kind of emergency."[89] Apparently,
the mail service and scant telephones were insufficient as quick and accessible
means of communication for most people in town. Only bureaucrats and the
wealthiest among them had phone lines installed in their offices and homes.

Fighting for Paternal Authority While Battling a Mysterious Disease

José's ability to reclaim his waning paternal authority in the family met a
new challenge when he realized that he faced a serious health problem. Unsure when or how to inform his sons, José disclosed his ailment when it
became too difficult to manage his regular routines on his own. It began
when, sometime in 1964, José began to notice trembling in one of his hands.
Unknown to himself, his family, and the many doctors in Mexico and the
United States who attempted to diagnose and treat him, José suffered from
the early signs of an incurable, debilitating disease—Parkinson's—an ailment
that would soon leave him unable to write, work, walk, or talk. Aware that
his uncontrolled movements had worsened, José said little to his sons until
December of that year. When his son José learned about the illness, he too
did not inform many people—family or friends—either in Imperial Valley
or Calvillo, including his girlfriend, Conchita. Within a few short months,
however, the mysterious affliction had progressed to the extent that it
was impossible to keep the many people who frequented the municipal
offices from noticing the increased trembling.[90]

  Like José, few in Calvillo or the rest of Mexico or even the United States
knew much about the disease, for significant research findings began to
emerge only in the post–World War II era.[91] Scant knowledge about the
ailment led some residents in Calvillo to rumor that his illness was a curse
from God, for in his capacity as a judge he had ruled against a local Catholic priest who had been charged with improprieties with a young female
parishioner. José, in contrast, believed his illness was a result of the anger—
coraje—he had experienced over Maura's relationship with José Soto as
well as her pregnancy. Those speculations would eventually be laid to rest,
for in the 1960s researchers figured out that Parkinson's was the result of
the lack of necessary levels of dopamine in the brain. That finding enabled

scientists to develop an effective treatment, namely, prescribing Levodopa or L-dopa. The immediate results were nothing short of miraculous, but over time scientists realized it was not a cure-all, as patients began to exhibit serious side effects. In time, investigators produced effective synthetic drugs helping patients control their bodily movements. Fortunately, for most Parkinson's sufferers today, if treated properly, the severity of the symptoms can be reduced for many years. Unfortunately, José would never see the benefits of those insights, as knowledge remained rudimentary in Mexico as well as in the United States in the 1960s.[92]

Within a few months of José's disclosure of his tremors, the disease had progressed significantly, interfering with his daily routine and casting a shadow on his outlook on life. As doctors later discovered, by the time the earliest signs of Parkinson's are manifest, 90 percent of the neurons producing dopamine have been destroyed, indicating that the disease appears slowly and goes undetected for a long time.[93] Complaining to Paco about the severity of his uncontrolled movements, which he believed was linked to nerve damage, José wrote: "In your house we continue poorly . . . my hand doesn't serve me anymore I have a strong neuritis, and it is only trembling, I am making the effort to see if I can improve, if not only God will know."[94] After two weeks brought little improvement, José's hope for recuperating had slowly but steadily deteriorated. José had recently visited a neurologist three or four times in Guadalajara, but the doctor had not provided much help other than suggesting brain surgery as a last resort. Wisely, José refused, for patients who had surgery to relieve the symptoms were at high risk for brain damage caused by human error and the rudimentary technology of the day. Not until decades later would surgical approaches become more effective, providing relief to patients; even today such operations are reserved for the most advanced cases.[95] José too was not sold on the idea. "I cannot agree," he said, noting that his hand "doesn't hurt or anything, only that it doesn't serve me much."[96]

Hopeless but not defeated, José set his sights on medical advances in the modern center of Mexico City and made plans to travel there to see a doctor. Though it is unclear who advised him about the possibility of treatment and how many times he went to the capital city looking for answers, it is clear that he went at least once, if not twice or three times, and his sons José, Paco, and Jesús took him to a clinic sometime in August or September 1965.[97] Apparently, Jesús had finally given in to his father's and mother's appeals for him to return home. For that trip, Paco and Jesús packed into a car in the summer heat and made their way south from San José to Brawley, where they picked up their brother José. From there, they continued their drive across the U.S.-Mexico border, heading south to Calvillo, approximately a 1,500-mile, thirty-hour drive.[98] Once in Calvillo, they picked up their father and pushed further south, driving another 345 miles to Mexico City, where they finally arrived at the clinic. After greeting them, the doctor carried out a series of rudimentary tests on José. For one, he used a thick metal fork and struck it near the patriarch's head, listening to the pitch or vibrations to rule out any masses or tumors in the brain. After a series of exams, the doctor could provide few answers about José's ailment, and they left empty-handed. Back in Calvillo, the sons left their father at home and continued the journey north without much delay, for most had to return to work.

As the disease progressed and José increasingly lost control of his most basic physical activities, such as signing the closing salutation of his correspondence, he became despondent and desperate for answers. In his last typewritten letter, which he was unable to sign, José reported to Paco, "I continue somewhat poorly, . . . for heaven's sake (sea por Dios). Look Paco I can't figure out what to do with this illness if you saw me you wouldn't recognize me how tired I am, and I am resolved to [go to] Guadalajara to see if it is possible to regain my health, and as soon as you all can don't delay in coming to see us," he implored. "I will continue to advise you the status of my illness."[99] Little did José realize that, as is the case for most Parkinson's sufferers, his initial tremor in his limb would be followed by stiffness, an increasingly stooped posture, and difficulty walking as well as increasing loss of muscle control. He would also suffer from the "masked face," preventing him from showing spontaneous facial expressions, giving him a faraway look, which many in his family and the pueblo misinterpreted as mental disability. In the end, like most Parkinson's patients, José would be confined to a wheelchair and soon be bedridden.[100]

With little hope of finding relief among medical doctors in Mexico, José set out to try his luck in the United States, where he had heard of a doctor, more likely a curandero (healer), with the ability to cure the disease. Apparently, José's youngest brother, Baudelio, a doctoral student of mathematics and well regarded in the family for his English-language abilities, informed him of a man in Houston, Texas, who was known for "extracting" the ailment from the blood. With that news in hand, José applied and received a tourist visa to travel to the United States and insisted that his sons take him for treatment, even though he did not yet know what disease afflicted him,

José Chávez Torres, the family patriarch, and Leovijilda Esparza Chávez ("Jilda"),
his wife, 1966, pose for a photograph to accompany their petition for a tourist
visa to the United States. The purpose of the trip was to find the purported
healer who extracted mysterious ailments such as the one that afflicted José.
Though the search was unsuccessful, they learned from U.S. medical officials that
José's deteriorating health was a consequence of Parkinson's, a little understood
disease.
Photograph in author's personal collection.

its source, or exactly where to find the healer. Apparently, the hope for a
palliative was strong enough to send them on the hunt across hundreds of
miles.[101]

José was not alone in his limited knowledge of Parkinson's, as scientists
had not yet developed a single test to identify it or to determine its cause,
and have yet to do so. Today, to determine the presence of the affliction, all
other diseases must be ruled out before medication can be prescribed, and
even then the patient's response to the medicine must be monitored to ensure a successful diagnosis. That process alone can take months, and sometimes years. Researchers also remain unsure about the causes of Parkinson's
but have suggested pesticides. Studies have found that people who live or
work near agricultural areas are seven times more likely than those who live
in urban areas to develop the malady. It is highly possible, then, that while
a farmworker in California, José was exposed to the pesticides dieldrin and

rotenone, which are often blamed for the ailment. Other causes include getting hit in the head and exposure to elevated levels of paraquat and aluminum, whereas heredity is no longer considered a factor. What is known is that no definitive answer existed in the 1960s.[102]

To accommodate the elder José's demand to travel to Texas, his sons Paco and José planned the trip for sometime in early 1966, assigning Paco to pick up their father, mother, and Baudelio—who would translate for them in the United States. The younger José, in turn, would then take them to Calvillo after the visit with the healer. About a month later, in March 1966, when the crew of four—José, Jilda, Paco, and Baudelio—finally reached Houston, they had no idea where to find the doctor, for they had no address, only the name of the suburb—Pasadena—where he was to be found. After a weeklong search and stay in a local motel (they had no friends or family in the area), they gave up hope and turned their attention to the Rice Institute, where medical researchers agreed to examine José at minimal cost. After the doctors performed an electroencephalogram and a battery of other medical tests, according to Paco, who recalled the details of the trip years later, they diagnosed José's ailment as Parkinson's, giving him little hope for treatment or recovery. For reasons that remain unknown, he did not receive any regimen of L-dopa or other drugs. Dismayed but not defeated, José insisted that they travel to San José, California, where his sons resided, with hopes of finding more answers there.

After they arrived in San José, Paco took him to a medical facility in Palo Alto, California, a few miles north, that offered some hope, but as Paco recalled years later in an interview, because they lacked medical insurance or the means to pay for expenses, the office workers shunned them, and they left the facility quickly. Paco then took José to the Santa Clara County Hospital, where he was treated for a month at Paco's expense. There the doctors evaluated him and gave him medical advice for controlling his diabetes but could not offer a cure.[103]

By July 1966, after three or four months in the United States looking for answers, they returned to Calvillo with few answers. A month later, when the younger José was in town to marry Conchita, he informed Paco that their father continued the same but had also developed stomach troubles. "Recently I took him to La Chona," a neighboring community, José informed Paco, "to see a nurse who is very good at curing and she gave him some drops but I think he continues the same."[104] A month later, their father remained unchanged, according to Jilda. "What are we going to do there is nothing we can do," she said hopelessly to Paco.[105]

By the end of 1966, the world the elder José had known had collapsed around him. Soon bedridden, he had long given up his work at the presidencia as well as socializing in the town plaza; though he did send his sons an occasional letter using a scribe or letter writer, he was less consistent in responding. On at least three occasions at the end of 1966 and early in 1967, the younger José told Paco that he had written home to their father but had yet to receive any response.[106] It is likely that their parents had received the letters but had no one available to write a response. In one of his last missives to Paco, written by a scribe, the elder José said little of substance except for the usual niceties and news about Juan's search for permanent work.[107]

By then the Parkinson's disease, as well as his diabetes and problems arising from poor dental work, had progressed to the extent that José had difficulty finding any pleasure in daily life, including his meals. Jilda explained to Paco that while José ate well, he remained unsatisfied. "We can't figure out what to give him look he drinks 4 eggs and 3 gelatins and milk cookies and a hotcake (*jacecui*) all good and nevertheless he says that he is not satisfied and everything so expensive . . . I can't figure out what to do."[108] José's declining physical health also seemed to contribute to his worsening mental health. As researchers have recently found, 50 to 80 percent of patients with Parkinson's eventually develop some form of dementia.[109] Though dementia takes ten years to develop in patients, it is likely that José's declining mental health began to become apparent at that time. According to Jilda, by March 1967, nearly a year after they had traveled to Houston, José's physical and mental health had deteriorated considerably. "Son I want to tell you that your father has days where he is worse and there are times that he doesn't even know what he says or what he wants, in a word, there are moments in which he seems to lose all awareness." Warning Paco of his ill health, Jilda continued, "I tell you this so that you are prepared if something comes to happen but I don't want you to disrupt your routine at work to come solely because he is ill."[110] In her distress, Jilda also reached out to José's aunt and her close friend, Andrea Torres, living in San José, California, informing them that his illness had not only worsened but brought on intense daily pain. Sad to hear the news, Andrea offered José her daily prayers for his recovery and sent Jilda, along with her letter, four dollars for necessities.[111]

Though little hope remained, his sons never relented in seeking a cure. In July 1967, José wrote to his brother Paco about the possibility of a cure by a local curandera. "Here in Mexicali there is a woman who cures many illnesses." "People come from very far with this lady and she has cured many,

I would say that it would be good to bring my father as she doesn't charge a lot."[112] Though Paco's response is unclear, the family was apparently unable to pursue that treatment, for no other details emerged about efforts to visit the healer.

By then, the disease had taken an emotional and economic toll on the family, with José asking his sons for continued support to pay for his medical costs, including bills for hospitalization, medicine, and checkups. The younger José, who was in dire straits himself, asked Paco to intercede. "Paco if you can send my father some 1–15 dls because he wrote to me telling me he needed some money I'm going to send him at least 10 dls and more later however I can I will help him."[113]

For Jilda, disabled and small in stature, the increasing severity of his disease was especially burdensome, for she bore the brunt of his frustrations with his declining health and influence in the household. Visitors to the home during the worst of his affliction recalled his difficult temper and personality. Pedro (Perico) Sánchez, Paco's close friend, recalled, "Yes, well, that happened when [José] became ill and the character of [José] became unbearable . . . because of his disease . . . because well used to being active all the time and then all of a sudden, bang, he couldn't move anymore, he couldn't do anything." Jilda endured his wrath. Sánchez continued, "She was not a happy person, as there are many people, but you could see that she wasn't upset about the situation, I can assure you . . . I never heard her complain, I would see her often." Indeed, Sánchez claimed he often ate dinner at their home.[114]

As José battled Parkinson's in the late 1960s and the 1970s, the women in the family found ways to secure resources that, along with the remittances from the sons, enabled them to support the household, which included a growing number of children from Maura's marriage. To earn pin money, Jilda hawked candies and other treats to neighbors from a stoop at her front door, while her daughter, Maura, earned a nice sum from a small-scale fee-for-phone service, which she ran out of their home after they had a phone line installed sometime in the mid-1960s at Jilda's insistence. Maura's telephone business not only served to connect loved ones across Mexico and the U.S.-Mexico border but also helped herself and the family. Shrewdly, Maura capitalized on the growing demand for phone service by family members of migrants left behind and the government's failure to expand communication networks among the rural population.[115] Not until a decade later would phone service become widespread in the pueblo and, in the process, cause Maura's business to decline.

During his final years, José demanded around-the-clock constant care and attention and did so primarily from Jilda. Many who visited the home recalled that when he called her name in a loud, booming voice, she moved as quickly as her injured hip allowed her to tend to his needs. The physical toll of the disease was indelible on his gaunt, immobile, and expressionless face on the day he died, February 16, 1978.[116]

JOSÉ CHÁVEZ TORRES'S BATTLE with Parkinson's disease, while devastating, was only one of the many struggles that he faced later in life. As his correspondence with his migrant sons indicates, he fought to maintain the remnants of his self-identity as the patriarchal figure of authority in the household as it stretched across the U.S.-Mexico borderlands. As one of countless Mexicans who stayed at home and was not simply left behind by family members who immigrated to the United States, José did not retreat into invisibility. Rather, he crafted a demanding personality and persistently implored his sons as well as his daughter to fulfill their filial obligations of emotional, moral, and economic support to the household. Though he advocated continually for their return or for at least word on their return, as well as monetary support, over time José could not battle against his sons' delayed visits and remittances or with his daughter's strong will. Within a matter of a few short years, José was forced to rethink and renegotiate his role and identity in the household—from its head to that of a common member of the family—and in the larger community. Though it is unclear how other residents of the town viewed his changing role or if they took note of it, they understood that he faced many new challenges. Ultimately, Parkinson's disease weakened his resolve physically but not his willingness to give up emotionally his role in the family.

José Chávez Torres was not the only member of the community in Calvillo who questioned his self-identity as a result of the extended emigration and absence of family members and loved ones. Asunción "Chonita" Alvarado, Paco's girlfriend, felt equally dismayed by Paco's migration, expressing deep emotional pain, heartache, and longing with his departure to el norte and the dry spells during which there was no contact. The next chapter demonstrates the significant role of communication and miscommunication as well as letter writing and chisme in maintaining relationships among migrants and sweethearts who stayed at home and the power of migration in renegotiating and remaking personal identities.

CHAPTER FOUR

A Dios

Migration, Miscommunication, and Heartbreak

In April 1963, after months of waiting for her boyfriend, Paco Chávez, to return home to Calvillo, Aguascalientes, Asunción "Chonita" Alvarado had given up hope. Initially, when Paco had left for el norte in September 1962, the two had communicated consistently through a series of passionate and stormy letters. Over time, as the epistolary exchanges slowed and gossip (*chisme*) in the town spread about their weakening relationship, Paco became suspicious of Chonita's fidelity and she of his commitment. For Chonita, the more Paco delayed in corresponding, the more doubtful and, soon, despondent she became, especially after Paco told her he would be unable to come to the annual *feria* (festival) in May in Calvillo, as he had promised. Crushed about the news, she nevertheless accepted his decision and promised not to broach the subject of his return migration again.

Two weeks later, unable to withstand the alienation, Chonita broke her pledge and sent him a missive in which she unleashed her pain and fury. "Look Paco don't think I am desperate or impatient because you don't come simply I tell you because in some letters you say you are coming soon and in the next [letter you say] you are not coming," she said. "I don't deny it that I wanted you to come now for the fiesta but now that you can't too bad I don't want to ask you the impossible" or, she continued, "infect you (*contagiarte*) with my sadness."[1]

Heartbroken but not dejected, she fired off a series of charges accusing him of wanting to hurt her purposefully by leading her on when he knew he would not return anytime soon. "By what I see . . . you have always wanted to . . . find a way [to] . . . hurt me and laugh at me, but this has finished I will not allow you to continue to treat me in the way that you do, you always infer that only I have interest in our relationship and for that reason I don't want to be a beggar (*una rogona*), and I even think that I make your life miserable (*pesada*)," she charged. "I consider our relations terminated, don't think I am mad I am telling you this without resentment I think this is the best for the both of us," she declared. "A Dios Paco," she said, ending the relationship.[2]

Though Chonita severed the courtship, she still cared for Paco, and he cared for her as well, as they maintained covert updates on each other's lives by corresponding with mutual friends and family members in Mexico and the United States. From letters written to Paco from his male friends (*cuates*) in Calvillo, he learned about her latest social and romantic relationships in the pueblo. She, in turn, learned about his experiences in el norte through the correspondence between her sister María Concepción "Conchita" Alvarado and Paco's older brother, José Chávez Esparza, Conchita's *novio* (boyfriend), who lived in Brawley, California, in Imperial Valley. The resourceful system of communication, though imperfect, allowed them to keep watch over each other's affairs as well as maintain hope about the possibility of renewing the *noviasgo* (courtship).

Paco and Chonita's on again, off again relationship suggests that maintaining intimate, romantic relations across the U.S.-Mexico borderlands was no easy prospect. Indeed, the rudimentary systems of communication and consistent miscommunication, distance and time-consuming transportation, gossip among the close-knit family and social networks, and shifting interests and personal goals proved too burdensome for them to maintain a long-term, cross-border affair. Though the noviasgo did not result in marriage, it allowed them to express their greatest hopes and dreams for their immediate and future circumstances, their gendered identities and expectations in and outside of courtship, and their everyday social and cultural experiences living between here (*aqui*) and there (*allá*). Like most Mexican male migrants, Paco longed for economic opportunity, masculine affirmation, and social stability for himself and loved ones left behind, including Chonita. Though she understood the importance of securing material necessities, Chonita was most interested in having a fulfilling relationship personally and emotionally with a partner at her side who could reassure her of his commitment.

To explore more deeply their longing as well as how and why the courtship disintegrated over time, this chapter opens with a discussion of the systems of personal communication available in Mexico and the United States in the early to the mid-twentieth century to Mexican migrants and those who stayed at home. Next, it probes how those systems—the postal service, telephone, and telegraph in particular—shaped the nature of Paco and Chonita's relationship across the borderlands. While initially they maintained consistent contact, over time they delayed corresponding, leading them to grow increasingly suspicious of each other's fidelity. As the correspondence indicates, they still remained emotionally attached and used their mutual acquaintances to carry out surveillance on each other's social relations in and outside of town. With the support of social and cultural mores that encouraged the regulation of women's bodies across local, national, and transnational spaces, Paco turned to many friends and family members in Calvillo to maintain watch over Chonita's latest moves. Chonita, in contrast, only had her sister to keep tabs on Paco, leaving her at an emotional loss for knowing fully his latest whereabouts and relations. Finally, the chapter demonstrates that, despite hanging by a thread, the relationship experienced a second chance when Chonita reached out to Paco for emotional support following her sister's migration to the U.S.-Mexico border, providing them with the opportunity to reignite the courtship. That reunion, however, disintegrated quickly, as they lacked consistency in maintaining close contact. Ultimately, the distance, infrequent communication, miscommunication, and shifting goals and interests proved too weighty for the relationship. Expressing her deepest sorrow in seeing the noviasgo fizzle, Chonita had no choice but to call it quits. Though the letters often worked to maintain relations, here they worked to destroy them as well.

Communication across the U.S.-Mexico Borderlands

For much of the early to mid-twentieth century, the letter and, later, the telephone remained the most accessible forms of personal communication available to the majority of *mexicanos*. While the telegraph developed earlier in mid-nineteenth-century Europe and spread rapidly to Mexico and the United States, its use was reserved primarily for government and business affairs. Ordinary people in urban areas did, however, use the telegraph occasionally to communicate urgent information when no other means were available, but most rural dwellers went without for much of the early to mid-twentieth century. Instead, most relied on the relatively inexpensive government-funded postal service to correspond with loved ones in and outside of Mexico.

That service, the Servicio Postal Mexicano, or Sepomex, first emerged in the 1870s and 1880s as part of President Porfirio Díaz's attempt to modernize and integrate the nation. Prior to that, for nearly 300 years, the mail served the Spanish colonial government's need to remain in contact with officials in the Viceroyalty of Spain. Under Díaz's regime, Mexico joined the International Universal Postal Union in 1875, allowing the country to expand its reach across the globe. To facilitate mail service, Mexico established the First Mexican Postal Code (Primer Codigo Postal Mexicano) in 1883 and quickly expanded its use. In less than twenty years, eighteen postal zones had been established as part of an attempt to make the service "agile and dynamic," with a commitment to "social, economic, and cultural service."[3] The broader goal remained making it available to all inhabitants of the country and the most popular form of national and international communication. To do this, the government established new offices, both brick and mortar as well as mobile, founded stamp shops, and hired and trained workers. Government officials also created new land, maritime, and air routes across the country and worked out postal service agreements with other countries, expanding the service across national and international lines.[4]

Initially, Sepomex maintained an adequate and reliable national and international mail service through much of the early to mid-twentieth century. With many of the deliveries facilitated by the development of railways in Mexico and in the U.S.-Mexico borderlands in the same period, by the 1950s and 1960s Mexicans in increasingly remote areas of the country steadily gained access to the network. Indeed, correspondence from Calvillo, Aguascalientes, to Guadalajara, Jalisco, in the 1960s took three days, while that sent from Calvillo to Mexicali, Baja California, arrived in five days. Mail service across the U.S.-Mexico border faced slightly longer delays, taking about five or six days in total. When airmail service was made available, the times for national and international delivery were reduced drastically. And while the costs of sending first-class correspondence stood at about forty *centavos* (cents) for regular ground mail at midcentury, the cost doubled to eighty centavos for airmail in the early 1960s. Despite the increase, many, if not most, residents continued to use the service.

While mail service to cities was widespread, door-to-door delivery was not available in Mexican pueblos and ranchos, forcing local residents and campesinos to travel to the nearest post office to pick up correspondence. Later, by the 1950s, letter carriers or *carteros* were hired to deliver mail to private residences in pueblos and nearby hamlets. When no street address appeared on the envelope or when the receiving party preferred to maintain discretion, carteros left mail at the postal station, where they appeared on the *lista correos* (mailing list) for personal retrieval.[5] For most Mexicans living in rural pueblos, such as Calvillo, the postal system worked efficiently, enabling residents to maintain close contact with loved ones throughout Mexico and the United States. Even those residents unable to read or write could send notes through the postal service. As long they found or hired a local scribe they could trust to pen the letters for them, they had a reliable and readily available avenue for corresponding.

The Mexican postal service, however, came crashing down in the 1980s and 1990s with the collapse of the economy, near-destruction of the basic infrastructure following massive earthquakes, and subsequent loss of confidence among the public that mail was being delivered efficiently and reliably.[6] The expansion of the Mexican economy in the early years of the twenty-first century has done little for the ability of Sepomex to recover or regain the confidence of Mexicans in and outside of the country. Today, few mexicanos who have the means to find alternatives use Sepomex. Comparatively, worldwide, Sepomex handles little mail compared to similar postal systems in countries such as Brazil, New Zealand, and the United States. Instead, Mexicans turn to some 4,000 private companies. For most impoverished residents in Mexico, speedy and reliable mail is out of reach, and they must rely on the national postal service, which can take up to two weeks or more to deliver mail from the United States.[7]

The modern mail service in the United States faces some challenges similar to those plaguing its counterpart in Mexico. The U.S. service, though, emerged earlier, established by the Second Continental Congress in Philadelphia in 1777, when it was inaugurated as the Post Office Department as part of the newly established U.S. government. Prior to that, the postal service primarily served the needs of the British colonial power, though it also provided delivery within and among the colonies. At that time, service was unevenly dispersed among communities and regions, depending on the social and economic needs of each locale as well as the presence of Native Americans who fought to maintain their territorial and cultural integrity. While delivery was relatively slow across considerable distances, government officials implemented the use of stagecoaches and horseback delivery to speed service and established first-, second-, and third-class mail, allowing for the mailing of letters, publications, and other material, respectively, at moderate rates. And though the service was rarely profitable, the government maintained it for the good of the public and kept prices below costs. That principle was put into practice when, in 1863, the government passed a law charging everyone the same price to mail letters across the United States regardless of the distance.[8]

The mail service made its way to California in the nineteenth century with the expansion of roads and railways following the wars and conquests of French, British, and Spanish colonies in the eighteenth and nineteenth centuries. Initially, in the 1840s and 1850s, mail heading from the East Coast to the West Coast was transported by steamships making their way to the Isthmus of Panama, a narrow strip of land between the Caribbean Sea and the Pacific Ocean. To get the mail on the steamships across the isthmus, workers loaded it onto canoes and mules, which transported it to ships on the Pacific Ocean bound for San Francisco. Though it took weeks to receive news, overland mail took even longer, up to several months. The completion of the transcontinental railroad in 1878, however, significantly shortened the delivery of correspondence and publications, to weeks or days. By the 1930s, nearly 10,000 U.S. railway post offices delivered mail across the country. As the cost of transporting mail escalated and alternatives, primarily airmail, took off throughout the United States, railway service was discontinued in favor of more efficient methods.[9]

As in Mexico, door-to-door delivery of mail was not readily available in the United States in the early years but emerged in the late nineteenth and early twentieth centuries primarily in urban areas, though it eventually spread to rural zones, such as Imperial Valley in southern California. To take advantage of postal delivery, communities had to provide basic infrastructure to allow letter carriers to reach residences, including sidewalks and crosswalks as well as lit and named streets and numbered houses. While carriers initially hand delivered to customers, they eventually turned to mailboxes as urbanization in the early twentieth century led to the expansion of populations in cities across the United States. When suburbanization increased in the postwar era, curbside cluster boxes became common, allowing for increased efficiency. In rural areas such as Imperial Valley, where residential demographics remained modest, single mailboxes and post office boxes were commonly used, as were hand-to-hand deliveries. There, rural carriers often functioned as traveling post offices, selling stamps and money orders as well as keeping customers informed about the latest rules and regulations.[10]

By the mid-1960s, the efficiency of U.S. mail service began to decline considerably, particularly in urban areas, as demand far outpaced the ability to serve customers efficiently. Financial neglect and fragmented control in the postal service created a bureaucratic nightmare that impacted delivery as well. Indeed, the lack of early mechanization and technological innovation prevented the development of a financially self-sufficient branch of government, leading it to become dependent on U.S. taxpayer subsidies and vulnerable to calls for budget cuts and, recently, privatization.[11]

Despite the growing troubles in the 1950s and 1960s at the Post Office Department, which was reorganized as the United States Postal Service (USPS) in the early 1970s, international mail service from the United States to Mexico remained within reach for most residents, including rural Mexican migrants living and working on U.S. farms in el norte. In 1964, first-class mail delivery of one ounce or less cost five cents and took about four days, allowing migrants in the United States to send up to two or three pages of news and personal information relatively quickly to loved ones across the border. Second-class mail, including greeting cards, cost a few cents less and took longer to arrive. That same year, in 1964, when airmail became available, delivery sped up considerably, yet the cost nearly doubled, to eight cents. The new service, though a bit more expensive, allowed for letters to arrive faster than by ground, enabling family and friends separated by the border to maintain intimate ties across transnational lines.

While the postal service remained the most accessible method of communication, the telephone also played an important role in keeping in contact, though the scarcity and expense meant that most had to go without or limit the time when they paid for the service. In Mexico telephones were first introduced in the late nineteenth century among government and bureaucratic officials and expanded in the early twentieth century as part of the celebration of 100 years of independence from Spain. Many of the lines established in the 1910s and 1920s, however, lasted only briefly, as rebels fighting in the Cristero Rebellion cut telephone lines in pueblos to hamper the government's attempt to suppress the role of the religious revolutionaries seeking to support the cause of the Catholic Church. As longtime residents of Calvillo recalled from stories they heard from their parents, after the Cristeros cut local telephones lines, the pueblo went without phone service for years. Government officials finally reestablished the system in the 1950s and 1960s, though they did so on a limited basis.

Indeed, when regular telephone service came to Calvillo, officials installed a few dozen lines or so around town, with the main operator of the lines functioning out of a small grocery store that doubled as a telephone station. Callers from other regions of Mexico, the United States, or elsewhere looking to speak with local residents phoned there. The intended recipient, if not readily available, was summoned by foot across town to take the call. Most residents who had the good fortune of having a phone were either wealthy or bureaucrats working in municipal government. Later, by the late 1960s and early 1970s, as the phone service expanded and costs decreased, more residents, including Paco's household in Calvillo, obtained the service, enabling them, as well as neighbors and residents in town with whom they shared the service for a small fee, to have increased access to local, national, and transnational communication.

Despite the widespread emergence of the phone in the 1960s and 1970s, letter writing continued as a popular mode of communication. In all likelihood, the limited accessibility and the cost of the phone service as well as the preference for the intimacy and material nature of the missive continued to draw ordinary Mexicans on both sides of the border to rely on correspondence to maintain relations with loved ones across the border. As Paco's and Chonita's correspondence would reveal, letters not only brought and maintained relationships but also tore them apart.

The Emotional and Physical Toll of Migration across the Borderlands

Chonita and Paco, like many Mexicans in Mexico and the United States, relied on the U.S. and Mexican postal services to nurture their relationship across the political divide, for the costs and limited availability of the telephone kept that form of communication out of reach. As their correspondence indicates, letter writing allowed them to maintain an even more intense and passionate courtship than that between Paco's older brother José and Chonita's younger sister Conchita.[12] In contrast to their respective siblings, José and Conchita, who also relied almost exclusively on correspondence to develop their relations, Paco and Chonita cultivated their noviasgo a few years before Paco's immigration to the United States in September 1962. In that time they spent together as novios in Calvillo, Paco and Chonita socialized regularly with friends and family over meals, attended the movie theater, and shared *refrescos* (sodas), allowing them to strengthen their social, emotional, and intimate bonds prior to their separation. José and Conchita, in contrast, had no such opportunity to cultivate their noviasgo, for theirs was primarily an epistolary-based relationship. Indeed, in the three years they wrote to each other, José and Conchita visited with each other only three times. When Paco made his decision, therefore, to head to el otro lado, Chonita faced an especially difficult time with loss and estrangement, for she knew that, like many friends and family members of Mexican migrants in the United States, it meant that she would be left behind and forced to wait until his return. For Paco, the move, though difficult, was necessary. Like most Mexican migrants of his day, he knew the limitations of the pueblo's educational system and economy as well as his family's ability to provide for his future. By going to el norte, as all his brothers and father had done before him, Paco rationalized, he had the real possibility of earning an income sufficient to maintain a household, which was essential to the ideal of Mexican manhood and affirming his masculine identity.[13] Though not an easy decision, he knew he had few other choices, for his family needed his support.

As Paco's correspondence to Chonita indicates, to reach el norte he left Calvillo for Mexicali, Baja California, from where he planned to apply for residency. With the support of extended family networks in Mexicali and letters of support from his older brother's employer, J. C. Reeves, a large farm owner and purveyor of agricultural products in Imperial Valley, Paco obtained his green card in less than three months, enabling him to venture to Brawley, California, and further north if he so desired. Though the process was relatively quick, as many migrants spent months or even years waiting for residency, for Chonita the wait seemed like an eternity, prompting her to inquire about his return. Paco was unable to do as she desired, however, for his limited means and job insecurity meant that he had to remain in the United States for fear of losing his position to others. His prolonged absence and sporadic communication as well as gossip that emerged in town about their personal lives soon strained the relationship.

Although the correspondence between Paco and Chonita is incomplete, as many of his letters are not extant, missives among family members and friends as well as the use of what David A. Gerber calls "double voice" indicate that, from the beginning of their epistolary relationship, the couple had difficulty with communicating clearly and consistently, particularly over his immediate return and future intentions.[14] "You had told me you would return the month before," Chonita wrote. "Please respond to me the soonest you can so that you can tell me when you will return (*cuando te vienes*) even though you might not believe it I have the desire to see you around here again."[15] Writing those words was no easy feat for Chonita, for they evoked emotional pain and anguish in considering that the relationship might not withstand the distance. Plus, as she stated years later in an interview, she infrequently displayed her emotions ever since she experienced deep loss after her father's sudden death—his unexplained murder—when she was a child.[16] "Well I think I am getting sentimental," she said to Paco in pouring her heart out. "There was no reason for you to lie to me . . . you can tell me if you don't want me to write to you please tell me I promise not to bother you any more."[17]

Unsure whether her direct approach might affront Paco, Chonita shifted her confrontational tone to that of a demure, insecure, and naïve young woman, suggesting apprehension in coming off too as demanding or "unladylike," given the patriarchal mores of the day, which taught women's

Aspiring to survival and opportunity in *el norte*, in 1962
Paco Chávez left behind not only his family—his father,
mother, and sister—but also his girlfriend, Asunción
Alvarado ("Chonita"), with whom he had a passionate
relationship. Though they attempted to keep the courtship
alive, the distance, miscommunication, inconsistent letter
writing, and suspicions of infidelity quickly dismantled
the affair.

Permission to reprint photograph provided by Paco Chávez.

subservience. Chonita's self-deprecating demeanor, while denigrating her sense of self-worth, was not uncommon among women of her day, as many female letter writers, her sister Conchita included, used such self-effacing, gendered language in their epistolary practices. Chonita's particularly dim view of her intellect, likely influenced by her knowledge that she had a limited, sixth grade education, in contrast to her younger sister's ninth grade education, might have also influenced her negative view of herself. "I beg you," she said soon after questioning Paco about his delay, "to forgive my silliness (*tonterias*) . . . believe me that I feel shame with you because I think it is a lot of work for you to read my writing which isn't really writing but a lot of scratches (*garavatos*) and many misspellings and . . . poorly dictated letters that I write but," she continued, "I expect you will forgive all of my errors because as you know I am an uneducated person (*una ignorante*)."[18]

In addition to her professed shortcomings, Chonita worried about boring him with her complaints, but, as she rationalized, she had every right to be upset. "I think I am writing you a newspaper on all this I don't think it will interest you much . . . as you didn't even tell me the truth about when you would return," she charged. Despite her harsh language, her letter proved to be more cathartic than didactic in nature, for she remained committed. "Goodbye from the one who cares about you," she ended. "And don't pay any attention to me they are jokes (*bromas*)."[19]

Chonita's letter, while conflicted and emotionally charged, compelled Paco to reply, for he dashed off a letter within days, leading her to respond quickly as well. Even though Paco's missive is no longer extant, her use of double voice indicates that he, too, was not only torn about their relationship but also worried about his reputation and honor as a male and his ability to ensure his girlfriend's sexual virtue while he was gone. Wanting assurances of her fidelity, which would, in turn, affirm his masculinity in the pueblo, even while he remained some 1,500 miles away, he asked about her love interests in Calvillo. Unphased, Chonita paid little attention to his suggestion of her infidelity, dismissing his concerns. "Don't worry about me finding another," she responded, "there is no one who pays attention to me in turn you tell me how many you have conquered (*conquistado*)."[20]

Apparently, Chonita was not troubled with Paco's concern for her sexual virtue, for she said few words in defending her commitment or in trying to hide any relations with other men. Instead, she changed the subject by responding to his interest in learning about her latest forms of entertainment. "Look," she answered, in response to his query about her favorite songs, "my favorite melodies are with the Sonora Santanera '*que te valla vien*' and with

Paco Cañedo 'how inhumane' as well as a number of other recent tunes by Miguel Angel, Sonia López, and Dioney Baldes," favorites among her siblings and friends as well. "Imagine," she told him excitedly, the bolero trio "*los tres Diamantes* were in Guadalajara on Saturday I was listening to them."[21]

Chonita not only shared musical interests but also photographs, as he requested. And though she poked fun at her images and her attempt to look more sophisticated with makeup, which she wore infrequently, she revealed her lighthearted personality and the intimacy she shared with Paco. "Today I send you my 'caricature' (*caricatura*) don't get scared as I promised you I lined my eyes and I look as if I am blind later I will send you another as they came out very bad (*muy mal*)." Despite her reluctance to share her photograph, suggesting a measure of unease with her physical appearance, she reminded him to send his. "Don't forget to send me your photo or if you don't want me to answer you don't do it," she said. She then signed off with "*tu peor es nada* [literally, your better than nothing] as they say in a silly manner seeing you is better than writing to you," indicating she continued to have a strong emotional attachment.[22]

Paco and Chonita's passionate and stormy letter writing did not relent. Two weeks later, on Christmas Eve, Paco wrote an ardent yet wistful letter to Chonita lamenting their separation and reassuring her of his commitment. Written after having imbibed one too many drinks during the holiday and missing his family, friends, and loved ones in Calvillo, as he admitted to several of his friends and family members, Paco expressed himself in a morose tone. "In reality I feel very lonely, hopefully and God willing, I will soon be in Calvillo, I miss you a lot, and I feel sorry for not having sent you even a card, but the present is a bearer of my feelings towards you," he said.[23] Responding directly to her doubts about his false promises, Paco explained he had no other choice. "Perhaps you think that I am very insincere (*muy falso*) in my promises, but if I don't go this year over there it is because in reality my economic problems prevent me from doing so, and believe me I want to be with you, primarily on this day the 24th."[24] Attempting to ease her doubts about his fidelity in particular and their noviasgo in general, Paco reassured her of her significance in his life and of his vulnerability without her. "I want to tell you like the last time, that you are the only one, and if by luck destiny has another path for us, I hope it is good, as my affection (*cariño*) has been for you, and if you came to ignore me believe me it would be the end of me." "You are the only who has been my happiness, and it is the only thing that gives me hope in continuing to live, and if God has something else for us, my happiness will be with you."[25] After professing his impassioned and unconditional pledge to the relationship, Paco's demeanor changed abruptly to one of distrust and accusations of betrayal.

Calling into question the integrity of her fidelity, Paco accused her of cheating on him with one of his friends in Calvillo. "I think I have placed too many hopes in you, as I believe you were betraying me with one of my friends, and I think it was somewhat brief when you deceived me, for a short time later you convinced yourself that it was difficult to entertain another affection . . . and what he wanted was simply to try his shot at love and betrayal." The deception, Paco noted, did not break him or taint his male honor, but instead tested his ability to withstand deception from those closest to him. "I'll know how to take care of myself from such things, for in my short life I've seen that the one most esteems (*aprecia*) is the first to betray," he wrote candidly about his so-called friend.[26]

Paco's accusatory tone then relented a bit, however, for he seemed to know or think that the alleged affair was not entirely Chonita's doing and that she had resisted the temptation of an underhanded man. The man in question was Alfonso "el Pinole" Lozano, Paco's friend and a distant family member as well as Chonita's second cousin. It was el Pinole, Paco wrote, "who attempted to carry out a dirty trick (*canallada*) that fortunately you were strong enough to rise above the temptation and you conserved yourself intact for me . . . and that is what gave me strength to continue to love you and have trust in you." Despite the breach, Paco held out hope for their relationship, signing off with "I'm yours until destiny decides."[27]

Unaware of the critical tenor of Paco's letter, which would arrive the next day, on Christmas, Chonita sent an emotionally laden note describing her despondency when she learned he would not return. Rather than pouring out her most intimate thoughts about missing him, she restrained herself. "If I start to tell you everything I have to say to you . . . it will not fit on the paper," she declared.[28] Instead, she sent him the brief missive and included a simple Christmas card and a photograph of herself and asked for one of his, likely hoping the images would help strengthen their unsteady and, at times, conflicted courtship.

Writing in response to his latest missive, in which he accused her of infidelity, Chonita said little about his allegations. Instead, in her letter to him, she brought attention to the infrequency of his correspondence and did so in a subtle manner, likely not wanting to sound desperate over not receiving word from him or powerless in the relationship. "Don't feel ashamed [about] not responding to me," she said, "do it at the hour that you wish don't feel sorry for me as I can see that is what you want." What she desired was lengthy, detailed letters. "Don't waste your money on a simple message," she told him. "I say this to you because mine are newspapers," filled with the latest developments in her life and in town.[29] Such elaborate communications, Chonita implied, were more valuable than those with thin news.

Apparently, Chonita's request for more detailed and lengthy missives went unnoticed, for Paco's forthcoming communication remained utterly too brief for her tastes. Two weeks later, at the end of January 1963, Chonita wrote another pointed missive about the brevity of his notes and questioned his commitment to maintaining their relationship. "It's not that you are not important to me but I think it's unjust what you do [in] sending me two or three words (*letras*) when I write to you up until the last line."[30] In her attempt to understand the brief nature of his correspondence, she thought perhaps he had misunderstood her last message when she had tried to explain herself using language laden with gendered and cultural meaning. Chonita noted that it was "nerves" or *nervios*—a mild state of anxiety—that had made her lose control over her mind and body.[31] In Mexico, an attack of nervios was (and remains) a commonly accepted, temporary emotional and physical state often associated with biological weakness among females. Some of her male peers, however, also experienced an attack of los nervios and did so in instances of extreme emotional and physical stress, as did Paco, as he confessed years later.[32] "Forgive me if I offended you in some way in the other [letter] but it wasn't my intention, I think I am very nervous that is why I commit so much error but you are kind and will know to forgive me."[33]

Notwithstanding Chonita's conflicted relations with Paco, she faced other difficulties at home further threatening her epistolary relationship with Paco. Chonita's mother, Natalia Loera, did not approve of her letter writing and took the opportunity to reprimand her for occupying her time with what likely seemed a frivolous practice. Chonita explained to Paco, "Well I won't write to you anymore because my mother saw me writing the letter and she is always scolding me and I don't know what it is that I am doing [wrong]."[34] In all likelihood, Natalia preferred to have Chonita, one of the two eldest daughters at home, assisting in the numerous domestic chores, which included tending to some ten to twelve younger siblings as well as washing, drying, and ironing loads of clothes with no modern conveniences or indoor plumbing. While the family had previously owned property and enjoyed a measure of wealth, in recent years the head of the household, Chonita's stepfather, had mismanaged the funds, leaving the entire clan nearly in the street. Much to her mother's chagrin, Chonita took time during the day to compose the intimate letters rather than tend to the many responsibilities in the household. To avoid her mother's wrath, Chonita asked Paco to send the letters to different addresses in town, which they did for a couple of months, until she declared it safe again to receive letters at home.[35] Despite the many challenges in maintaining the noviasgo, Chonita ended her letter idealistically. "That's all for today . . . goodbye from your girlfriend who will never (jamas) forget you."[36]

Chonita's pledge of commitment was apparently insufficient for Paco, for he remained insecure about his status as her boyfriend and her ability to fend off the males in town who knew of his recent departure. According to the gender ideologies of the day, women had weaker moral, physical, and intellectual constitutions than men and succumbed easily to bodily temptations, which was particularly dangerous to the stability of families and the larger community. To contain and control women's impulsive, irrational behavior, social prescriptions held that they needed to be monitored by family and social networks and, as needed, by custom and the law. Women who violated gender norms of sexual morality and domesticity, in particular, risked punishment, including social criticism at best and confinement at worst.[37] To assure himself that Conchita followed the gender norms of the day, by remaining faithful and upholding his reputation as an honorable man, Paco asked his cuates, with whom he also corresponded, to send him word about Chonita's latest whereabouts and potential love interests. When Paco received news of her interactions with other men in town, he asked her pointedly to explain her affairs. Chonita could not, however, readily challenge those observations, for Paco rarely disclosed his sources of surveillance. Rather, Paco seemed to level general accusations, prompting her to respond in kind. Within a few months of leaving town, Paco queried about her relations. "The person I speak with sometimes is with el maldito Che (I mean 'Perico')," or Pedro Sánchez, a mutual friend, Chonita explained, "but I heard that he said he was going to marry me and for that reason I hardly speak with him because I feel shame you know how bashful (chiviada) I am." Though it is unlikely Perico intended to pursue her hand in marriage, for he never mentioned it to Paco or anyone else in his correspondence or in an interview he gave years later, Chonita expressed firmly that she had no interest in him. But in a lighthearted tone she reminded Paco to remain guarded about Perico's intentions. "Don't be too sure because he's after my bones (huesos)."[38]

Somewhat reassured of her fidelity in the short term, Paco nevertheless remained suspicious of the influences shaping her consciousness and correspondence, for he suspected—and rightly so—that her sisters Sanjuana, the eldest, and Conchita, her closest confidante, read the letters either with or without her knowledge. Chonita tried to assuage his doubts. "Don't even worry about your letters I have them underneath the mattress," Chonita explained. "I can't assure you that they are complete because the bed bugs have already taken them away." As subsequent correspondence revealed, Chonita was not altogether truthful or aware of the fate of her missives, for her sisters meddled in her epistolary relationship with Paco and sometimes intercepted and read the notes without her knowledge. To diminish Paco's suspicions even further, Chonita denied being angry or upset with delays in his correspondence, though they did seem to bother her. "I wasn't upset because you hadn't responded to me I thought mine had not arrived because I thought I had not put your name on it and I was thinking that it was going to be returned to me." She was distracted, she explained, "with the fact that they were only reprimanding me I didn't recall until later." To prove further that she was committed to him, Chonita explained to him that every time she went to the ice cream shop (*paletería*) she played his favorite tune on the jukebox as a reminder of him.[39]

To feed the intimacy they had cultivated as novios in Calvillo, Chonita turned to poetry, sending Paco a series of published poems about migration, life, loss, death, and peace—written using precise penmanship on the front and back of a single lined piece of paper. The pieces, transcribed lovingly and patiently from an unnamed book of poetry, seemed to resonate with Chonita's emotional state of longing for Paco's return. Much to Chonita's dismay, however, Paco questioned the integrity of the poems and her ability to compose them neatly on the page. Upset at his doubts, Chonita wasted no time in firing back. "Paco I don't understand why you said I didn't do the other [letter] I want to think that you were very drunk to come out with that one." Probably it was, she reasoned, "because I made the lettering small so that the darn (*mentados*) poemas would fit." Nevertheless, she implored, "Stop thinking that I have someone do it for me."[40]

Despite Chonita's attempt to settle the integrity of her letter writing as well as her fidelity, she found herself defending her sexual honor repeatedly, for Paco's friends continued their surveillance and reports to him about the men interested in pursuing a noviasgo and, eventually, marriage. To remove all doubt, Chonita explained in detail her affairs, particularly with one fellow who would not take no for an answer. "Look I'm going to tell you what I am sure they have already told you that they see me talking with a man who wears a cowboy hat (*un gorrudo*)." "I am telling you this," she continued, "because your brother [Juan] saw me" with him. "He is so stubborn," she said in an irritated tone about her admirer, "that I cannot even go out the door because he is waiting for me and the error was in telling him I don't like having a boyfriend and I can't love anyone." Though she thought he would not bother her anymore, she said, "I think that every day it is worse." He says, she explained, "that one day I can grow to love him." Chonita reassured Paco that she had not led him on. Rather, she tried to get rid of him many times. "I give him good '*cortones*' and he continues with the same he says I have to marry him in reality I don't know how to get rid of this plague." "He rattles my nerves (*me pone de nerbios*)," she confessed.[41] Chonita then ended her missive to Paco by telling him she longed to see him and hoped he would return in May for the yearly community celebration.

Paco's commitments, however, kept him from returning to Calvillo, for nine days later and nearly six months since he had left for el norte, Chonita continued to voice frustration waiting for his return. "I had a small hope that at last you would be able to come," she said at the end of March 1963, "but I think I am going to be waiting all my life, I hope not to bother you anymore." In Chonita's view, Paco's failure to return was a personal choice and not one dictated by economic or family hardship. Though dejected, Chonita had a glimmer of hope that he would return and soon, for the pueblo was going to celebrate with festivities at the end of the following month. "Regardless I will tell you the date of the fiesta it is the 23rd [of May.]"[42]

Paco, though, had no plans to return anytime soon. Instead, he asked her when she might travel to the United States to join him. "Any day now I will go," to the United States, she responded. "Only don't say that I am a show-off (*presumida*)," she wrote, attempting to impress him, "but I too already have in what to travel don't think that only you have it." Apparently, Chonita, like Paco, had access to a car, perhaps the family's or a friend's car, giving her the ability to travel to el norte if she so desired. Though it is difficult to verify Chonita's words, it is clear she was lashing out in pain at having been left behind and, in her view, ignored and forgotten. She remained, however, heartbroken and longed to see him, feelings she could not hide. "I bid you farewell," she ended, "and I'll keep waiting that one day you'll be able to come even though I told you I would not speak about this anymore."[43]

Chonita's willingness to wait proved short-lived, for a few weeks later, in April 1963, after Paco confirmed he would be unable to return for the annual fiesta, she severed the relationship with her declaration of "A Dios." Nevertheless, Chonita's decision to end the noviasgo was difficult, for she continued to care for Paco and he, in turn, for her, as they informed their mutual friends and family in Calvillo.

Spies, Lies, and Surveillance in the Borderlands

Despite Paco and Chonita's split, they remained attached emotionally, for they asked close friends and family members to carry out surveillance as to each other's physical whereabouts and social interactions. Paco had an advantage over Chonita, however, for he had far more reporters beating the pavement in Calvillo keeping watch over her body than she had in el norte keeping watch over his. Most of Paco's cuates responded readily with chisme, telling him what they heard about Chonita or had seen firsthand in the pueblo's streets, movie theater, and central plaza, among other public spaces. Contrary to popular belief, chisme, or social intelligence, was not (and is not) solely a female activity; males ascribed to it too. In correspondence between his friends, Paco's buddies confessed to exchanging chisme willingly and joyfully, demonstrating that engaging in gossip did not compromise their sense of masculinity or what it meant to be a man in Calvillo. The implications of gossip, also used as a form of entertainment or a form of influencing others, however, are highly gendered, as Joanna Dreby has argued. In her research on contemporary Mexican migrants, Dreby finds that "transnational gossip morally evaluates mothers to a greater extent than fathers."[44] In other words, women who were subjects of Dreby's research suffered harsher consequences than men from gossip.

While both Paco and Chonita set out to determine each other's commitment to the relationship during and after the courtship, Paco was less trusting of her sexual virtue than she of his, a reflection of the double standard of male and female sexuality. According to Mexican cultural and moral strictures, women who engaged in sex outside the confines of marriage were dishonorable, while men who did the same faced little social and cultural censure. Dishonor came to men when their wives, daughters, or sisters engaged in dishonorable acts such as having sexual relations with men who were not their spouses. A widow's, mother's, or daughter's dishonor, in contrast, did not result from a male family member engaging in sex outside of marriage but, rather, from women's sexuality being deemed threatening to the stability of marriage and the family (including the transfer and inheritance of property) and the larger community.[45]

Among the friends and family members who spent the most time and effort as well as ink monitoring and relaying Chonita's relationships was el Pinole, the "canalla" whom Paco had accused of attempting to seduce her shortly after his emigration. Curiously, neither Paco nor el Pinole broached the attempted seduction in their subsequent correspondence, suggesting that Paco preferred to ignore it altogether or else risk losing a valuable source of information, though he could not always guarantee its veracity. What Paco could guarantee was el Pinole's sustained interest in Chonita. Indeed, in the letters he wrote to Paco about Chonita, he launched quickly into what he called "los chismes" of the day, which almost always began with an update on her latest relations. In the first letter he sent to Paco shortly after the latter departed in September 1962, el Pinole reassured him that Chonita was heartbroken over his emigration. "Look in the first place I am going to tell you about Chona she is sad and inconsolable (*desconzolada*) as she needs her *teporocho* (in this context, slang for boyfriend) and here she is in my house which is also yours and she says she hopes you come for December."[46] Doubtless el Pinole's update brought Paco some relief, as it settled the concerns he may have had about her commitment, though it also likely raised questions as well, particularly with her presence in el Pinole's house in her vulnerable, distraught state, as Pinole had described her. To counter any suspicions of his intentions by having Chonita over at his home, el Pinole implicitly reassured Paco that he had no interest in her by reporting on the latest "mango" (a sexually attractive woman) of the pueblo and his long-term plan of marrying his girlfriend. Whether Paco felt reassured by el Pinole's sexual interests in other women in town is unclear, though it is clear that all he could do was remain hopeful that their relationship could be revived despite the social influences and physical distance keeping Chonita away.

Three months later, depressed and lonely, Paco wrote to el Pinole telling him he was unsure of Chonita's fidelity, indicating that, even though they had already parted ways, he felt entitled to monitor her social relations. Attempting to uplift his spirits, el Pinole moved swiftly to ameliorate Paco's anxiety. "Regarding your *Lombricienta* (slang for worm-like or thin girlfriend) I am going to tell you . . . the truth," he said. "I have not seen that she is betraying you and that is the pure truth."[47] El Pinole's report was reinforced by that of Perico, who wrote less often but nevertheless provided updates. Perico intimated that Chonita remained loyal despite the efforts of local men to pressure her into relationships. "Look when I was at the fiesta" of the *guayaba* (guava), Perico said, "I was standing talking to the guys (*la raza*) in the plaza when your TEPOROCHA walked by accompanied but at the moment that I saw her he left and he didn't give me the chance to say he was going to pay for it," presumably for attempting to muscle in on Paco's ex-girlfriend. According to Perico, she then said, "CONCEITED MAN HE DIDN'T WANT TO LEAVE!" To Perico, Chonita's public exclamation meant explicitly that she wanted the public to know she was uninterested in other men and implicitly remained committed to Paco. Given her loyalty, Perico warned Paco about maintaining his own fidelity, "Don't be the one who plays rude with her."[48]

Likely relieved to hear the news from Perico, Paco nevertheless seemed unconvinced and asked el Pinole if he should continue to write to Chonita. El Pinole responded affirmatively, encouraging him to communicate with her, especially because he had spied her socializing with a man of whom neither he nor Paco approved. "Every night she spends time talking with that *sangrón* (conceited man) that one who annoys you so much and sometimes I think she is betraying you with *el batito sangrepesada* (the annoying dude) that one who also annoys me the son of his granny."[49]

Though el Pinole failed to explain why he questioned Chonita's loyalty to Paco given their separation, he informed Paco that she faced family pressure, particularly from her sisters Conchita and Sanjuana, to dissolve permanently any relationship with Paco and form a socially and economically advantageous one in the pueblo. Paco was not surprised, for he, too, suspected that her sisters encouraged her to rethink her cross-border relationship. In March 1963, el Pinole wrote, "Look Paco, Chona loves you in truth but she finds herself between a rock and a hard place, and it is because you know how her sisters are that they only make fun of the people and they don't pay attention to themselves, as they say around here the fox doesn't see his own tail." El Pinole continued, "They tell her not to be dumb (*taruga*) and that she should find another around here and if he loves her a lot why doesn't he send word to you that he [will] come for her and marry her, and that way the difficulties will end."[50] El Pinole's insight on the sisters' influence, though not altogether verifiable, likely helped explain why Chonita vacillated drastically in her demeanor toward Paco and the noviasgo. In many of her letters, she expressed both a lifetime commitment and a will to end it swiftly with little remorse.

While el Pinole's words and surveillance of Conchita's affairs provided Paco with hope, two months later reuniting seemed a far-off reality.

Apparently, el Pinole had seen Chonita with "el batito sangrepesada" in town. "I became aware of when your darned *spatula* (slang for thin girlfriend) started cheating on you (*hacer 'guey'*) and since then she has not directed a word to me," likely knowing he communicated with Paco.[51] "She played hard to get but then all the draculas my apologies her sisters told her that [he] was in her best interest and then she stopped playing hard to get." As a consequence, el Pinole continued, even the family welcomed him. "Now you have that coarse guy (*pelao*) standing well with the family. His name is, well I don't think his name would interest you but he's a son of^#%* Antonio Flores," a local ranchero.[52]

A few weeks after el Pinole had dashed Paco's hopes for a reunion with Chonita, el Pinole offered promising news based on his latest surveillance. Even though Chonita's suitor, Antonio Flores, had pursued her relentlessly, she was simply not interested. Instead, she longed for Paco. "Look compadre, you know that I like to speak the truth respecting girlfriends and I think that the young man (*señorito*) . . . has a lot of interest in getting married but frankly she does not appear for a moment to have forgotten her better than nothing and perhaps has the smallest of hopes that when you return you will tell her . . . well you already know what . . . or no?" El Pinole could report little more on Chonita, he told Paco, as she (and her mother as well) continued to keep her distance from him, likely knowing he would eventually inform Paco what he had seen and heard. El Pinole, however, encouraged Paco to cheer up and find another girlfriend as an alternative. "Try not to get depressed so much find another girlfriend (*jiotosa*, slang for rash-like girlfriend) when you can and that way you forget about sad things."[53]

Despite el Pinole's encouragement that Paco find another girlfriend, a month later he reported that Chonita continued to love Paco. El Pinole became aware of her sustained passion when he informed Chonita, after she had asked him, that Paco would return to Calvillo sometime soon, in fall 1963, nearly a year after his departure. "Well you know brother . . . it looks like your ex-girlfriend doesn't forget for a moment her better than oranges (*su pior es naranjas*) . . . because now she speaks to me . . . and she asked me when you were going to come and I told her . . . after September and she started neighing like a mule out of sheer joy and said that perhaps she loves you more than before." El Pinole wrote to Paco that he was unsure why she had a change of heart but that it seemed genuine because she "asked me to show her the letters that you send me, to see how you express yourself of her respectable person."[54] For Chonita, like many letter writers of the nineteenth and twentieth centuries, including the British immigrant authors identified by Gerber, the correspondence constituted the self. By seeing Paco's written words, the paper, the envelope, and especially the photographs, Chonita was reminded of his physical and emotional presence in her life, even though he resided in el norte, some 1,500 miles away. "Well you know that I just showed your letter to your ex-girlfriend and she said you had turned out very well in the photos, only that you seemed thinner but that you were still as handsome as before and she says she has a crazy urge (*ganas locas*) to see you and she told me to ask you if it is true that you are coming," el Pinole informed Paco.[55] El Pinole ended by saying the words that Paco likely wanted to hear. "She says she loves you very much that hopefully . . . you don't forget her ever that she even though far is always is close to you and close but very close to your heart, even if you don't love her."[56]

Paco's suggestions of returning soon did not, however, materialize. Paco's inability to return to Mexico during the holiday season, an expected ritual of most Mexican male migrants, did not crush the potential for renewing the courtship, as María del Socorro Salazar, another mutual friend based in Calvillo, informed him. In March 1964, a few months after his last communication with el Pinole, Paco asked Socorro about Chonita's latest intimate relationship. "Paco you ask if Chona has a boyfriend well yes, yes she has one but it is only to pass the time because she told me so." Chonita still cared for Paco, according to Socorro, as she wept when she heard from Juan, Paco's older brother, that he planned to marry sometime soon. "You know finally she cried for you when your brother told her that you were going to get married with a woman from la Chona," a nearby community, "is it true or is not true[?]" she asked.[57] Unsettled by the news, Socorro told Paco that, in the company of Chonita, Conchita, Perico, and several other friends, she had asked el Pinole what he knew about Paco's future plans. "Last night when we came out of the movie theater we asked Toño [el Pinole] if it was true and he told us that he was not aware of it, but I think you can remove our doubts 'or no.' "[58] Though his response is unknown, it is probable Paco told her he had no plans to marry and that his brother's words were suspect, for he never mentioned any love interest or engagement in his correspondence with family and friends.

Unlike Juan, Socorro was not interested in completely severing Paco and Chonita's relationship, but rather restoring it. Two months later, in September 1964, Socorro delivered more welcome news. "Look Chona cut her hair, and she looks more beautiful, and she says that if you want you can write to her and she will be happy to reply and she says that she sends you a hug (*un abrazo*) on her behalf . . . that is what she said that you write to her first."[59] According to gender conventions for female letter writers of the day, males wrote letters of courtship to females first. Women did not initiate such correspondence. Despite Socorro's news and the upbeat tone for the future of their relationship, Paco's queries about Chonita's whereabouts grew less and less frequent, resulting in the unofficial death of the relationship by the end of 1964.

Playing "Teléfono Descompuesto" (Broken Telephone) in the Borderlands

Chonita, like Paco, was interested in knowing about his latest relationships as well as any remaining interest or commitment he might have to the noviasgo. Chonita, however, had few friends or family members in el otro lado who could keep an eye on Paco, as he did with her, and report any potential intimate relations. Plus, given the gender ideologies of the day, she probably knew she could do little to stop him from engaging in sexual relations outside of marriage with other women. In fact, the correspondence of one of Paco's male friends suggests that during his time in the border region attempting to adjust his migratory status, Paco paid for sexual relations with an unnamed woman in San Luis, Sonora, about fifty miles southeast of Mexicali, Baja California. How often he did this is unknown, for no other reference emerges verifying or denying that incident or subsequent ones.[60] It was not uncommon, though, as Ana E. Rosas's and Deborah Cohen's research demonstrates, for migrant farmworking men of the era to visit prostitutes or establish brief as well as long-term relationships with women in the United States while they had sweethearts, wives, and children waiting for them at home in Mexico.[61] Mexican women, in contrast, were expected to remain chaste while waiting for their boyfriends and husbands to return, even though many men failed to do so for years at a time, while others simply disappeared. Determined to find out Paco's current relationship, if any, Chonita used her confidante, Conchita, and her epistolary relationship with José to keep tabs on Paco. Conchita, it seems, was happy to oblige, for she not only inquired about Paco with Chonita's knowledge but also without it.

Chonita's and Conchita's approach to determining Paco's social relations was secretive and clever. Rather than query José about Paco's acquaintances and raise suspicion about her interest in Paco, Conchita asked José to relay messages to Paco to find out his current living and working conditions. In a message sent in January 1964, a little more than six months after Chonita had ended her relationship with Paco with the simple "A Dios," Conchita sent José a missive that ended with: "P.S. Send my greetings to Paco and tell him please if it is not too much of a bother to please write to me. If you can do me the favor."[62] Unaware of the women's ploy, José answered innocently. "P.S. Paco is not here or else I would gladly give him your message, he is in San José, Calif., he left for over there since July of last year."[63] With that news, Conchita and Chonita now had a better sense of Paco's locale in northern California, and likely knew he was living with his older brother, Jesús, who had lived in that city for a number of years, as was well known to family and friends in Calvillo.

José, however, was not completely blind to Chonita's desire in reuniting with Paco and broke his custom of rarely speaking about their courtship to uplift her spirits by relaying a message to her through Conchita. "Greetings with much affection to Chonita and tell her that if I could make it so that she and Paco would reconcile I would do that with pleasure," he said. "Tell her not to lose hope as I know that Paco loves her at least when he was here he told it to someone with whom he has a lot of trust (*confianza*)."[64] Whether José relayed the news to win favor with Conchita is unclear, but it is clear that Conchita wasted little time in relaying that insight to Chonita, who, in turn, responded quickly to José through Conchita's correspondence. "'Chifis' says thanks for your words of inspiration that she hopes it will be as you say," Conchita wrote to José.[65] A week later, José affirmed his wishes when he wrote to Conchita, in English—in his attempt to impress her with his English-language skills, "Tell Chifis I really wish some day she and my brother get togother [*sic*] and get Mariage [*sic*]."[66]

After seeing that José was amenable to relaying messages, the sisters boldly asked José to act as an agent to probe deeply Paco's relationships. The ruse began later that month, in April 1964, when Chonita became worried that Socorro, their mutual acquaintance with whom Paco had corresponded recently and with whom Chonita had a rocky friendship, had communicated falsehoods about her or had slandered her person to Paco. Initially, Chonita had asked Paco what Socorro had said about her, and Paco responded that he had not yet received her reply, which was true, as Socorro delayed more than two months in answering his letter. Chonita, however, was not convinced, fearing the worst. To determine what Socorro had relayed to Paco, Chonita took advantage of José's frequent communication with Conchita and asked her to ask José what he knew about Soccorro's latest missive. As Conchita explained to José, "It would be better if you told [Paco] that I asked you or let's see how you figure it out because I think my little sister distrusts too much that girl (*esa niña*)."[67]

José drew the line in meddling in Paco's affairs, however, refusing to follow through with the request, even though it might jeopardize his relationship with Conchita and Chonita as well. "I wanted to tell you that I am sorry to say that I cannot tell Paco what Chifis wants as I do not know how to go about it and believe me that I am really sorry and you know why because I think that if I write to Paco and I ask him he is going to think . . . why am I interested in him and Chifis," for "very few times we have dealt with such matters."[68] Sensing her mistake, Conchita apologized for the request and ended her note with a "thousand regrets" and asking him to "forget about it."[69]

Despite overstepping the bounds of communication, Conchita did not relent in relaying news to José about Chonita's relations in town, hoping, perhaps, that José in turn would share the information with Paco. Though it is unclear what role Chonita played in Conchita's attempt to play matchmaker, no doubt they both hoped that José would pass along the latest word to Paco. In an attempt to stir Paco's attention, Conchita related to José that their older brother, Juan, had attempted to impress Chonita by speaking to her about love and by telling her that Paco had never loved her in order to tarnish his reputation with Chonita. While Conchita thought it was funny (*chistoso*), to José his older brother's comments were no laughing matter. "I don't even want to think what you say about my brother [Juan] it was distasteful and hopefully Paco doesn't find out for Juan only wishes to be like him."[70]

Despite Conchita's six-month attempt to mend the relationship, Paco and Chonita's noviasgo remained at a standstill. By early 1966, Chifis had found another boyfriend. To Conchita, Chonita's new boyfriend seemed an odd fellow. She and her older sister found his rural mannerisms and speech comical. For Chonita, though, he brought a measure of emotional relief. "She says that at least so she won't spend her time so sad," Conchita informed José.[71]

Reaching Out and Rekindling the Flame across the Borderlands

More than two years following Chonita's fateful "A Dios," Chonita and Paco rekindled their relationship after she reached out in distress over her sister Conchita's quickly planned marriage to José in August 1966. More distressing to Chonita was Conchita's sudden, but not unexpected, departure with José to Mexicali, from where they planned to migrate to California. Despite gender conventions of the day, Chonita wrote to Paco relating feelings of abandonment and loss that Conchita's move had stirred. Chonita was, in fact, losing her *media naranja*, her other half. For most of their child-hood, Chonita and Conchita, who were born two years apart, had re-mained the closest of friends, and Chonita, who had few others in similar roles, remained fiercely loyal. Chonita displayed that loyalty a few months before her sister's marriage to José when she interceded on Conchita's be-half, defending her from a local woman who attempted to tarnish her rep-utation. In June of that year, at the annual feria, while Conchita and Chonita enjoyed a refresco and listened to a *conjunto* (band), a visibly drunk woman from a nearby town interrupted their diversion. The ine-briated woman, who apparently knew of Conchita and José's long-distance relationship, told Conchita that her boyfriend was going to find out about the sisters' night out. While Conchita found her threats amusing, Chonita did not appreciate the surveillance, especially coming from another woman. Chiding the onlooker, Chonita retorted angrily, "Who commissioned you to watch us?"[72]

Conchita's nuptials and swift departure from the household were, indeed, difficult for Chonita, prompting her to plead for Paco's assistance. "Well as you probably already know of the stupidity that our siblings have just com-mitted I feel summarily depressed (*abatida*) because as you might know Concha apart from being my sister she was to me my only friend . . . with whom I counted on even though we always lived like . . . billiard balls fight-ing and always together."[73] Though Chonita rationalized Conchita's depar-ture from the home as inevitable, believing that one day she would marry and leave the household to form her own family, Chonita had difficulty dealing with the emotional impact of that sudden loss. Rather than confess to her own anguish and pain, Chonita expressed concern about Conchita's mental health, as she explained to Paco, wondering if she was content or depressed and perhaps hoping that she might regain her senses and leave José and return to Calvillo. As Asunción admitted years later in an inter-view, she opposed the idea of her sister's marriage to José, for she knew that Conchita neither loved him nor had a proper courtship, as she understood it. "*No tuvo noviasgo, no tuvo noviasgo, solo las cartas* (She didn't have a court-ship, she didn't have a courtship, only the letters)." Chonita was right about Conchita's emotional state, for the latter never consented verbally—said "yes"—to the marriage. Rather, she went along with José's plans, knowing marriage was the best solution for her and her household, given its dire eco-nomic circumstances. During Conchita's wedding ceremony, Asunción recalled years later, she suppressed the urge to call out, "*No te cases, no te cases!* (Don't marry, don't marry!)"[74]

Chonita embracing her younger sister, María Concepción
Alvarado ("Conchita") on the latter's wedding day, in 1966.
Distraught at the idea of losing Conchita, her confidante,
and conscious that Conchita was not in love with José,
Chonita felt compelled to yell out during the ceremony,
"*No te cases, no te cases!* (Don't marry, don't marry!),"
but kept her composure. The marriage went off without
a hitch.
Photograph in author's personal collection.

Though Chonita knew it was too late to dissolve the marriage—an annulment in the Catholic Church occurred rarely—she turned to Paco to provide the latest news about her sister's emotional and physical state and thereby offer a palliative to her grief. "As soon as you see them write to me because I have also become quite worried about Concha for when she left here she was in a very lamentable state of spirit (*estado de animo*) and I'm very worried that she may even get sick as a result of the drastic change (*golpe tan duro*) she has endured in having to leave behind everything that was a part of her." Chonita qualified her statement by explaining that Conchita probably missed their mother the most, though doubtless Chonita hoped Conchita missed her as well.[75]

All was not lost, however, for Conchita's departure provided Chonita with an opportunity to seek Paco's emotional support. "Taking advantage of your trust I would like to ask if it is possible for you to go soon where they live so that you can inform me how they are doing for I am sure that if I write to her to Concha or she writes she is not going to tell me the truth," Chonita wrote. "That is why I turn to you and knowing what a happy disposition you have I am sure it will give her much pleasure that you go and visit her." Chonita qualified her request by assuring Paco that she valued José, his brother and Conchita's husband, and his role in the household but knew that he was in Brawley, across the border at work for most of the day while Conchita stayed at home in Mexicali. "Don't think I think that José is not going to put everything on his part so that she is not so depressed (*aguitada*)," but Paco's visit, she said, "will make her feel a little more like she is not so alone."[76]

Anxious to know about her sister, Chonita was cautious in soliciting Paco's assistance, as she wanted to avoid appearing emotionally needy. "I think that with so much admonishment (*remendación*) you probably think that I like you for a babysitter but you . . . are in your right in not to help me with what I ask you." Leaving the door open for him to deny the request, she added, "If it is that way I beg you to forget that I have bothered you and you pretend that I did not write to you and sent you so much silliness (*mensadas*)." "Nevertheless do not forget that if one day you need my help even if it is little in what I can help don't hesitate for a moment as I am here to assist you and yours." Chonita ended by saying she appreciated "everything you can do for my sister," though the request was for her peace of mind as well.[77]

Apparently, Paco was not only willing to assist Chonita in maintaining ties with her sister across the borderlands but also interested in rekindling their relationship. Indeed, in no less than a month, Paco and Chonita had picked up the passionate and stormy nature of their affair, as reflected in the correspondence. Though Paco's response is no longer extant, Chonita's double voice indicates that he responded enthusiastically, telling her about his present and future plans and sending her his most recent portrait, a symbol of his interest in strengthening the bond. Thrilled to receive his letter and image, she opened her letter by praising his portrait. "*Chulopon* (gorgeous man) you don't know the joy you bring every time you write and even more today that you sent me your photo in which you look very good."[78] In response to the news about his studies, she asked him for details. "I want to ask you something if it's not too much indiscretion ¿what is it that you are studying?" Using self-effacing language, as was her custom, she added, "Of course if you don't want to say for a particular reason too bad I will have to live with it and remain in the dark." Impressed by his motivations and accomplishments, which included supporting his ailing father, Chonita wished him luck. "You know I would be very happy that all your dreams of grandeur came to be it would be a motivating satisfaction for you and all yours, I can only admire you for being so studious and at the same time hard working and ... being such a good son."[79]

Following the praise she showered on Paco, the tone of Chonita's missive suddenly changed to one of self-loathing. Apparently, Chonita's reflection on Paco's reformulated self-identity, as conveyed in his letter, as an ambitious, education- and goal-oriented migrant, led her to cast aspersions on her life in the pueblo. Using harsh words to describe herself, she wrote: "In turn I go from bad to worse every day I think that never in my dirty life I am going to amount to in anything I have always been an uneducated person as you know but too bad, I have confidence that one day you will relay to me a bit of science and that is if I take it like medicine to see if I improve a bit."[80]

Concerned by Chonita's conflicted letter, Paco responded, reminding her of the intimacy they shared and encouraging her to speak honestly and directly, free from the influence of others. "Don't ask me questions like that," about what he was studying, he wrote in English. "It makes me feel so bad that I think we are strangers, if you want to know something tell me but don't say 'if I can' do you understand me?" Switching to Spanish, he continued, "I want you to speak to me with trust not as if we were simply friends." Believing that her sisters continued to read the correspondence and shape her thinking about the relationship, he reiterated the need to keep it private between the two of them and not allow others who might misconstrue its meaning to see it. "That is why I want ... you [to] destroy them," the letters, "and that nobody sees them." That way, he explained, "what you say is what you feel and nobody misinterprets my words I want . . . you [to] love me more than you love me now." Paco knew, however, that it would be difficult to negotiate the influence of her family in their affairs. "If one day you don't love me or you don't care for me let it be your decision not of another person who can do it only with the end of laughing at you."[81] As Paco's words inferred so eloquently, letters could not only build and maintain relationships but also destroy them, especially when in the wrong hands.

Delighted to receive his honest and open response, Chonita nevertheless questioned his commitment. "My heart you had me very preoccupied with your delay in responding I didn't know what to think." "I thought," she said, "you had found a *chancluda de por acá* (girl from other there)." Her doubts about Paco's faithfulness, however, dissipated almost instantly the moment she opened his letter, for it brought her joy and wonderment and an opportunity to escape her reality. "I don't know what happens to me," she wrote; "every time I receive news from you it is as [if] everything changes quickly I see the colors more vibrant, the sun more luminous the trees more beautiful well everything seems more lovely even on the days when I [am] most fatigued and most upset with solely thinking of you or rereading your letters everything disappears at the moment." She confessed, too, that she had not burned the letters, as he had instructed. Instead, she guarded them. "But don't worry nobody sees them unless it is me," she reassured him. His absence, however, continued to make her feel empty. "Are you visiting in December?" she asked. "I want to see you so badly that I think I will never see you." Demonstrating her continued commitment, she ended by writing, "*Te quiero, te quiero, te adoro* (I love you, I love you, I adore you)."[82]

Despite Chonita's passionate confession, Paco failed to respond promptly, leading her to send another letter within a few weeks, suggesting that she sensed a growing disconnect and powerlessness in the relationship.[83] Chonita's intuition was not incorrect, for Paco's response indicated that he too questioned the viability of the relationship, given his changing circumstances in el norte as well as his dreams and desires. Writing during the holiday season, Paco opened by apologizing for the delay and reflecting on his desire for "Santa Claus"—a sign of his adaptation to U.S. consumer culture— to bring him a new car for the holidays so that he could go to Calvillo to see her. He doubted it would happen, he joked, because he had misbehaved. "What did you ask [Santa Claus]" to bring you? he queried Chonita.

"I think I can almost guess and I imagine that he is a gorgeous young man (*chamacón*) almost like me. Or no?" he said in a lighthearted tone.[84]

Reflecting on the physical and growing emotional divide between them, Paco's tone became serious. Relating a bittersweet experience at the holiday dance at the adult education center he attended, he lamented her absence at the event and in his life generally. "I enjoyed myself tremendously only that you did not come, well what happened that you made me wait and wait, how I would have enjoyed it but you refused to budge (*te pusiste tus moños*) and didn't come." Apparently, Paco had invited her to visit him for the holiday season but for reasons that remain unknown she had refused or been unable to travel. He lamented her inability to accompany him but resigned himself to their growing cross-border alienation. "Too bad," he said, "hopefully one day not too far off we will see each other again."[85]

Confessing his daily longing for bridging the gap between here and there and for Chonita's presence in his life, Paco told her he saw her reflection in the women he met on the streets. "When I get out of work I come across a young woman who looks like you and I have the urge to speak to her thinking it is you but then I realize it is not you and well I don't speak to her."[86] Chonita's absence was proving too much to bear. Wishing her a joyful Christmas, he signed off with "yours forever."

The distance separating Chonita and Paco, while seemingly unbridgeable, contracted significantly in the following months when she moved to Mexicali, Baja California, to accompany Conchita, who, recently married, needed help during a difficult pregnancy. Chonita's proximity to the U.S.-Mexico border and San José, California, more specifically, where Paco resided, did little to reinfuse the relationship, however, for he failed to visit her, despite his intentions to do so. In a mournful tone, she sent him a letter lamenting their continued separation and imploring him to visit her: "You don't know how much I would have liked [to have seen you]," she said in March 1967.[87] Three months later and still no word from Paco, Chonita was exasperated and at a loss to explain his deafening silence. Resigned to risking the relationship, she penned an ultimatum and sent it special delivery, ensuring that it would reach his hands. Please respond, she said, "in the name of the love that one day you told me you had for me . . . because you know a *desengaño* is preferable a thousand times than to be with the *incertidumbre* (uncertainty)." "I assure you," she concluded, "that after you say the last word I will never bother you again."[88] True to her word, Chonita stopped sending letters, for Paco never replied to that missive as well, officially ending what had long ago died.

Chonita and Paco's five-year on-again, off-again epistolary relationship demonstrates that migration impacted not only those who went north in search of economic opportunity, gendered affirmation, and social stability but also loved ones who stayed behind. As Chonita's correspondence indicates, she endured tremendous personal sacrifices, emotional suffering, and conflicted views about her changing identity over the course of the long-distance, cross-border relationship. Indeed, Paco's departure and his new-found identity as a risk-taking, street-smart, worldly migrant enjoying the material comforts, cultural advances, and, potentially, the *chancludas* (women) of el norte, altered her sense of self-identity as a young woman living in a rural town. While she often expressed disdain for her lack of education, onerous domestic responsibilities, and life in Calvillo, she was unwilling to leave everything and everyone behind, as Paco had. As a female, Chonita did not face the same kind of social and cultural pressure males confronted in proving their gender and sexual identity as "men" who had the ability to provide for themselves and their families. Paco's emigration, nevertheless, shook her sense of who she was, where she belonged, and what she had planned for the future.

Chonita's correspondence demonstrates too that she violated many of the rules Gerber identified among nineteenth-century British immigrants in the United States who sent letters home. While most letter writers Gerber encountered practiced one-for-one reciprocity, Chonita was unable to honor that protocol, for she could not endure Paco's long silences and longed to communicate with him. Sensing her growing powerlessness in the relationship, as did many Italians in the immigrant experience to Canada, as Sonia Cancian has found, Chonita fired off letter after letter, to no avail, attempting to redeem her position and the courtship.[89]

Chonita was not the only individual who was left behind and impacted by the migration of young men such as Paco. Chapter 5 illustrates the ways in which migration and the lure it offered every potential migrant male proved powerful in pulling many young men north, despite the odds against them. For Rogelio Martínez Serna, Paco's friend from Calvillo, dreams of "pockets full of dollars" kept his eyes locked on the prize of migration and, eventually, earning enough money to return and settle comfortably in Mexico. Migration, as he soon learned, was no easy prospect. For Rogelio, that experience led him to suffer physical and emotional scars in his attempts to journey across the U.S.-Mexico borderlands.

CHAPTER FIVE

A Toda Madre (ATM)

Migrant Dreams and Nightmares in El Norte

In August 1962, Rogelio Martínez Serna, an eighteen-year-old migrant originally from Calvillo, Aguascalientes, living and working in Los Angeles, California, dashed off a letter to his childhood friend Paco Chávez, residing in Mexico. Exasperated, Rogelio had been waiting for Paco's communication that he would soon join him in the City of Angels. "Look I've been waiting for your letter and nothing at all. What is going on?" Paco apparently had not yet solidified his plans to emigrate to el norte. To convince him to come, Rogelio extolled Los Angeles's pleasures, including leisure, work, and sexuality. "Here you can have a fabulous (*chevere*) time," Rogelio told him. "I for the moment have settled in a restaurant in the center of Los Angeles" at the Hilton Hotel. "I am not full time I work 3 or 4 days a week I make 1.25 an hour." Wage labor (which was essential to Paco's journey and affirmation of manhood, according to Mexican gendered and cultural understandings of the day), Rogelio bragged, was relatively easy to find as long as he was resourceful. "Look the day I arrived I obtained a job (*jale*) as a bus boy in Woolworth's but I couldn't because I lacked the social security and now I have it and I can work wherever I want it is the only thing they ask, the S.S." Rogelio was correct about the ease in obtaining a social security number. Prior to 1973, anyone, including those without permanent residency or citizenship, like him, could apply and receive one within days.[1] Young women abounded, too, Rogelio said, giving young men, presumably heterosexuals like their female counterparts, the opportunity to affirm their masculinity in a new cultural and social space. "Here you should see there are millions and they all pull more than their weight."[2]

Immigration policies and practices at the U.S.-Mexico border were lax, too, Rogelio informed Paco, as he crossed with little fanfare. "I came through Tijuana as you know and there was no trouble (*vorlote*) not even a bit, I'm going tell you ... if your immigration papers (*papeles*) are not moving along better to come to Tijuana there you can obtain your local crossing card (*mica*) and you are already here in Los Angeles." Moreover, Paco need not worry about *la migra* (the border patrol) in the city. "Here the migra doesn't bother you ever because almost all are Chicano here." In the early 1960s,

Chicanos or Mexican Americans, as Rogelio smartly observed, outnumbered the Mexican immigrant population, particularly the undocumented sector, a trend that would begin to reverse with the end of the bracero program and increased demand for cheap labor in the service sector and the construction industry as well as tighter immigration restrictions from Mexico with the passage of the Immigration Act of 1965. Trying to persuade him, Rogelio said, "C'mon (*animate*) Paco here the scene (*movida*) is more than good . . . it is enormous you cannot even imagine."[3]

Rogelio's portrayal of his experience in Los Angeles was not altogether truthful, however. Indeed, as he later confessed to Paco, being away from family and friends left him feeling lonely and insecure, especially living in the shadow of the law. What Rogelio longed for was the familiar sights of there (*allá*) in the new environment (*aquí*). What he needed as well was insight—social remittances—about resources and opportunities available in el norte, and he continually asked Paco for tips on negotiating life in the United States.[4] Paco had yet to migrate and had no firsthand experience but did, however, have some knowledge about life in *el otro lado* (the other side) from his older brothers, father, and uncles who had migrated years before him. "Paco," Rogelio wrote before signing off, "I hope you will answer me soon and that it is some five pages of correspondence to know how la movida is over there" in the United States.[5]

Within a few weeks, still having received no word from Paco, Rogelio had apparently had enough and departed the City of Angels and returned to the border city of Ciudad Juárez, Chihuahua. There, in Ciudad Juárez, where he had resided since the age of fourteen after migrating from Calvillo looking for social and economic opportunity, he joined extended family and community members from his hometown, hoping to obtain his residency to work lawfully in the United States. Dejected but hopeful, he submitted his application, resigned to waiting for his fortunes to turn. After waiting nearly a year and seeing Paco migrate to California relatively easily with the assistance of his brother in September 1962, Rogelio became impatient and decided to depart to Tijuana as soon as he was able to save some money for his passage. Within a few months, by early 1963, he had secured enough to get him to the Golden State, where he was sure he could find work. But after suffering a harrowing crossing and finding only backbreaking, poorly paid employment, Rogelio was ready to call it quits in el norte and head home.

Rogelio's experience with migration was not uncommon for Mexican males seeking to immigrate to the United States in the 1950s and 1960s. Like

Residing temporarily in Mexicali, Baja California, in late 1962, waiting for the approval of his petition for permanent residency, Paco Chávez (*right*) relied on a cross-border social network of family and friends of the family, including Jesús Hernández (*left*), as well as U.S. employers, to facilitate his lawful migration to the United States. Not all migrants, including his friend Rogelio Martínez Serna, had access to such networks, making the journey difficult, if not impossible.
Permission to reprint photograph provided by Paco Chávez.

the contemporary braceros, or contract laborers from Mexico, Rogelio sought employment, a livable wage, and the opportunity to save money and eventually return to Mexico, where he hoped to make a life for himself as the head of a household. Mexican men not under a contract soon discovered, however, that they faced a number of legal and economic challenges with migrating. Their inability to cross the border lawfully not only forced them to cross unlawfully as *mojados* (wetbacks), a misnomer given to undocumented persons, but also eroded their sense of manhood. As Ramona Pérez, Deborah Cohen, and Cristina Rosas have found, for Mexican men and boys, migrating across the U.S.-Mexico border forms a rite of passage in proving oneself a "man," who, in turn, then has the ability to support his family.[6] Those unable to cross, as a result of being detained, denied, or obstructed, must deal with that immediate failure (*fracaso*) as well as the long-term implications for their identity as "men." For Rogelio, setbacks with attempting to migrate were, indeed, low points personally and emotionally. Despite the temporary defeats, Rogelio, like many of his migrant peers, took his chances with crossing into the new environment, as he longed to find new opportunities and adventures that affirmed his sense of manhood. Yet, doing so in a social and cultural context that erased the complexity of his masculinity and rendered him an insignificant laborer and beast of burden would not be easy, as he soon discovered.

To understand migrants' longing for opportunity allá in the United States and long-term stability aqui in Mexico, this chapter traces Rogelio Martínez Serna's experience—and that of his peers—across the U.S.-Mexico borderlands and his attempts to achieve an economically, personally, and emotionally stable family life. The chapter opens by examining Rogelio's desire as well as his effort to migrate lawfully across the U.S.-Mexico border following his brief time in Los Angeles. It shows that his motivation for migration was stoked by economic need as well as Paco's recent successful journey to and settlement in California. Like his peers back home, Rogelio imagined Paco living in the United States, earning pockets full of dollars, riding around in a flashy car, and attracting women. Inspired by Paco and not easily defeated, Rogelio developed ingenious plans to make it across *la linea* (the line). Even when faced with roadblocks, as he was repeatedly, Rogelio pressed on with his larger aim in mind: migrating to California to work and save enough money for a secure life in Mexico.

But life as an undocumented worker in the Golden State was anything but golden for him. Indeed, the harsh labor, measly pay, and constant threat of la migra led him to retreat quickly to Ciudad Juárez. Rogelio, however, never lost sight of his aims, especially with peers providing practical, emotional, and economic support for how to lead the life of a successful male Mexican migrant with his masculinity and manhood intact. As Rogelio's experiences and those of his peers make clear, migrants relied on each other—and the broader social networks—to achieve lawful migration and obtain employment, housing, and transportation as well as familiar forms of entertainment and companionship, facilitating their transition to the new environment and enabling them to bridge the best of both worlds.

The Hardening of the U.S.-Mexico Border in the Twentieth Century

Rogelio Martínez Serna's challenges with crossing the U.S.-Mexico border in the early 1960s were not an anomaly. Rather, they reflected the hardening of the border line over the course of the twentieth century. For Mexican migrants decades earlier, in the late 1800s and early 1900s, traversing the border was a relatively simpler process than it was for Rogelio and his peers in the 1960s. As Manuel Gamio and George J. Sánchez have shown, passage to el norte in the early twentieth century was uncomplicated, for migrants simply provided their names to border inspectors, sometimes paid a small fee (usually pennies) or nothing at all, and walked across the line to their final destination. Mexicans faced few difficulties in doing so largely because of the increased demand for cheap labor in the expanding agricultural and industrial global capitalist economy of the Southwest and the decreasing supply of Asian and southern European laborers, which resulted from restrictive policies and practices aimed at curbing what were seen as competitive laborers driving down the wages and opportunities of white workers. Indeed, border inspectors, and later border patrol agents, were most concerned with detaining and deporting Chinese immigrants—not Mexicans—and smugglers of contraband. Not until the passage of the Immigration Acts of 1917, 1921, and especially 1924 did Mexicans face mounting obstacles on their way north. Those obstacles were largely the result of rising fears over European foreigners and the "enemies within" stoked by World War I as well as paranoia over infectious and inheritable diseases threatening to pollute the national body in the late 1910s and early 1920s.[7]

Initially, in the early 1900s, U.S. officials—with pressure from U.S. employers—overlooked the limitations placed on migrants when it came to Mexican laborers. Despite the acts of 1917 and 1921, stipulating literacy tests and visa fees, border inspectors exempted Mexican workers, facilitating their crossing. That approach began to shift, however, when diseases identified with the Mexican border emerged in the U.S. public arena as particularly dangerous and deadly. As Alexandra M. Stern has shown, the outbreak of typhoid fever in El Paso in 1917 and the deaths of four people, including an American doctor, resulted in the medicalization of migrants of Mexican origin and the move to enforce the barring of any person "likely to become a public charge" or thought to be carrying a contagious disease. Equally significant for Mexicans was the establishment of the U.S. Border Patrol, as stipulated in the Immigration Act of 1924, and their new classification as "alien others." Charged with the surveillance of criminal activity and the apprehension of offenders (including persons crossing the border without inspection) across a vast, rugged landscape nearly 2,000 miles in length, the border patrol was ineffective in enforcing immigration policies, particularly with its limited personnel of 450 agents and its $2 million budget. And while Mexican immigrants found themselves up against a new adversary in their attempts to migrate across the border freely, most still managed to cross the borderlands without much difficulty, as they took advantage of the open terrain, poorly constructed fences, natural waterways, and the services of the new entrepreneurs or guides known as coyotes (smugglers), mostly small-scale mom-and-pop operations, all of which facilitated unsanctioned cross-border migration.

Though most Mexicans had relatively little difficulty migrating across the border through the early 1920s, the onset of a series of severe economic downturns in California and across the United States resulted in an unprecedented near-closing of the U.S.-Mexico border in the late 1920s and early 1930s. Launched in response to the Great Depression and an effort to reserve employment, public assistance, and sustenance for those identified as deserving (white) Americans, Mexican migrants and U.S.-born Mexican Americans faced local, state, and federal efforts to repatriate persons of Mexican ancestry, regardless of citizenship. In violation of the U.S. Constitution, Mexican immigrants and Mexicans Americans were "encouraged" to return voluntarily as well as being detained and repatriated forcibly to Mexico. Some U.S.-born and naturalized American citizens of Mexican descent, as Marla A. Ramírez has found in her research, had their passports confiscated, making it difficult, if not impossible, ever to return. Mexicans looking to cross the border into the United States faced equal hostility and were denied entry on the likelihood of their becoming public charges. By the time the program ended at the federal level in 1933 and was eventually discontinued at the state and local levels a few years after that, some 500,000 or more persons of Mexican descent had been subject to repatriation or expulsion. Though the Mexican and Mexican American communities in the United States remained intact, the effects of the legal injustice and targeting of Mexican people within and without the United States as an economic threat and a racial problem proved to have long-term effects. Confused, unwelcome, and outcast, many Mexicans and Mexican Americans retreated to their neighborhoods, feeling scapegoated, rejected, and silenced as to their role in the United States. Not until a generation later would significant numbers of people of Mexican descent claim their rightful place in U.S. society.[8]

Notwithstanding the alienation of Mexican and Mexican American people, the onset of World War II and U.S. involvement in the war beginning in the early 1940s led to an increased demand for labor at home and abroad, resulting in expanding opportunities for Mexicans such as Rogelio Martínez Serna to migrate for employment. With the enlistment and deployment of thousands of U.S. men in the armed services abroad and the rapid expansion of the war economy on the home front, the United States experienced a shortage of laborers willing to work in the poorly paid, backbreaking industry of agriculture. While white women and racial and ethnic minority men and women found new employment opportunities in the war industries, few workers sought to toil in the fields for little remuneration. With the prodding of large-scale farmers and agribusiness capitalists and their demand for cheap, dispensable labor in the United States, the U.S. State Department and the Mexican government negotiated the bracero program, the labor importation program, which lasted twenty-two years.[9] While 2 million or more Mexican men participated (no women were allowed for fear they would bring their families and remain permanently in the United States), emigration to el norte remained relatively difficult for Mexican males such as Rogelio who were not under contract or who lacked the support of a potential employer.

To immigrate to the United States, Mexicans had to fulfill the stringent stipulations of the McCarran-Walter Act of 1952, also known as the Omnibus Immigration and Naturalization Act. Carried out in light of fears of communism in the post–World War II era, it not only stipulated the detention and deportation of persons linked to or influenced by communist organizations but also maintained the national origins quota system. As Mae Ngai notes, that quota system was based on racial preferences for white northern Europeans and placed limits on persons from southern European as well as African and Asian countries, as stipulated in the immigration acts of 1921 and 1924. Though Mexico was not subject to the quotas, Mexicans were often denied entry through the public charge exclusion. The act of 1952, Ngai states, "was less an overhaul than a hardening of existing policy," for it "retained the numerical ceiling of 155,000 quota-immigrants per year based on the . . . formula of 1924" despite the increase in the U.S. population since then.[10] The 1952 act also imposed a quota for occupational "preferences" for skilled laborers, mandating that half of each country's quota be set aside for those persons with specialized skills in short supply. Second and third preferences were reserved for the parents of U.S. citizens and for the spouses and children of permanent residents. As Ngai stresses, the law not only favored persons with education, skills, and family ties in the United States but also limited the migration of people of color.[11]

Under those stringent provisions of the new law, persons from Mexico seeking to migrate had to show proof of a specialized skill or an employer's promise of support. As Rogelio and many Mexicans already knew and stressed repeatedly, they needed *cartas de sostenimiento* (letters of support) showing that they had an employer willing not only to hire them but also to maintain them when work slowed or ceased all together. Rogelio also needed to pay fees, between twenty and forty dollars, and sometimes more, to have his paperwork processed at the U.S. consulate in Ciudad Juárez. Though these were simple requirements, many Mexicans did not have such skills, nor did they have sufficient money to pay the costs, as work opportunities in Mexico yielded few pesos to the dollar. The restrictions left many Mexican men, especially those with few skills or contacts and little education, with few options other than to migrate without inspection and live as undocumented migrants in the United States until they could find an alternative to adjust their immigration status.

Dreaming of Green Cards, Pockets Full of Dollars, Women, and Cars

Neither working under contract in farm labor nor living the life of a mojado appealed to Rogelio.[12] He tried repeatedly to obtain the coveted green card and work in urban areas, which, in the 1960s and 1970s, had expanded, with increasing employment opportunities for service workers to meet the personal needs of educated, highly paid, skilled workers in the growing technology and information sectors of the emerging global economy. As he knew and as his friend Paco later confirmed, work was increasingly available in restaurants, hotels, car washes, and dry cleaners in urban areas, alongside the steady employment found in the agricultural fields of the Golden State. For Rogelio, however, making it across the U.S.-Mexico border lawfully was the first order of business and a task not easily achieved.

In February 1963, six months after his stint in Los Angeles as a busboy and, later, as an attendant at a hotel, Rogelio found himself in Ciudad Juárez, working at his uncle's cozy barbershop. Though it had only four chairs, it boasted a steady clientele. He spent his time, he told Paco, who had recently settled with his older brother, José, in Imperial Valley in California, "more or less well (*suave*)." What concerned him most was his application for residency. "Look I have already submitted my application to the consulate and they already sent me the first notice I am only waiting for them to call me to go and present myself even though I don't have the letters neither the one of support nor the one from work." Knowing that Paco had recently migrated successfully with the assistance of José's employer, J. C. Reeves, a farm owner and agriculturalist, Rogelio asked Paco for his advice. "Hopefully and you would give me direction (*un norte*) more or less where to obtain them" (the letters of support). At the moment, Rogelio was not interested in restaurant or similar kinds of work. "Better," he said, "if it is to work in *el campo* (farmwork)," where Rogelio would not be expected to speak English, a language he had yet to master.[13] Rogelio also had the possibility of reaching out to relatives in El Paso and Los Angeles, he told Paco, but these family members were unlikely to provide any kind assistance, as they were unsupportive (*son muy hojos*). For that reason, he implied, he had no other option than to turn to Paco.

While Paco's response is unclear, for his correspondence is no longer extant, it is clear that he was unable to assist Rogelio with the letters needed to secure residency. In all likelihood Paco's recent arrival to el norte meant that he, too, faced uncertainty and had not yet obtained the confidence of his employer. Paco, nevertheless, encouraged Rogelio's efforts to migrate and provided him with social remittances about the migratory process in particular and about life in the United States in general. Rogelio welcomed Paco's missives, for he was consumed with the idea of migrating to el norte, as he provided frequent and detailed reports of his latest efforts—and setbacks—to make it across the border lawfully. Within a few months, Rogelio had become so desperate, he told Paco, that he had even asked barbershop clients—many of them U.S. residents from El Paso seeking inexpensive personal services in Ciudad Juárez—for their assistance. "Here as you know many residents come and I have asked them for the letters, but you know without knowing them" they were unwilling to take the risk with the U.S. immigration authorities of vouching for him.[14]

What Rogelio longed for most was to be in el norte, working and discovering new places, themes he wrote about repeatedly in his correspondence. "Look I would really like to have my papers so that I could be with you over there in various places of the U.S.A. but look too bad (*lastima*)," he wrote, adding that he thought that "at least 2 or 3 months more" of waiting for a response to his petition would be needed.[15] Wanting to know more about Paco's experiences in Brawley, California, a small agricultural town with no more 12,700 residents spread out in the heart of Imperial Valley, Rogelio asked him to relay details about that community and the broader region.[16] Rogelio seemed to imagine Brawley as an exciting place, full of opportunities for young men like himself and Paco. "Tell me how is everything here (*aqui*) in Brawley, Calif., well I can only imagine it."[17] Before signing off, Rogelio again asked Paco to describe life in the Golden State, a query he repeated in almost all his missives. In all likelihood, he wanted Paco to confirm the abundant opportunities he dreamed about in the United States. Curiously, Rogelio forgot about or chose to remember selectively his experience in Los Angeles, which, he claimed, had afforded him many adventures despite his status as an unauthorized migrant.

Rogelio was not the only Mexican man fantasizing about the abundance of el norte. Several of Paco's male friends, who wrote to him frequently and knew he had emigrated, also longed to hear stories of migrant success at work and play. Antonio "el Pinole" Lozano, a longtime cuate from Calvillo, like Rogelio, wrote to Paco within days of the latter's migrating to Brawley and asked for details of his successful adventure. "I expect you to write to me to tell how suave it is in el norte," he stated.[18] Jesús Lozano, el Pinole's younger brother and another of Paco's friends from Calvillo, asked him too about life in el otro lado and about the possibility of following in his footsteps by traveling to Mexico's northern border and emigrating from there. "You know I have the urge to go to Mexicali but I don't have the will what do you advise I should do?"[19] While it is unknown what words of advice Paco offered, for his response is missing, it is clear that Jesús did not seriously consider moving to the border region. Instead, he remained in Mexico and continued to correspond with Paco yet never again broached the subject, at least according to the surviving correspondence.

Like Jesús and el Pinole, Alfonso Martínez, a Calvillense who resided in Mexicali and with whom Paco had lived while waiting for his residency, consulted with Paco on migrating successfully across the border. Alfonso, however, requested more than insight about el norte. What he wanted was cash. Indeed, Alfonso needed money to complete his application for residency and asked Paco repeatedly for support, presumably believing that Paco's migration had resulted in his earning a significant of amount of income. Alfonso was correct, but only partially. Paco had landed poorly paid agricultural work in Brawley, and later in the service industry in Silicon Valley. Jobs in restaurants, car washes, and the personal services sector paid only slightly more than those in Imperial Valley.[20] Despite Paco's low wages and difficulties with his employers, which his cuates knew little about, his friends imagined him living in el norte in a land of abundance. While it is unclear if Paco relayed exaggerated details of wealth in el otro lado, as too few of his letters have survived to make a definitive analysis, it is likely that his friends heard the stories from family and friends who had traveled or lived in the United States.

Narratives of streets "paved with gold" and the power of those tales to pull people north were not a new phenomenon. Indeed, since the early twentieth century, when Mexican migration to the United States increased significantly, those who had traveled to or lived in el otro lado communicated about the riches and opportunities with those who stayed at home. Manuel Gamio's interviews with Mexican migrants in the 1920s indicate that those cross-border narratives circulated regularly through word of mouth as well as through letters sent back and forth across the border. Later, in the 1940s, 1950s, and 1960s, those narratives were reinforced through the visual images circulating in wildly popular Hollywood movies that made their way throughout Mexico, including Calvillo. For years, even during Mexico's "golden age" of cinema from the late 1930s through the 1950s, U.S. English-language films were the most popular source of entertainment in movie houses.[21] Years later, Paco recalled that, as a young man in Calvillo in the late 1950s and early 1960s, he saw a variety of American films in the local theater as well as in the larger, more cosmopolitan city of Aguascalientes. The flicks included *El diablo es una mujer* (*The Devil Is a Woman*, 1935), *Lo que el viento se llevó* (*Gone with the Wind*, 1940, among the most dominant films in Latin America), *La tunica* (*The Robe*, 1953), *Oro de Napoles* (*Gold of Naples*, 1953), *Rica, joven y bonita* (*Rich, Young and Pretty*, 1953), and *Una grieta en el espejo* (*Crack in the Mirror*, 1960). The movies, along with the exchange of correspondence and oral stories, doubtless helped to stir the imagination and led to the migration of thousands of Mexicans to the United States.[22]

In response to Alfonso's request for money for residency, Paco sent him some ten or twenty dollars in January 1964, within weeks of arriving in Imperial Valley. Apparently, that sum was not enough. A few months later, Alfonso wrote again, requesting thirty to forty dollars to obtain his Mexican passport, which he needed to apply for the green card. Alfonso was close to making it across, he told Paco, for a *ranchero*, a local farm owner, had provided him with letters of support but could not guarantee any employment. Plus, his usual source for loans in Mexicali, he explained, was not available, and his father also was unable to provide much. And while he worked picking cotton in Mexicali, the measly twenty-five pesos (roughly two dollars) he earned in a ten-hour workday was not enough. "Is that just?" he asked Paco.[23] Apparently, Paco was moved to help his friend and sent him some cash by the end of May 1964 and, along with the twenty dollars Alfonso had managed to save, he had enough. "Thank you Paco, thank you very much," Alfonso wrote in June 1964.[24] Much-needed repairs to Alfonso's household as well as other family expenses, however, consumed the hard-earned money earmarked for his residency. Nevertheless, Alfonso maintained his hope of earning and saving enough to obtain his green card, allowing him to join Paco in el norte.[25]

Whether Alfonso managed to cross the border with or without inspection is unknown, but what is known is that Paco's friends, including Rogelio, continued to imagine him a successful migrant with pockets full of dollars. Indeed, Pedro "Perico" Sánchez, a longtime friend from Calvillo who stayed at home, sent Paco a missive soon after he had left Calvillo with praise about the prosperity he reportedly relished. "I've heard that you've enjoyed success, you don't know how happy I am," Perico wrote. "P.S. Tell me where you work and if it's true that you've had a good experience."[26] A year later, el Pinole went so far as to fancy his friend a wealthy man when he wrote, "Hoping that as you receive this [letter] you enjoy good health and your pockets full of $$$$$$$$$$$$$$."[27] Two years after that note, Paco received praise from José Luis López Velasco, another cuate from Calvillo. Believing Paco had disposable means, José Luis asked him for some 100 to 150 pesos, or eight to twelve dollars, for his girlfriend, as she was "ill" or pregnant.[28] While many of Paco's male peers sought to borrow money—*dolares* they would likely be unable to repay anytime soon—Rogelio rarely, if ever, asked for any. What Rogelio wanted most were the social contacts for and access to stable employment, among other opportunities for economic relief and stability, which he believed Paco could provide. Though Rogelio, José Luis, el Pinole, and Pedro came to Paco with different needs and concerns, they could all agree on one thing: he had achieved the migrant dream.

Indeed, Rogelio as well as the majority of Paco's friends not only pictured him with pockets full of dollars but also with access to women, as they believed migrating to el norte was the path to accessing young women and affirming one's manhood and masculinity, despite the economically marginalized status of most recent Mexican migrants in the United States. In December 1962, three months after Paco's departure to el norte, José Luis wrote, sending him greetings to all "the girls" presumably in Paco's company. Not satisfied with only imagining Paco's encounters with women, José Luis urged him to relate the details of his many sexual conquests. "Tell me (*platicame*) how many girlfriends you have over there, if you have already made your first communion or not yet."[29] In other words, he wanted to know if Paco had engaged in sexual relations with women in el norte. Whether he meant *norteamericanas* or *mexicanas*, U.S.- or Mexico-born, is unclear. Nevertheless, in his friend's view, Paco had likely gained such experience and as a consequence was believed to be a much more sophisticated and worldly man than he had been in Calvillo. Still, some of his friends liked to test what they saw as Paco's new and enhanced sense of masculinity.

Among the friends who wanted to hear the most about his sexual encounters with women was el Pinole, who was also the most explicit and denigrating in his language and conceptions of women, femininity, and female sexuality. "I expect that when you come over here you will surprise us with the news that you are no longer afraid of the *jiotosas* (slang for rash-like females) and that you come ready and willing for everything ... but don't worry don't confess that you are *tarugo* (dumb) with the *cucarachas* (slang for females and, literally, cockroaches)."[30] Rather than admit his limited knowledge of sex with women, el Pinole advised Paco to portray himself as a sexually experienced man.

El Pinole's contempt for women was not reserved for those in Mexico and extended to those in the United States. In Mexico in the 1960s and 1970s, many characterized American or white women as loose sexually and morally and accessible to the men who wanted them. Those ideas, which were likely reinforced by popular media, were not new but rather deep-rooted, as they circulated freely among the Mexican migrant population in the early twentieth century. In his interviews with migrants in the southwestern United States in the 1920s, Manuel Gamio found that Mexican men and women held a deep disdain for North American women whom they believed affronted gender norms Mexicans held sacred. Gamio's informants characterized norteamericanas as too frivolous with money, too free (*muy libres*) in their social conventions, and too independent in their gender relations, for many of the women controlled their spouses and divorced them too easily, as they had the protection of the law. American women were also more apt than Mexican women to affront cultural beliefs of dishonor and shame by displaying their bodies in public and did so, as one woman of Mexican origin noted, by bathing freely at the beaches.[31]

Similar ideas persisted among Mexicans decades later, as el Pinole's advice suggested. El Pinole expected Paco to take advantage of the modern sexual norms and the women who subscribed to those ideals in el norte. El Pinole seemed most interested in the "Go-Go" girls, the scantily clad dancers popular in nightclubs in San Francisco, California, and, later, in locales as far away as Japan and Vietnam. "Tell me if you have any news, a girlfriend or at least a *garbanza* (female chickpea), because I know the *piojosas* (flea-infested females) of the *nueva ola* (new wave) are in abundance over there, those that they call the a Go-Go and that they don't hold back, therefore you should have at least one to *ruletear* (spin)."[32]

Alfonso, Paco's friend living in Mexicali, was as explicit as el Pinole in fantasizing about Paco's sexual rendezvous with women, including the ladies of the night. "Hey Paco 'do you know the bad women (*mujeres malas*) of San José,'" he asked, "or maybe you don't know the secrets like in San Luis Sonora do you recall when you went that's what I'm referring to send me word," he implored.[33] Rogelio, too, queried Paco about his female relationships but did so less explicitly and less frequently than either Alfonso or el Pinole. "I expect you have your girlfriends around here . . . hopefully . . . you have some 15 or more."[34] Whether Paco confirmed Rogelio, Alfonso, and el Pinole's imaginings about his intimate and abundant relationships with women in the United States is unclear. What is clear is that his friends rendered him a Mexican male migrant with an enhanced masculine sexual identity.

In addition to having access to women and heterosexual relations, Rogelio and other friends of Paco's envisioned him riding around in his fashionable convertible car, which he had purchased shortly following his emigration. He lovingly called it "*el poderoso* (the powerful one)," as he told them soon after buying the used automobile.[35] Paco knew that the car was not only useful for transporting him quickly to and from the agricultural fields but also an important symbol of physical and economic mobility as well as masculinity. To his friends, having this mode of transportation made it possible to travel to el norte to find work and earn a decent paycheck and to journey south to Mexico on a whim or as needed to visit ill relatives or attend a family gathering, giving one greater flexibility and control in carving out one's immediate future. The car also symbolized access to places of leisure frequented by young heterosexual male Mexican migrants of his day, enabling him and his friends to attend local dances, indoor and drive-in movie theaters, concerts, or eateries and to meet eligible heterosexual Mexican females. Those adventures pleased Paco, especially his attendance at live music venues. In one of the few extant letters he wrote to el Pinole in 1965, Paco mentioned attending concerts with well-known Mexican artists. "[I] enjoyed one with your uncle Juan guess guess Mendoza the very one . . . take a look at the artists, I also saw Irma Serrano," a well-known ranchero-style singer.[36] Paco could not understand why others—particularly U.S.-born Mexican Americans, with whom Mexican immigrants sometimes clashed over cultural and ideological differences, particularly the use of the Spanish language—could not appreciate such musical tastes. "That's what makes me angry with these Chicanos," he said, "that they don't appreciate the good music."[37]

Alfonso, Paco's friend in Mexicali, knew the benefits of mobility and access to women as well, and hoped Paco would allow him to use the car to travel to "Calvis, Ranch (Calvillo) to see Juanita," presumably his girlfriend.[38] Two weeks later, Alfonso continued to daydream of Paco's ride, believing it would affirm his masculinity. "You with a *carrito* (little car) it will be easier to go see the *chavalas* (girls) you got ahead of me already but no matter and then we will even go together to 'Calvis, Ranch.' And hopefully I can bring from that little town a *cherita* (girl) as I already [had relations with] my girlfriend," he said, boasting of his exploits. "Therefore, we need to taste (*probar*) from another side let's see what luck I have."[39]

Equally important to the affirmation of Paco's cuates' masculine identity was the material wealth and economic mobility that the car symbolized. For a relatively poor migrant or would-be migrant male like Rogelio or Paco, owning a car meant an incremental rise from poverty or the working class to the lower middle class, proving a man's ability to support a family. El Pinole understood the significance of Paco's new car and his masculinity when he begged Paco to show him a photograph of el poderoso next to his well-formed, firm, and masculine body. "I want to meet it and in addition to see you to see how muscular (*ponchado*) you are with the exercise."[40]

Rogelio, too, realized the many benefits of an automobile and eventually owned a car as well, but he did so by pooling his resources with other friends from Calvillo, including Rafael Martínez, who pitched in to purchase one they called "*el cacheton* (the chubby-faced one)." Apparently, Ro-

A rendering of Paco's amorous relationship with a female acquaintance, possibly a coworker at the restaurant where he washed dishes in the 1960s. The illustration speaks to the masculine image his friends on both sides of the border had of him in *el norte*. Imagining him as having pockets full of dollars, access to "liberated" women, newly acquired sexual prowess, and a powerful convertible car, Paco's friends pictured him as a successful migrant. Little did they know that he suffered from economic instability as well as personal and emotional stress.

Digital image in author's personal collection.

gelio and Rafael's car was not as reliable as Paco's, as it repeatedly had flat tires, as it did one morning in August 1964. "Forget it, that tire will have to be fixed," Rogelio said to Paco.[41] A week later, Rogelio wrote again, saying the car was still not doing well. Paco's auto, though, seemed destined for greatness, at least in Rogelio's eyes. "Greetings to your 'super carr' and hopefully it behaves even better every day."[42]

Though it is difficult to know all the details Paco reported to his friends to feed the dream of his success with physical and economic mobility as well as leisure, entertainment, and women, given that his letters are no longer extant, it is known that he relayed sufficient news to keep them interested in his adventures. Paco told them, for instance, about his studies in auto mechanics as well as English. While few of his friends commented on his educational pursuits, those who did were impressed with his attempts to adapt to the local culture and expand his opportunities. "I congratulate you for studying more than for the diplomas or trophies you will be able to secure in your studies," el Pinole wrote in 1967, a short time after relocating to Mexico City. "I too would like to study, but you can't imagine the problems that can originate trying to realize such a goal here in the capital."[43]

Paco was not alone among his friends in fueling the dream of el norte. Like thousands of Mexican migrant men who came before and after him, Rafael Martínez, Paco's childhood friend, communicated similar ideas to his friends in the United States and Mexico. But Rafael was more deliberate than Paco in portraying the enchanted life of the migrant. In his correspondence with Paco, Rafael related his successes in various fields. Labor in the agricultural fields of Lindsay, California, a small town in the northern Central Valley of the Golden State, where Rafael resided and worked picking a variety of fruits, was often slow, he admitted, but plentiful when the harvest came in, enabling him to fill his pockets full of dollars.

Adaptation to the local culture was also relatively easy for Rafael, as he demonstrated by writing to Paco in English. Though his command of the English language was imperfect, and Rafael knew it, doubtless his capacity impressed Paco and his peers, who had yet to master much of the dominant language in the United States. "Mr. Pac. Dear Friend: ~~I am ansering the your's there I~~ (Excuse me, that's no right.) I received your letter, and I am answering it wishing for you and Rogelio the best of helth, me 'a-t-m' (*a toda madre*, doing great) thanks to God our Lord."[44] In addition to demonstrating his strong command of English, Rafael bragged about his sexual exploits with women in Mexico and the United States. In October 1964, he told Paco he had plans to travel with a friend to Tijuana to "spend

100,000,000.00 of his abundant fortune on *la mujeres de la* street," prostitutes.[45] Rafael also related stories about his intimate relationships with local young women who seemed enthralled by his masculine sexuality. "Look in Lindsay I secured 2 girlfriends and with the 2 of them I kissed a lot; one of them has 18 lovely springs and the other is going to turn 15 and the 15 year old is the master in the art of the kiss, she would give me only French kisses. I have a ton of moves (*movidas*) that I have to tell you about; but right now I cannot recall more. *Es todo por* (that's all for) now," he wrote in Spanish and English.[46]

Despite migrants' communications about their experiences of success in el norte, the reality was that life was hard as a single, migrant Mexican male, particularly for those who crossed the border without inspection and resided in a land with few family or social networks buffering the largely foreign language and culture. Paco, like many migrants, including his older brother José, communicated those sentiments to many of his friends, including María López L., el Pinole's girlfriend, who had recently relocated to the United States to work and join family members, much to el Pinole's chagrin. In response to Paco's correspondence with María, in which he described his heartfelt misgivings about life in el norte, María urged him to visit her in Los Angeles, presumably for camaraderie and companionship. "Paco you tell me you find yourself lonely and sad well look make the effort and really come over here."[47] Though she wanted him to visit, she could only make herself available during the weekends, as she worked during the week. Whether Paco visited María is unknown, but in all likelihood her correspondence gave him some reassurance of the larger social network supporting him and his fellow migrants.

La Migra and Crossing the Border

Migrant dreams of women, cars, dollars, and green cards proved powerful for Rogelio, who waited patiently to cross the border lawfully a few months after Paco had migrated to the United States in December 1962. Though Rogelio's application for residency was delayed, he remained hopeful, working in the barbershop and adapting to the local culture, which included perfecting *caló*, a vernacular slang and mix of English and Spanish popular among working-class youths, including *pachucos* and *pachucas*, in the El Paso–Ciudad Juárez border region of the 1940s and 1950s. Rogelio recalled years later that he picked up the language by listening, practicing, and perfecting the words and phrases uttered by his new companions, whom he befriended at the local *mercado* (market) where he worked as a young man luring customers to the stalls.[48] Though Rogelio reveled in using the language, not everyone welcomed such youth culture, particularly the middle class and elite of Mexican society.[49] While Rogelio developed a strong affinity to border culture, he grew restless waiting to hear from the consulate about his residency.

Desperate, Rogelio dashed off a pointed missive to Paco, pleading for help. "Tell me Paco if you might be able to obtain the letters in case they call me, . . . I will . . . later buy some *cahuamas* (large, thirty-two-ounce beers)."[50] Unfortunately for Rogelio, Paco was in no position to request a letter of support from Reeves, for Paco's relationship with his employer remained tenuous. Despite Paco's inability to assist Rogelio, a month later, after paying a visit to Calvillo, Rogelio still had his sights set on migrating to the United States and turned to Paco again, hoping this time he might come through. In his latest missive, Rogelio confided that he was in love and had contemplated marrying his "girly frend," as he wrote in English, in Ciudad Juárez, but he knew he was broke and unable to fulfill his role as head of household, a gendered responsibility that came along with marriage. Rogelio was not ready to take on that obligation. "I don't know what to do, get married no, . . . I think the best thing to do is to go somewhere far from her, tell me how it is here where you are, if there is *chansa* to join you around here."[51]

Rogelio, however, like Paco and other migrants, confessed he had mixed feelings about being alone, away from friends and familiar sights and sounds. "In Los Angeles one feels sort of sad you should see and one needs someone with which to joke around and pass the time, to not feel so far from the *terre* (homeland) well you understand me."[52] Plus, he continued, as an unauthorized migrant, he faced risks. "Look Paco if I go for it and manage to cross with God's favor, it is to have a good little time with you and then leave." In thinking about Paco's residency and the privileges it afforded, Rogelio fantasized about doing the same: "How great it is to be with your papeles." Rogelio knew he daydreamed, though, for the local border economy was weak and the need for relief was great. The Border Industrialization Program of 1965, with its promise of foreign investment and assembly and manufacturing industries as well as employment for local Mexicans, had yet to materialize in the border cities of Tijuana, Baja California, and Ciudad Juárez, Chihuahua. "You know my passport is still a long time in coming for they have not even responded to me, as there is a lot of people without work here in El [P]aso and vicinity." Before signing off, Rogelio asked Paco again for his assistance. "Then in all seriousness Paco if you see that it's possible for me to go well just tell me, because in all honesty Juárez doesn't do it for me anymore in the conditions that I find myself . . . respond soon Paco please," he begged.[53]

Undeterred from obtaining residency but in need of making a living, two weeks later Rogelio came up with a new plan for earning extra income. In light of slow sales at the barbershop, Rogelio turned to selling U.S. contraband merchandise (*fayuca*) in the local market in Ciudad Juárez, where a few years earlier he had found work after migrating to the city. Engaging in *fayuquear*, a common though unlawful practice, seemed to bring only minor consequences as long as one paid the appropriate tax, or bribe (*mordida*), to the authorities. "I bought a car to falluquiar here I'm going to bring in fruit from the other side to the market here hopefully and I will learn the way (*modo*) of this job."[54] Rogelio was not alone in his new endeavor, however. He had two associates (*socios*), originally from Calvillo, whom he could presumably trust. Ciudad Juárez, as Rogelio later confirmed in an oral interview, had a large expatriate community from Calvillo looking for similar social and economic opportunities. "Here in Juárez today almost all of Calvillo is here if you only saw how many people there are here from the homeland over there."[55] Calvillenses were not the only recently transplanted Mexicans in the northern region. In the 1950s and 1960s, tens of thousands of rural migrants from Durango, Guanajuato, Michoacan, and Jalisco made their way north to the border states of Chihuahua, Coahuila, and Baja California, looking for opportunities, but the local economy as well as the municipal infrastructure was simply unable to absorb them, as Rogelio had discovered.[56] Notwithstanding Rogelio's optimism for his new line of work, his venture soured quickly, as his main means of transport broke down, leaving him and his associates unable to carry out the cross-border buying and selling of merchandise. "My car broke down and I hit the mat (*me fui a la lona*) worse than a knockout."[57] Rogelio's only recourse was to find another car, but he had little luck buying one he could afford.

Three months later, penniless and unable to travel to Calvillo in December for the holidays, as did many expatriates from that pueblo, Rogelio spent Christmas and New Year's in Ciudad Juárez, planning to try his luck again in Los Angeles by using his local crossing card to reach his destination. Rogelio knew, however, that by doing so he invited difficulties with la migra as well as the winter weather, which could be harsh in the high desert area of that region. "I am nevertheless going to give it a shot we'll see how it goes."[58] Rogelio had good reason to risk the move: his business had failed, and work at the barbershop was slow. Trimming hair, he reported, left him with "not even enough for *tamales de miercoles*" (literally, tamales for Wednesday, but here "miercoles" is used as a euphemism for *mierda* or shit). Rogelio had grown desperate. "Look . . . I've already spent a year with my application and they haven't given me even the tiniest of hope." He had no other alternative, he told Paco, "than to enter as a mojado if I am lucky I will get to work if not too bad."[59] Though his spirits remained high, a week later he confessed that his limited options weighed him down emotionally. "I am walking around like a lost soul (*bala perdida*) here in Juariles (slang for Juárez)." In a few days, he told Paco, he planned to be in Tijuana and then cross the border. Rogelio's trip was not without forethought, however. He had planned it so that when he arrived in Tijuana he would reach a barbershop where he would work for a bit "to lighten his situation and enter through the main door."[60]

With few resources and no word from the U.S. consulate about his migratory status, Rogelio boarded a bus to Tijuana. Taking a minute to dash off a missive to Paco on a torn piece of paper, he told his friend about his final decision to risk crossing as an undocumented migrant. He saw no other recourse, he explained, for he could not afford the letters of support on the black market. "Well my passport too bad it couldn't be done they tried to sell me the letters for 300.00 dollars," or 3,750 pesos, an astronomical figure in 1964, especially for mexicanos who earned pesos—pennies on the dollar. "Like that can you believe it when do I cross?" Not knowing what to expect in el norte, specifically in San José, where he hoped to land with Paco and other compatriots from Calvillo, he pleaded with Paco to respond to him in Tijuana quickly. "Tell me how everything is there," he implored, "and now, if God wills it, we will see each other over here." He was ready to move forward, too, he told Paco, for his relationship with his girlfriend had ended. "Too bad, rest in peace."[61]

As much as Rogelio kept up his spirits, he was dealt another blow attempting to migrate. This time it was a physical blow. "Look," he told Paco nearly two weeks later, in March 1964, "I've spent 10 days here in Culiacan we crashed on this side of Durango about 100 kilometers." Rogelio reported no deaths but serious injuries. He was among the fortunate, he implied. "I only dislocated my right arm."[62] Fortunately, his father sent Rogelio money to get him to Tijuana, but it was only enough to get him on board a low-budget busline. Not letting the situation defeat him, he resigned himself—"*ai se va* (it goes that way)." Rogelio's troubles were not yet over. While in Culiacan, a thief stole his local crossing card, some *centavos*, and photographs.

"Well if I told you all the *desmadre* (chaos) that happened to me along the road, you would cry I had better not tell you."[63] When he eventually reached Tijuana, he encountered a harrowing experience crossing the line. "I was able to cross but you cannot imagine how I struggled I was in Tijuana for 12 days suffering *la pena negra* (a pitiful shame)."[64]

Rogelio's difficulties with crossing the Tijuana–San Diego border in the early 1960s suggest that traversing the line was far more difficult to do than he had indicated initially and that scholars have suggested recently. By most scholarly accounts, the Immigration and Naturalization Service (INS) at the time was a largely ineffectual, underfunded government agency with a budget smaller than many city police departments. In contrast, ten years earlier, in the 1950s, the INS Border Patrol, responsible for enforcement, had served up impressive apprehension rates with Operation Wetback (1954), detaining more than 1 million undocumented persons, most of them Mexican laborers. Yet, in subsequent decades, in the 1960s and 1970s, it received little support to halt migrants crossing without inspection, especially following the end of the bracero program in 1964 with the continued demand for cheap laborers. Peter Andreas argues that the policing was so lax that the majority of crossers engaged in self-smuggling, or, in the case of vulnerable populations such as women, children, and the elderly, hired a local border guide to get them across safely. The fencing at the border, though limited to urban areas and constructed of ten-foot-high chain-link fences, did force migrants to try to their luck further east through the harsh deserts and rough mountains, which could and often did lead to exposure to dehydration in the summer and hypothermia in the winter and, in some cases, death. But those barriers, which pale in comparison to those that would emerge in the 1990s and beyond, seemed unable to stop most people from crossing.[65]

How and why Rogelio was deterred at the border remains unknown, for he said nothing more in his letter to Paco, nor could he remember—or perhaps chose not to remember—years later the details of that attempt to cross. Rogelio did recall, however, that crossing at Tijuana was especially difficult in those years because of the want and desperation in the Mexican border city, which could offer few employment opportunities to the increasing Mexican migrant population. With few options, many migrants, like him, attempted to make their way across the U.S.-Mexico border with meager resources. Years later Rogelio also recalled sleeping in the Tijuana bus terminal on many occasions, as he lacked the funds to purchase a ticket. On those occasions he remembered, too, he sometimes had to sleep on cardboard and use that same material to keep him warm. While Rogelio was able to make it across the border using his local crossing card, he had to travel beyond the checkpoints along the way. That was no easy feat. He remembered that, on another occasion, he was nearly apprehended and returned to Mexico at the inspection point in San Clemente, California. Fortunately, though, he devised a successful ruse, explaining to the agent who pulled him over that his trip north to Los Angeles was for the day to catch a Dodgers baseball game. When asked for more details, Rogelio provided the name of the opposing team. Luckily, he explained in an oral interview years later, earlier that day he had seen the morning newspaper with the details of the event, allowing him to convince the agent of his intentions. Satisfied, the border patrol agent allowed him to continue on his way and wished him well, but not until rattling Rogelio's nerves about migrating successfully, residency or no residency, to the United States.[66]

Rogelio's later attempt to reunite with Paco in San José proved equally successful, though his circumstances were less than ideal. Once across Tijuana, following his difficult ordeal, Rogelio traveled about 100 miles north to Stanton, California, in present-day Orange County, where he found agricultural labor picking strawberries. Work was plentiful but strenuous and poorly paid as well as precarious given his undocumented status. Uncomfortable and unhappy in Stanton, he queried Paco once more about the possibility of employment in San José, as he knew Paco had recently landed some promising positions in the service industry, including washing dishes in a Mexican restaurant and scrubbing cars at the Miracle Mile car wash. At the car wash, Paco had managed to ascend to lead worker, overseeing the work of fellow mexicanos as well as gringos. Paco's fortunes gave Rogelio hope. "I work in whatever is available even as a manager," Rogelio joked. "I have a week here picking strawberries but we work 7–6—or 8 hours and they pay us $1 . . . as such I don't think that is just." Plus, as a mojado, Rogelio relayed, he had to watch constantly for the immigration authorities, who frequently raided the job site. On one occasion, he nearly fell in their trap, but fortunately, he was away in Los Angeles when they arrived. "I am not comfortable here because of la migra frequently they show up," he related. "This Monday I went to Los Angeles to obtain a social security and luckily the migra came when I was in Los Angeles and I escaped like a cat (*como gato*)."[67]

Though Paco's response is unknown, it is known that he failed to respond to Rogelio's query, for a week later Rogelio wrote to Paco again about employment in San José, for he was once more in desperate need. "Look

[P]aco I hope . . . there would be work here in San José I work in whatever is available look I am really in debt and there you have that I even want to get married but without money no cigar (*sin manis ni piri*)," he wrote in caló. Reaching San José would not be easy, however. He needed at least sixteen dollars for a round-trip fare on "Greihound." He kept his hopes alive, though, as he was resourceful and could adapt to the local culture, as he knew some English. "I hope there would be work I with a bit of broken (*machetiada*) English can make myself understood." Rogelio was interested in making it to San José not only for economic security but also for the camaraderie with his most intimate friends, including Paco. Many of their friends from home, he told Paco, had recently crossed at Tijuana and reached Los Angeles, and what Rogelio longed for most was to share his experiences—both the difficulties and rewards—with his cuates. "P.S. I really would like to see you so that we can have a long talk of some 100 hours, 'you know.'"[68]

After a few weeks of onerous labor and no word from Paco about job openings, Rogelio called it quits in Stanton, even though work abounded at the rancho. He returned to Ciudad Juárez dejected but not completely hopeless. Once home, he wrote to Paco telling him he still had dreams of obtaining the letters of support he needed for residency, but if unable to do so he would not even waste his money in completing the application. Instead, Rogelio rationalized, he would have to use his local crossing card to enter the United States, as he had done several times before. Once across, he had plans of working as a "houseman, and B[u]sboy as they are my strongest suits."[69]

Rogelio's expectations were dashed, however, when he reached the consulate in Ciudad Juárez and learned that his application had stalled. "But what can you do there is nothing more than to continue trying and see if it works out." The consulate gave him four months, he told Paco, to provide the letters, and since he knew it was nearly impossible to do so he had lost hope. Rogelio contemplated returning to Calvillo, for he had apparently tired of Ciudad Juárez, but he lacked the means to make the 820-mile journey. "If you only saw how difficult and ugly it is here in Juárez," he wrote in caló, "well the truth is that I want to return to the rancho," that is, home.[70]

Not one to give up easily, six weeks later Rogelio was on his way to California, with hopes of reuniting with his friends. While Rogelio planned to surprise Paco, he did not have enough money to cover the costs of his trip to the city and traveled only as far as Tijuana. He was in Tijuana, he told Paco, "working and saving the little that can be to go for it." Rogelio continued, "Find me a job well I mean if I manage to get there if I don't well in the name of God." Rogelio then asked Paco for his telephone number and "God willing the next week I will land there if God [wills it]."[71]

A month later, Rogelio had made it to northern California but not to San José. Instead, he ended up in Rio Oso, near Sacramento, employed as a farmworker along with some expatriates from Calvillo, working his fingers to the bone picking peaches in the intense summer heat and humidity of the region. "Mr Paco," he wrote, "I hope you find yourself *a.t.m.* (*a toda madre*)," in great condition, "we here well I don't know if we are of meat and bones or of water. Well look yesterday I sweat 1 liter and ¼ of water or rather of sweat."[72] For the strenuous labor of picking one box of fuzzy peaches, which cause severe irritation to the skin when handled for long periods of time, they received $3.75, and on an average day Rogelio managed to fill two and a half boxes and sometimes nearly three, except on slow days when they worked only a few hours. He did well, he implied, but the best picker among his fellow workers, he confessed, was Rafael, the cuate from Calvillo who was popular with the local young women. The peach season would not last long, he informed Paco, for there were a lot of workers and much of the harvest was green and not ready for picking. Given the scarcity of long-term work, he hoped to reach San José, where he believed opportunities were plentiful. "Hopefully . . . when I receive your response you will have work for me for I think that it is much better in San Chepo, than here where we are."[73] He had plans to arrive soon in San José, he told Paco, for he had access to el cacheton, the car he and his coworkers owned and shared. Rest assured, he told Paco confidently, that as soon as he and his compatriots received word from him about the possibility for employment, they would be in the city. In the meantime, they would continue to pick peaches, which he described as *jodidón* (tough), "el 'dura'-sno" (literally, "tough"-one, peach).[74]

Besides dealing with brutal working conditions, Rogelio had to protect himself from the immigration authorities, which he knew frequented the rancho. To do so, he changed his full name from Rogelio Martínez Serna to "Rogelio Martínez V., my new surname you know," he explained to Paco.[75] Avoiding detection was not an easy prospect, as he soon learned. A few weeks later, the migra caught up with him and some of his coworkers. However, they were not detained or deported, even though he lacked his papers. It was a frightening experience, he said. "Look the other day they scared the living daylights out of me, the border patrol for they caught us in the bathroom and that is what saved me (*balentío*)." Rogelio wanted nothing more than to leave that work behind for better opportunities and companionship in San José. "You already know Paco as soon as there is work

Rogelio Martínez Serna, sometime in 1964, at Alum Rock Park in San José, California. After numerous failed attempts to migrate and reunite with his pal Paco Chávez in *el norte*, Rogelio finally made it. Photograph by Paco Chávez.
Permission to reprint photograph provided by Rogelio Martínez Serna.

we will peel out of here at the first chance hopefully it would be soon for I am here scared out of my wits (*con el 'chico' en la mano*)."[76] Nine days later Rogelio remained in Rio Oso, though he had hoped to be in San José. Work had slowed, he explained to Paco. For three days, they picked no peaches and on the fourth day one box the entire day. "This is not working anymore."[77] Dejected, he made plans to leave for San José as soon as possible.

After months of wanting to land in San José with his cuates from Calvillo, Rogelio finally made it by September 1964 and remained there until December. Though no correspondence exists detailing those experiences, Paco recalled years later in an interview that Rogelio lived with him and some buddies from Calvillo in a two-bedroom apartment near the home of Paco's aunt in San José. There, the guys made a home life while they worked in various service industries. Rogelio managed to obtain a job working in a restaurant for a boss named "Mr. Rocky." Within walking distance of his new home, he set out for work washing dishes and preparing basic meals. But for reasons that remain unclear, Rogelio left the job somewhat abruptly.[78]

Leaving the Promised Land

After a few months working and living in San José, Rogelio was back in Ciudad Juárez by January 1965. There, he was ready to marry a new sweetheart but knew he needed to earn money to maintain the household and his role in the family. To do so, he and his new wife planned to take their honeymoon in San José, where he could take advantage of employment possibilities at the same time. "I see it is the only way to be able to save in order to later return to establish ourselves in Chihuahua," he explained.[79] Rogelio then called on his social network, in this case, Paco, to inquire with his former boss, Mr. Rocky, about the possibility of working for him again, as he had already contacted him and had received no response. Apparently, however, Rogelio had left his work with Mr. Rocky under strained conditions, as he later hinted to Paco.[80] Rogelio implored Paco again to help him with employment in the United States: "Hopefully Paco you are the only one that can help in this matter if you would be able to find in one place or another work please, tell me if you are still with Don Nazario in the restaurant."[81]

Undaunted by the uncertainty of his economic situation, a few weeks later Rogelio wrote to Paco informing him of his upcoming wedding. By then Paco too was out of a job. "You tell me you are not working," Rogelio commented, "well too bad (*caray*) this is precisely what I was telling you about in my previous [letter] about Mr Rocky . . . for work for me." Regardless of the scarce work opportunities, Rogelio still planned to return to the United States to earn and save money, and then eventually go back to Mexico. But in the short term, Rogelio was flat broke. As he explained to Paco, he had almost obtained his green card on the black market, as he had given a down payment, but lacked the forty dollars to finish paying it off. Rogelio confessed that he also needed funds to pay for his wedding. "Well you cannot even imagine I don't even have enough for my ceremony well nevertheless in the name of God let's see how this turns out."[82] Rogelio's decision to marry without economic security troubled him, but apparently he was confident in his ability to provide for his family in the future, enabling him to continue with his marital plans.

Two months later, in March 1965, Rogelio's wedding went off without a hitch in Ciudad Juárez, but he was still in need of a job. Rogelio worked in the border city, but he longed for opportunities in San José, as work was "hard and you don't earn much."[83] Two weeks later, he wrote, "I was [working] in pecans but they finished and now I am at the barbershop but the work is a bit difficult but we are managing little by little." Rogelio never lost hope, however, of migrating to the United States and making a life for himself and his new wife. "I on the first opportunity will go with all my will to work for a while."[84] Sending greetings to his friends in San José, Rogelio signed off his final letter to Paco.

Fortunately for Rogelio, as he indicated years later in an oral interview, his new wife had permanent U.S. residency, allowing him to adjust his migratory status within the year. That process brought much relief and satisfaction, as it allowed him and his wife to travel to the United States for much-needed employment and opportunity. To this day, Rogelio counts his blessings and the fifty-one years since he acquired his lawful status, marking the day he fulfilled one of his greatest hopes and dreams. Today, Rogelio continues to move with ease north and south across the border, crossing several times a year, reuniting with friends and family aqui y allá, demonstrating his fluid identity as an emigrant of and migrant in the U.S.-Mexican borderlands.[85]

ROGELIO'S REPEATED EFFORTS to migrate lawfully and successfully across the U.S.-Mexico border and to find a source of stability for himself and his family in order to fulfill his gendered obligations as a Mexican man demonstrate his tenacity in achieving his hopes and dreams for personal, emotional, and economic fulfillment. Inspired by Paco's migratory success, whether real or imagined, Rogelio, like thousands of migrants before and after him, was willing to risk his personal safety and security to make it across to what he saw as the promised land. And though he met setbacks throughout his journeys across la frontera, his determination to carve a better life for himself and his new family motivated him to continue taking those chances.

Ultimately, as he saw it, he had no other choice at his disposal, as economic opportunities in Ciudad Juárez as well as in Calvillo were scarce. Not until the development of the Border Industrialization Program and the launching of the maquiladora industry in 1965 would a semblance of relief—in the form of poorly paid industrial and assembly line work—come to the inhabitants of the border region. Until then many border dwellers relied on tourist dollars and tourism as well as the business of contraband, or falluqear, to cover their basic necessities. Calvillo, in contrast, had even fewer opportunities, as Rogelio likely knew. Men could engage in poorly paid agricultural and livestock pursuits, while women could pursue equally low-paying needlework or embroidery or sell prepared meals—dinner (*cena*) primarily—from their homes, as many did to make ends meet.

Despite the odds against Rogelio and many migrants like him, he never relented in his efforts to take on new opportunities, always believing he would have the chanza, as he and his fellow migrants often repeated in their personal letters, to cross the border lawfully, gain steady employment, and establish a stable household, allowing them to claim a masculine identity. When in flux, he struggled mightily to find any form of employment available to him, relying on friends and family networks and leaving it up to fate or a higher being, namely, God, to provide him with the opportunities to forge ahead. Rogelio and his male buddies were, however, neither victims nor passive agents in the process. They were, too, oppressive in their views of women, gender, and female sexuality. When needed, the men used women's bodies to assert their masculinity and manhood as well as their heterosexuality.

As Rogelio's correspondence attests, he confronted many challenges and did so with hope and humor as well as creativity and resiliency even while he faced some of his darkest moments. To pass the time, he learned caló, signaling his adaptation to the local border culture and the remaking of his self-identity from that of a Calvillense to a pachuco-inspired *norteño* (northerner). Never one to miss an opportunity or succumb to defeat, Rogelio searched for opportunities to establish roots and a build a home in the new environment. All these complex layers of his identity and that of other migrants must be weighed in evaluating their struggles and accomplishments in and across the U.S.-Mexico borderlands.

Conclusion
On the Significance of Letter Writing and Letters

In today's culture of communication, handwritten or typed letters are largely irrelevant forms of producing, sending, and receiving information. The Internet, social media, e-mail, and cell phones and the ability to transmit and receive messages instantaneously have replaced correspondence and corresponding and made them nearly obsolete. Yet, as I have found in my attempt to recover a slice in the life of my family's history and link it to broader patterns of migration, gender, intimacy, identity, and courtship across the U.S.-Mexico borderlands, the creative art of letter writing and 300 plus letters written in the 1960s and 1970s at the heart of this study have proved an invaluable source of insight on the past and present world around us. Indeed, the intricate and detail-laden missives provide a window onto the ways in which immigration policies and practices impacted the everyday lives of migrants and those left behind. They demonstrate, too, how migrants and nonmigrants alike built, nurtured, and sustained intimate, emotional, and social relationships across vast distances, including nation-state divides. Despite the ability of distance and time to weaken, at best, and destroy, at worst, personal, family, and community relations, the notes indicate that migrants pursued their hopes and dreams and sometimes nearly lost and shattered them altogether. Embedded in a richly textured social, political, economic, cultural, and historical context, the notes provide a unique lens onto the lives of ordinary people negotiating extraordinary circumstances in their attempts to establish transnational lives that could sustain them and the loved ones who stayed at home.

As snapshots of a moment in time, the letters reveal the thought processes and actions of individuals as a particular idea or event unfolded in a moment of time. Unlike oral histories, which Lynn Abrams reminds us are living memories and changing interpretations of those memories years after the episodes transpired, correspondence focuses primarily on the here and now.[1] Admittedly, the frozen or static nature of notes may distort how we understand or interpret a letter writer's personal, emotional, and intellectual frame of mind, as they do not provide insight on the evolution of the author's understanding or perceptions on life. However, if we pay attention to letter writers' changing representation of the self as well as their interactions with the world around them, we can see their maturing outlook on their lives and the larger society. Personal letters, complemented with oral histories, music, films, newspapers, material culture, and government records, as I have attempted to show, have the power to bring into clearer focus the people, ideas, events, and structures shaping their relationships.

A close reading of the hundreds of personal letters at the core of this study demonstrates, as well, that migrant longing was an emotional, mental, and physical response to living in the borderlands. For migrants such as José, Conchita, Paco, Chonita, José the elder, and Rogelio, among others, the desire to bridge here and there (*aqui y allá*) and, effectively, to weave a seamless border, though a contradictory concept, made perfect sense, for it entailed integrating the familiar with the foreign. For them, living in a space with the cultural relevance of home was essential to maintaining their identity and sense of who they were as Mexican men and women, mothers and fathers, sisters and brothers, and well-known members of the community. For José, a former bracero and recent U.S. permanent resident featured in chapter 1, it also meant having a wife with whom to carry out intimate relations, establish a household and a family, and save enough money to build a second home in the *terre* (homeland) where he could visit his extended family and friends and revisit the memories of his childhood. As José and many Mexicans of his generation understood, despite claims of the "Mexican Miracle" of the 1940s, 1950s, and 1960s, Mexico offered few opportunities for economic prosperity, particularly in rural areas like Calvillo, Aguascalientes. While most farmers and farmworkers who migrated from the countryside took their chances in Mexico City, with its burgeoning industries, many others, like José and his brothers and their father before them, opted to try their luck at migratory labor in *el norte*. When that failed to provide the stability José desired, he established roots in the United States yet continued to long for companionship and romantic love to round out his life.

For Conchita, whose story is related in chapter 2, her longing signified more than bridging here and there. Rather, it involved helping to provide her increasingly impoverished family with the basic necessities as well as relieving her mother's personal and financial burden of caring for the family with little help from a spouse who treated her poorly. While Conchita was most interested in pursuing an education, visiting with her friends, and viewing the latest popular American and Mexican films, her family's shrinking opportunities obliged her to pursue various avenues of support. In her young life, Conchita worked in the household, accepted positions in sales, took on poorly paid needlework, and, finally married José and migrated to the borderlands, hoping she could provide her family with some relief.

For Chonita, Conchita's older sister, the subject of chapter 3, her emotional longing to bridge here and there included, as well, maintaining the passion and romantic love she felt for Paco, especially after he left for el norte. What she wanted most was to reconcile their physical separation and be included in the migrant experience. When Paco neglected to return home or correspond, even after she did so consistently and passionately and pleaded with him to do the same, she felt a deep void as well as emotional pain that left her vulnerable to the instability of the long-distance, cross-border relationship. Given her conflicted state of mind, her sisters, her closest confidantes, convinced her easily to question his interest in sustaining the relationship and his motivation in leaving her behind. Within weeks or months, the courtship began to crumble. Contrary to Chonita's beliefs, Paco had not forgotten his "better than nothing" (*peor es nada*). Rather, he had to fight his own demons in *el otro lado*. That included finding employment and economic stability for himself and his family, which counted on his remittances for some of the most basic household necessities, as well as maintaining his honor and masculinity, which focused on providing for himself and his family and ensuring his girlfriend's fidelity while he was away.

The longing of José the elder, as revealed in chapter 4, was perhaps the most conflicted among the family members and friends situated across the political divide. While he lamented his four sons' absence in the household and their failure to return regularly or at least annually, he blasted their failure to provide remittances and to heed his paternal admonitions. In other words, José wanted them not only at home but also abroad earning enough to provide for the costs of repairing the family home and feeding the family as well as his gambling pursuits. The tension, while difficult, if not impossible, to reconcile, consumed most of his time and energy, leaving him at an emotional, physical, and psychological loss about what to do or say to get them to obey what little was left of his patriarchal authority.

Rogelio, like José the elder, at the center of chapter 5, was relentless in his attempt to bridge here and there, despite the numerous emotional, physical, and economic barriers he encountered in his migratory journey. His goal was the most iconic of all among Mexican migrants: make it across the

U.S.-Mexico border, find employment, and save enough to build economic stability in the homeland to live a life of comfort, not unlike one in the United States. Rogelio's migrant dream, however, as personified by Paco's apparent success with his green card or residency, pockets full of dollars, convertible car, and access to women, quickly turned into a nightmare when he suffered setback after setback. Not one to relent, Rogelio pressed ahead, confident that the few resources and networks at his disposable would be sufficient to achieve his transnational dream of living comfortably in both worlds.

The correspondence shows, too, that migrants not only sought to bridge the physical, emotional, and psychological divide of the borderlands but also employed a variety of ingenious strategies to end their longing. For José, the ability to draw upon a repertoire of cultural tools, such as penning perfect handwritten letters, employing the English language, and highlighting his interests in the latest popular music and films, among other creative approaches, proved successful. He not only managed to present himself in his correspondence as a sophisticated, experienced, and cosmopolitan man but also to win Conchita's hand in marriage. For Conchita, alleviating her longing was tied to giving up her hopes and dreams for a career and agreeing to marry and migrate to find ways to provide for her mother and siblings. Though she never said yes to José's marriage proposal, she eventually went through with the hastily planned and humble ceremony. In time, however, as her correspondence reveals, she developed romantic feelings of love and companionship for José.

In contrast to Conchita and José, the elder José was the least successful in alleviating his patriarchal longing. As the correspondence indicates, José attempted to do so by using the force of paternal authority, as constituted through the letter, to get his sons to return home for a visit or at least send remittances. When that approach failed to elicit a response, he turned to guilt, admonishing his sons for neglecting their filial obligations to him as well as their mother's basic needs and those of the household generally.

Equally distraught over the absence of a loved one, Chonita wasted little time in seeking to end her longing and heartbreak after her boyfriend Paco migrated to el norte and, seemingly, cast her aside or simply forgot about her. To get him to return or at least correspond with frequency, she threatened to cut off their relationship on more than one occasion, hoping to elicit a response and renew the intimacy they once shared. When that failed to work, she turned to her sister Conchita, recently married and residing in the borderlands, to provide clandestine reports about his whereabouts, giving her the smallest of hopes that he might still have feelings for her. That approach, however, proved ineffective.

Unknown to Chonita, Paco still cared for her, but his longing to establish a semblance of economic security was paramount, leading him to focus his energies on finding stable employment, adopting a trade, and learning the English language. Equally important was maintaining his masculinity, which was linked to her sexuality. To ensure her fidelity and his honor, Paco turned to his friends—a social network of surveillance—in Calvillo to watch her every move and report any sign of betrayal. The regulation of Chonita's sexuality, however, did little to reconcile the trust and honesty that had been unable to withstand the emotional, physical, and geographic scale of the cross-border separation.

Rogelio, like Paco and countless other migrants, also turned to social networks to achieve his dreams and desires for migration, economic security, and companionship when his attempts to do so on his own failed repeatedly. As Rogelio's letters to Paco indicate, his business pursuits in a barbershop and, later, selling contraband produce in the Mexican border town of Ciudad Juárez, Chihuahua, where he was based, went south quickly after the local economy slumped and his automobile died, preventing him from earning enough to pay the costs of U.S. residency and lawful entry. Despite those setbacks, Rogelio remained undeterred. With no other option, he crossed the border without inspection. His repeated brushes with *la migra* (border patrol), harsh working conditions, and little pay, however, proved too hard to bear, prompting him to return to Ciudad Juárez. Rogelio, nevertheless, remained resilient and optimistic. Soon after arriving in the border town, he redoubled his efforts to access what seemed to him limitless opportunities in the United States.

These narratives of migrant longing and making and remaking of self-identity, as revealed in the art and practice of personal letter writing, provide a unique opportunity to delve deeply, richly, and widely into the range of emotional and intimate thoughts and feelings driving and guiding migrants across the U.S.-Mexico borderlands. As the correspondence attests, economic insecurity, household instability, negligible opportunities at home, and the need for personal and emotional fulfillment often drove Mexican men and women to migrate to try their luck in el norte. Unfulfilled personal relationships, unfinished business, and household and familial responsibilities, as well as longtime friendships and intimate relations, often called—and sometimes pulled—these same migrants home. Life was not easy for these migrants, who sought, at once, to be here and there, enjoying the best of both worlds. They did what they could, however, in splitting the self by maintaining multiple identities, social networks, residences, and lives across the border. In doing so, they proved creative, resourceful, and resilient in navigating an inhospitable world for the future of their families and communities.

Acknowledgments

Many generous people shared their most intimate and personal archives to help bring together what I call an attempt to map a slice in the life of my family's history across the U.S.-Mexico borderlands. First and foremost are my *tío* Paco Chávez and his late wife, Beatríz Chávez, the keepers of the letters. Without them, this history would not have been preserved, and it would not have been possible for me to tell the story. As I recount in the narrative, when all seemed lost in 1981, after my parents died in a car accident, they took my brother, Juan G. Chávez, and me into their home and, along with their two younger daughters, Alicia and Gloria, raised us as best as they could with the resources at their disposal. I am forever grateful for their sacrifices. Second, I want to thank all the family and community members as well as intimate friends, *comadres*, and *compadres* who shared their memories. They include Asunción Alvarado, Juan Alvarado, Maura Chávez Esparza, Juan Chávez Esparza, Baudelio Chávez Torres, Guillermina Gallegos Díaz, Alicia González Torres, Eligio Hernández, Raúl Jaramillo, Rogelio Martínez Serna, Steve Reeves, Dolores "Lola" Salazar Rodríguez, Pedro "Perico" Sánchez Martínez, and Rebeca Serna Macías. My cousin, María Magdalena Gallegos Alvarado, as well as my brother, Juan, my parents' numerous siblings, extended family members, and friends in Calvillo, Aguascalientes, Brawley, California, and San José, California, among other places, also helped fill in many gaps and shared many memories. *Mil gracias a todos.*

Colleagues at UC Davis and UC Santa Barbara who heard early ideas for this history and encouraged me when I encountered rough patches along the way include Sasha Abramsky, Inés Hernández-Avila, D. Inés Casillas, Karen Lunsford, Emiko Saldívar, Julie Sze, and Barbara Walker. I thank, too, my invaluable undergraduate research assistants, who helped scan and preserve the letters, retrieve books and articles, and move the project along in the early stages. They include Adela Contreras, Zuleima Flores-Abid, and Cristina Prado. As I delved into the personal family letters and tried to make sense of the material and situate it in a broader context of migration, gender, and identity, I had the invaluable assistance of experts in the field, including José Alamillo, Deborah Boehm, Deborah Cohen, Sergio de la

Mora, Katharine M. Donato, Alice Echols, Laura E. Enríquez, Lori Flores, Donna R. Gabaccia, David A. Gerber, Lisbeth Haas, Kevin R. Johnson, Alan Kraut, Natalia Molina, Judy Tzu-Chun Wu, and all the junior scholars who participated in the Developing the Field of Gender and Migration conference at UC Irvine in 2016. They advanced my thinking in so many ways, especially about the methodology, subjectivity, and significance of the study. I also thank the *Western Historical Quarterly* and former Senior Editor David Rich Lewis and the anonymous reviewers for their rigorous feedback for an essay that forms parts of chapters one and two. As a result of that feedback, that article, originally published as "Migrant Longing, Courtship, and Gendered Identity in the U.S.-Mexico Borderlands" in the *Western History Quarterly* in Summer 2016, was awarded the 2017 Judith Lee Ridge Prize for the best article by any member of the organization from the Western Association of Women's Historians and the 2017 Bolton-Cutter Award for the best article in Spanish Borderlands history from the Western History Association. I thank, too, the *Women's Review of Books* and Editor-in-Chief Amy Hoffman for the opportunity to explore the "intimacy of the archive"; the UCLA Center for the Study of International Migration and Director Roger Waldinger for giving me the opportunity to share my findings with peers; and my colleagues in the UCSB Department of History who provided valuable insights on early drafts of this study.

I am especially grateful to the many individuals who provided support as well as criticism at all stages of the project. Without them pushing me to rethink the analysis and framing of the narrative, this work would be less developed than it is now. I especially want to acknowledge my personal and intellectual confidantes, Catherine Ceniza Choy, Natalia Molina, Lorena Oropeza, and Alexandra Minna Stern, for their unflagging support throughout the years. I would be remiss, too, in not acknowledging the selfless mentors who have taught me so many invaluable lessons throughout my career: Ernesto Chávez, Norris Hundley, Kevin R. Johnson, Vicki L. Ruiz, and Denise Segura.

I also want to thank the former UCSB Dean of Social Sciences, Melvin Oliver, and the current UCSB Dean of Humanities and Fine Arts, John Majewski, for their financial support of the research and the book's publication. The UCSB Chicano Studies Institute also provided funding for a workshop on "Gender and Intimacy Across the U.S.-Mexico Borderlands" that allowed me to develop my ideas in a broader conversation with colleagues from across the country. I thank the CSI and my cofacilitator and colleague, Verónica Castillo-Muñoz, for helping me work through my analysis.

A special thanks as well to Clay Stalls, Curator of California and Hispanic Collections, Huntington Library, San Marino, California, who has made the preservation of these family letters possible. Fortunately for my family and future generations, the correspondence now makes up the Chávez Family Papers and is accessible to anyone who visits the archive.

Last but not least, I want to acknowledge my biggest fans: my spouse, Ebers García, whose artistic talents continue to enhance my scholarship; my daughter, Eliana Aliyah, who keeps me grounded; and my son, Evan Abraham, for challenging me to be a better person. I thank them for putting up with the long days, evenings, and weekends at work on this project and the many missed events and days spent traveling to share this history. I am forever grateful that they have supported the project and joined me along this journey in recovering our history.

Notes

Abbreviations Used in Notes

AA	Asunción Alvarado
AGT	Alicia González Torres
ALE	Alfonso "el Pinole" Lozano Esparza
AST	Andrea S. Torres
BCT	Baudelio Chávez Torres
CFP	Chávez Family Papers (Correspondence), 1962–1971
DSR	Dolores "Lola" Salazar Rodríguez
EH	Eligio Hernández
GGD	Guillermina Gallegos Díaz
IH	Ildefonso "Alfonso" Hernández
JA	Juan Alvarado
JC	Juan Chávez Esparza
JCE	José Chávez Esparza
JCT	José Chávez Torres
JGD	Juan Gallegos Díaz
JLE	Jesús Lozano Esparza
JLV	José Luis López Velasco
JS	José Soto
LE	Leovigilda Esparza
MCA	María Concepción Alvarado
MCE	Maura Chávez Esparza
MLL	María López L.
MSS	María del Socorro Salazar
PCE	José Guadalupe "Paco" Francisco Chávez Esparza
PS	Pedro "Perico" Sánchez
RM	Rafael Martínez
RMS	Rogelio Martínez Serna
RSM	Rebeca Serna Macías

Introduction

1. Not all the correspondence has survived. A close examination indicates that some letters are missing. The entire collection now resides at the Huntington Library, San Marino, California.

2. D. Cohen, *Braceros*, 181. For more on remittances, see Zong and Batalova, "Mexican Immigrants in the United States." In 2016, for the first time, remittances formed the top source of foreign income, reaching $26 billion.

3. Braceros found many creative ways to pass the time. D. Cohen, *Braceros*, 118–39.

4. Echols, "Orphans in the Storm."

5. My analysis has been shaped by Gerber, *Authors of Their Lives*; Gerber, "Acts of Deceiving"; Elliott, Gerber, and Sinke, *Letters across Borders*; Cancian, *Families, Lovers, and Their Letters*; Earle, "Letters and Love"; Doss, "Affect"; and Breckenridge, "Love Letters."

6. The discussion of the "Mexican Miracle" comes from Niblo, *Mexico in the 1940s*; Joseph, Rubenstein, and Zolov, *Fragments of a Golden Age*; Joseph and Henderson, *The Mexico Reader*; Cross and Sandos, *Across the Border*; Navarro, *Los extranjeros*; Sanders, *Gender and Welfare*; and Raat and Brescia, *Mexico and the United States*. On the uses of culture to promote revolutionary nationalism, see Rubenstein, *Bad Language*.

7. Niblo, *Mexico in the 1940s*, 2.

8. Ibid., 1–4, 16; quote from 3. On Alemán's proposed changes to Article 27, see ibid., 183–86. On ejidos, see Joseph and Henderson, *The Mexican Reader*, 461–62; and Cross and Sandos, *Across the Border*.

9. Joseph and Henderson, *The Mexican Reader*, 461.

10. Niblo, *Mexico in the 1940s*, 21, 89, 91, 115.

11. For more on the commodification of Mexico through tourism and entertainment, see Fein, "Myths of Cultural Imperialism."

12. Niblo, *Mexico in the 1940s*, 223–25, 255–303.

13. Quoted in ibid., 224. See also ibid., 170–73, 189–90, 198, 222–25.

14. On films that discouraged emigration, see Maciel, *El Bandolero*; and Claire Fox, *The Fence and the River*, 106–18.

15. Niblo, *Mexico in the 1940s*, 42, 51–52. For the role of Alemán in promoting nationalism through film, see Fein, "Myths of Cultural Imperialism," 161–66; and Fein, "From Collaboration to Containment." For more on Mexico's golden age of cinema, see Berg, *The Classical Mexican Cinema*; and Irwin and Ricalde, *Global Mexican Cinema*.

16. Niblo, *Mexico in the 1940s*, 45.

17. Monsiváis, "Cantinflas and Tin Tan," 51.

18. For more on Cantinflas's influence, see Pilcher, *Cantinflas*.

19. For more on "Los olvidados," see Acevedo-Muñoz, *Buñuel and Mexico*, 57–79.

20. Literacy rates in Mexico in the 1940s and 1950s are unclear. See Niblo, *Mexico in the 1940s*, 37, 57–58. For the prohibition of dubbing Mexican films, see ibid., 353; and De Usabel, *The High Noon of American Films*, 182–90.

21. Schmidt, "Making It Real," 45. For the role of illustrated magazines in forging a national identity, see Mraz, "Today, Tomorrow and Always." Many scholars, including Monsiváis, have argued that cinema served in the project of modernizing Mexicans. See Schmidt, "Making It Real," 45–46, and Green, "Cablevision(nation)," 420.

22. Niblo, *Mexico in the 1940s*, 363.

23. Ibid., 4.

24. Zolov, "Discovering a Land," 234–35.

25. PCE Interview, San José, California, 20 April 2008.

26. Pilcher, "Mexico's Pepsi Challenge," 78–79.

27. Niblo, *Mexico in the 1940s*, 15.

28. Ibid., 32; PCE Interview, San José, California, 20 April 2008.

29. Niblo, *Mexico in the 1940s*, 15–20, 361–63.

30. Statistics on migratory trends in Mexico come from Unikel, as cited in Bachelor, "Toiling for the 'New Invaders,'" 315–16, fn2. See also Cross and Sandos, *Across the Border*, 32–33.

31. On population growth, see Niblo, *Mexico in the 1940s*, 1.

32. Quoted in Bachelor, "Toiling for the 'New Invaders,'" 309.

33. For more on industrialization and urbanization in Mexico City, see Joseph and Henderson, *The Mexico Reader*, 461; and Bachelor, "Toiling for the 'New Invaders.'"

34. Niblo, *Mexico in the 1940s*, 30. For more on braceros' personal experiences, see the hundreds of oral histories archived at the Bracero History Archive, http://braceroarchive.org.

35. Durand, Massey, and Parrado, "The New Era of Mexican Migration," 519; Cross and Sandos, *Across the Border*, 36–46; and, García y Griego, "The Importation of Mexican Contract Laborers to the United States, 1942–1964," 49. The exact number of braceros is difficult to know given that many signed multiple contracts while in the program.

36. Niblo, *Mexico in the 1940s*, 28–31; and D. Cohen, *Braceros*, 10, 35–38.

37. Lytle Hernández, "Crimes and Consequences," 425.

38. The 4 percent statistic comes from Brown, "The Impact of U.S. Work Experience," 1, cited in D. Cohen, *Braceros*, 232, n4. For more on the bracero program, see, for instance, ibid.; Loza, *Defiant Braceros*; Flores, *Grounds for Dreaming*; Sifuentez, *Of Forests and Fields*; and Weise, *Corazón de Dixie*; Calavita, *Inside the State*; Mitchell, *They Saved the Crops*; Waldinger, *The Cross-Border Connection*; and Cross and Sandos, *Across the Border*, 36, 43, 45.

39. Cross and Sandos, *Across the Border*, 33.

40. For more on the history of maquilas and gender, see Salzinger, *Genders in Production*; Davidson, *Lives on the Line*; and Fernández-Kelly, *For We Are Sold*. For excellent documentaries, see "Not a Drop to Drink" in Mathew Snedden and Paul Espinosa's *The Border*; and Vicki Funari and Sergio De la Torre's *Maquilapolis*. For more on the history of vice and tourism, see, for instance, Bender, *Run for the Border*; Schantz, "From the Mexicali Rose to the Tijuana Brass"; Arreola and Curtis, *The Mexican Border Cities*; and Martínez, *Border Boom Town*.

41. My use of "common people" refers to Light's conception of family history. Light, *A Common People*.

42. References to wetbacks and wire crossers appear in the newspapers of the day. See, for instance, *La Opinión*, 3 May 1950. The paper also refers to them as "*braceros ilegales.*"

43. Schmidt, "Making It Real," 37, n69.

44. Waldinger, *The Cross-Border Connection*, 6–37, 41–45; Hoffnung-Garskof, *A Tale of Two Cities*; and R. Smith, *Mexican New York*. For more on migration globally, see, for instance, Cabana and Clark, "Introduction"; and Sassen, *Expulsions*. As Sassen observes, the increase in "human mobility and expulsion is now recognized as a

defining feature of the twenty-first century." Quoted in Nail, *The Figure of the Migrant*, 2.

45. A. Rosas, *Abrazando el Espíritu*. While studies on courtship in mid-twentieth-century Mexico are scarce, such studies within a U.S. context are available. See Bailey, *From Front Porch to Back Seat*; Lystra, *Searching the Heart*; and Matsumoto, "Courtship in American History."

46. Pérez, "Crossing the Border"; C. Rosas, "El desafío de ser hombre y no migrar"; and Castellanos, "Building Communities of Sentiment." Also see D. Cohen, "From Peasant to Worker"; and A. Rosas, *Abrazando el Espíritu*, 276–80. For calls for more studies on gender and migration, see, for instance, Castellanos and Boehm, "Introduction"; and Donato et al., "A Glass Half Full?"; Hondagneu-Sotelo, *Gender and U.S. Immigration*; and Segura and Zavella, *Women and Migration*.

47. For more on the policing of women's roles and relations, see Abrego, *Sacrificing Families*; Dreby, "Gender and Transnational Gossip"; Sorensen, "Narratives of Longing"; Hondagneu-Sotelo, *Gendered Transitions*; and Hondagneu-Sotelo and Avila, "'I'm Here but I'm There.'"

48. Boehm, "'Now I Am a Man and a Woman!'" For more on masculinity, migration, and emotions in Latin American contexts, see Gutmann, *The Meanings of Macho*; Broughton, "Migration as Engendered Practice"; and Montes, "The Role of Emotions in the Construction of Masculinity."

49. Berlant, "Intimacy"; Berlant, *Intimacy*; and Zelizer, *The Purchase of Intimacy*, 14–15.

50. Parrenas, "Long-Distance Intimacy"; and Parrenas, *Children of Global Migration*.

51. McKay, "Sending Dollars Shows Feeling."

52. Ibid., 179.

53. Stoler, *Haunted by Empire*, 16.

54. Studies that do make extended use of letters include Orozco, *Receive Our Memories*; and Guzmán, "The Transnational Life and Letters." For the most recent literature, see Borges and Cancian, "Reconsidering the Migrant Letter."

55. Gerber, *Authors of Their Lives*, 67–68.

56. Ibid., 32, 51–52.

57. Ibid., 91, 158.

58. Cancian, *Families, Lovers, and Their Letters*, 8.

59. Gerber, *Authors of Their Lives*, 27–28.

60. Ibid., 108.

61. Insights on oral history come from Blackwell, *!Chicana!*; Abrams, *Oral History Theory*; and Gerber, *Authors of Their Lives*, 325.

62. Gerber, *Authors of Their Lives*, 57; and Cancian, *Families, Lovers, and Their Letters*, 115–16.

63. Gerber, *Authors of Their Lives*, 67–68.

64. Gamio, *El inmigrante mexicano*, 98, 101.

65. D. Cohen, *Braceros*, 81–82.

66. Gerber, *Authors of Their Lives*, 2.

67. PCE Interview, Calvillo, Aguascalientes, 8 September 2014. For more on the postal service in Mexico, see, for instance, Martínez Rodríguez, *El correo en México*; Gojman de Backal and Bonilla, *Historia del correo*; and chapter 4 in this work.

68. On the censorship of braceros' correspondence, see A. Rosas, *Abrazando el Espíritu*.

69. Gerber, *Authors of Their Lives*, 317, 321.

70. Gerber, "Acts of Deceiving," 315–30; and Gerber, *Authors of Their Lives*, 99–101.

Chapter One

1. JCE to MCA, 27 December 1963, CFP. "[M]e vine muy encantado con su modo de ser y todo como es usted[.]"

2. Ibid. "Yo no le encuentro ningún sentido a un noviasgo como dijo Ud. 'De lejos' sin el principal objetivo . . . matrimonio[.]" "[N]o le pido me corresponda inmediatamente sino que cuando Ud crea poder sentir cariño por mi[.]" "[P]uedo asegurarle que la llegaré a querer como nadie la haya querido." The Spanish-language terms "corresponda" and "correspondo," while conjugations of the verb "corresponder," to correspond, have multiple meanings depending upon context. In the letters, José used the words primarily to talk about requited love, that is, to describe the kind of reciprocal love, affection, and intimacy he sought. He also used them to describe what or who he believed belonged to him and would, in turn, reciprocate. "Corresponder" also means to correspond, to write to each other, which is not how he is using it here, but it is fitting for the way in which he employed letters work to cultivate the relationship.

3. Ibid. "[L]a vida me parece distinta todo me parece mejor que antes[.]" "De una manera especial quisiera pedirle me diga si puedo seguir escribiendole aunque no me corresponda luego quizá mas delante cuando le platique como soy y lo que me gusta o sea como soy en la realidad, me llegue a corresponder." "Mil perdones por la letra pues hay veces que ni yo le entiendo lo que escribo." On educational gains in Mexico, see *Necesidades esenciales en México*, 25, 46.

4. Gerber finds that letter writers he studies are careful not to violate the sequence of one-for-one correspondence, which was crucial for organizing and maintaining relationships. Gerber, *Authors of Their Lives*, 102–5.

5. JCE to MCA, 20 January 1964, CFP. "Conchita perdone que la enfade o moleste pero hace 3 semanas le escribí una carta y no se si la resivió o nó pues no he resivido contestación alguna tampoco se devolvio la carta[.]" "Yo le suplico . . . que por favor me conteste aunque me diga lo que sea. Mire Conchita no tengo palabras como explicarle mis sentimientos, si es que realmente no quiere tener aunque sea amistad con migo[.]"

6. Ibid. "Si por algún motive le regañaron en su casa por haberle escrito a su domicilio puede indicarme otro . . . U otra cosa Conchita si es que la haigan dicho algo de mi puede decirme con confiansa que le diré no tengo nada que me avergüense[.]"

7. MCA to JCE, 28 January 1964, CFP. "Boy hacerle sincera como creo que Ud lo fue conmigo, mire yo no siento quererlo de una manera que nos llevara hacer algo

mas que amigos[.]" "[S]erá por el poco tiempo que tenemos de tratarnos que casi se puede decir que apenas nos conocimos[.]"

8. Ibid. "[S]in embargo si siento un afecto muy grande y un profundo agradecimiento ... Mire sígame escribiendo me gusta para que sea un buen amigo y como dice Ud despues Dios dirá."

9. Gerber, *Authors of Their Lives*, 116–17.

10. JCE to MCA, 4 February 1964, CFP. "Conchita quisiera encontrar las palabras mas bonitas para expresarte mi alegria que siento pues me imaginé que no me contestarias[.]" "[C]ierto es que apenas nos conocimos fisicamente pero podremos conocernos mas intimamente escribiendonos y hablando con la verdad entonces puedes decir lo que tu corazón te dicte."

11. For more on farmworkers consorting with prostitutes, see D. Cohen, *Braceros*; Loza, *Defiant Braceros*; and Alamillo, *Making Lemonade out of Lemons*.

12. Quilodrán, "México: Diferencias de nupcialidad por regiones"; and Parrado and Zenteno, "Gender Differences."

13. In early to mid-twentieth-century Mexico, children began and ended their schooling at an older age than in the United States. See *Necesidades esenciales en México*, 18.

14. José's employment history comes from PCE Interview, San José, California, 20 April 2008; and AGT Interview, Aguascalientes, Aguascalientes, 10 February 2009.

15. Mitchell, *They Saved the Crops*. For more on the early history of the valley, see Andrés, *Power and Control*; Collins, "The Imperial Valley and Mexicali"; Volman, *Imperial*; and Round, *The Impossible Land*.

16. The literature on the bracero program is vast. The sources used for this study include Alarcón, "U.S. Immigration Policy"; Calavita, *Inside the State*; Mitchell, *They Saved the Crops*; D. Cohen, *Braceros*; Lytle Hernández, *Migra!*; Loza, *Defiant Braceros*; Flores, *Grounds for Dreaming*; Weise, *Corazón de Dixie*; and Sifuentez, *Of Forests and Fields*.

17. For more on the use of terms such as "illegal" and "wetback," see Abrego, *Sacrificing Families*.

18. PCE Interview, San José, California, 20 April 2008.

19. Women, however, did provide invaluable support to the program's stability and success. See A. Rosas, *Abrazando el Espíritu*; and Arredondo, *Mexican Chicago*.

20. For details of the recruiting station at Empalme, Sonora, see the documentary *Harvest of Loneliness*; A. Rosas, *Abrazando el Espíritu*, 7, 161–62; and D. Cohen, *Braceros*.

21. Conditions cited in Nettie Brown, "The 1961 Imperial Farm-Labor Dispute: A Prize-Winning Feature," *Imperial Hometown Review*, 21 June 1962, 1–2. See also Munson J. Dowd, "History of Imperial Irrigation District," 2, cited in Durazo, "Capitalist Development," 45.

22. Durazo, "Capitalist Development," 45; and Collins, "The Imperial Valley," 3.

23. For more on the economic development, see Andrés, "Invisible Borders"; and Fernández, "Race and the Western Frontier."

24. Herrera, "Before the Waters"; and Bolton, *Anza's California Expeditions*, 5 vols.

25. Established in 1907, Imperial County included the municipalities of Calexico, Imperial, Dixieland, Brawley, and El Centro. Durazo, "Capitalist Development," 45–46.

26. For views of Mexicans as ideal agricultural laborers due to their biology, see D. Gutiérrez, *Walls and Mirrors*; and Guerín-Gonzales, *Mexican Workers*. For first-person accounts of working conditions in the early 1900s, see Gamio, *El inmigrante mexicano*.

27. For more on Asian exclusion, see, for instance, Ngai, *Impossible Subjects*.

28. *Harvest of Loneliness*. See also Mitchell, *They Saved the Crops*.

29. Durand and Massey, "Mexican Migration," 22; and Reichert and Massey, "Patterns of U.S. Migration." On the role of social networks, see Durand, Massey, and Parrado, "The New Era of Mexican Migration," 519.

30. Collins, "Imperial-Mexicali Valleys," 4; and Durazo, "Capitalist Development," 46–50.

31. For firsthand accounts of braceros' exploitation in Imperial County, see Yellen Papers, boxes 1–3.

32. JCE to MCA, 27 July 1965, CFP. "[A]demás el patrón es buen amigo[.]" Steve Reeves Interview, Brawley, California, 15 October 2015.

33. JCE to MCA, 1 August 1964, CFP. "[Y]o tengo (aunque esté mal decirlo), la preferencia quiero decir que me toco el trabajo mas libiano y sencillo[.]"

34. My comparison of braceros to black sharecroppers comes from Wilkerson's *The Warmth of Other Suns*.

35. "Income tax statement, 1962," José Chávez Esparza, Route 2, Box 164, Brawley, Calif. In author's possession. For poverty rates for 1962, see United States Census Bureau, "Poverty Thresholds 1962," http://www.census.gov/hhes/www/poverty/data/threshld/thresh62.html.

36. Massey et al., *Return to Aztlan*, 117, 308.

37. Lytle Hernández, "Crimes and Consequences." For more on earlier campaigns, including ones involving repatriation, see M. Ramírez, "Contested Illegality"; Balderrama and Rodríguez, *Decade of Betrayal*; Sánchez, *Becoming Mexican American*; and Johnson, "The Forgotten 'Repatriation.'"

38. For Conchita's request to José, see MCA to JCE, 3 May 1964, CFP; for José's refusal, JCE to MCA, 10 May 1964, CFP. "[P]ero entre nosotros muy pocas veces nos hemos tratado de estos asuntos."

39. JCE to MCA, 4 February 1964, CFP. "Saludos para los de tu casa y especialmente para tu hermana y perdona la discreción pero no me acuerdo como se llama, savia que era novia de mi hermano pero creo que no se su nombre; me lo dices por favor?"

40. PCE Interview, San José, California, 12 December 2016.

41. Ibid. According to Paco, Reeves owned several homes he made available to farmworkers at no charge.

42. D. Cohen, *Braceros*, 118–39.

43. JCE to MCA, 1 August 1964, CFP. "El domingo pasado fuimos a un paseo, Celevró Juan R. su cumpleaños y nos fuimos a un 'Pee Nick' dia de campo, bueno estuvo mas o menos bien nos divertimos algo en lo frio porque saves aqui en el valle

hace algo de calor pero como a 75 kmos o sea en el cerro esta muy fresco el lugar esta por la carretera que ba a San Diego, tambien el año pasado fuimos al mismo lugar y el 4 de julio dia de la Independencia era aqui fuimos a Ensenada B.C. y tomamos algunas fotos."

44. See, for instance, JCE to MCA, 22 April 1964, CFP.

45. Gerber, *Authors of Their Lives*, 102.

46. JCE to MCA, 16 February 1964, CFP. "[N]o estoy triste tengo fe que pronto resiviré carta tuya y con eso tengo para estar contento además tengo fe que me correspondas ojalá y sea pronto."

47. Ibid. "[A]penas nos conocimos pues es cierto[.]" "[E]res muy bonita por lo cual no me animaba a hablarte[.]" "¿[R]ecuerdas que el dia que me dijiste que no habias sido tu a la que le hablé que habia sido tu prima? pues todavia no lo creo, cierto que me habia tomado unas copas pero no handaba borracho solo me habia deshecho un poco de el miedo de declararteme, pues desde que te vi por ves primera senti deseos de hablarte pero como yo no soy de esos que tienen la facilidad para hablarle a las muchachas y saves por que es que creo . . . que soy feo[.]" "[Q]uiero que sepas que no te defraudaré si me correspondes[.] [Y]o te ofresco todo mi cariño que es mucho y muy cincero."

48. Ibid. "[D]ije hoy tengo que resivír carta de 'Shelly' (asi estaba escrito lo traduci al Ingles . . .) y si no resivo no le buelvo a escribir hasta que no me escriba S[h]elly y ese dia resivi tu carta."

49. MCA to JCE, 28 February 1964, CFP. "[A]unque no lo creas no díspongo de mucho tiempo con eso de que estoy estudiando y demas quihaceres que tengo se me pasa el tiempo." "Pero sí tu dispones de mas tiempo que c[r]eo que no es así, y si lo es haslo tu que llo en cuanto pueda te las contesto."

50. For an example of José's difficulty with using palabras de amor, see JCE to MCA, 28 January 1965, CFP. "[A] pesar de que cuando hablabamos nunca nos dijimos cosas romanticas creo que nos queremos mucho[.]" "Even though when we spoke we did not say romantic things to each other I believe we love each other very much."

51. PCE Interview, San José, California, 6 March 2015. My thinking on affect, emotions, and intimacy has been shaped by Doss, "Affect"; and McKay, "Sending Dollars Shows Feeling."

52. JCE to MCA, 22 March 1964, CFP. "[S]iento que son 10 años." "[T]e escribo para decirte que no me olvido de ti . . . ya quisiera que tu también pienses en mi, si supieras cuanto deseo que me llegues a querer pues es lo que mas hanhelo[.]"

53. Ibid. "[H]oy fue domingo y me tocó trabajarlo estuvo el dia feo hizo viento y me la pasé recordando de ti y me sentia contento porque parece que te veia y como espero resivir carta de ti pronto es lo que me hacia sentir contento y me decia a mi mismo no importa cuanto espero con tal de que no te olvides de mi[.]" "Mira ahora que te conoci me siento feliz no se como explicarte pero es que antes vivia sin fe o sin esperanza no savia que hacer queria irme para Calvillo y no volver mas aqui. [A]lgunas veces se lo dije a mi papá y me aconsejo que aqui me estuviera que despues quedria venirme de nuevo[.]" "[C]reeme que no defraudaré tu cariño . . . en mi vida he soñado con casarme con la muchacha que me corresponda a mi cariño y dedicarle

toda mi vida a ella, en todo y por todo y esa muchacha quiero que seas tu tienes todo lo que yo apresio y deseo[.]"

54. MCA to JCE, 24 March 1964, CFP. "[M]ira llo te quiero con un cariño muy distinto al amor, bueno (habersi me entiendes) llo quisiera poder corresponder a tu sentimientos, pero lla vez que el corazón no se manda." "[L]lo tampoco nunca me he enamorado creo que porque no se me ha llegado mi tiempo o porque tengo un consepto muy malo de los hombres, quizas no todos son igual excepto algunos[.]" "[T]u eres . . . uno de los pocos hombres en realidad que se le puede decir hombres y no solo porque usen pantalones, cuando menos ese consepto tengo de ti." "La carta puedes romperla o leerla como quieras pero no me la mandes."

55. JCE to MCA, 14 June 1966, CFP. "[D]espues de que todos los dias que llegava a la casa y no encontraba carta de ti sentia feo y ese dia desde la mañana parece que savia que iva a resivir carta tuya soy un poco adivino[.]"

56. JCE to MCA, 10 May 1964, CFP. "Me platicas también que fiesta le hicieron a las Madres en éste dia pues hoy es 10 saves que todo el dia lo pasé acordandome de allá de todo de mi mamá, de ti de la fiesta bueno de todo[.]" "[S]aves que aqui me la paso triste porque no se porque no me gusta el ambiente aqui ahora el dia 5 celebraron fiesta unos clubs que hay pero no fui pues estuvo muy feo el tiempo y tuve que trabajar bueno lo que yo creo que me pasa es que quisiera estar allá[.]"

57. JCE to MCA, 2 June 1964, CFP. "Shelly Siento deseos de preguntarte de algo que no quisiera que mal interpretaras o que no sea de tu agrado . . . hay esperanzas de que me quieras, saves yo no puedo mentirte, para decirte que siento quererte no se cuanto pero siento que aun puedo quererte mas quiero decirte algo asi como que desde que te conoci me pareciste (como te dije antes) Marabillosa pues eres muy bonita e inteligente y cincera bueno no puedo pedir mas y a lo mejor ni meresco tanto pero si me llegas a quere te aseguro que no te defraudaré[.]"

58. JCE to MCA, 30 June 1964, CFP. "[I]va a telefonearte hoy . . . para felicitarte." "[A]unque no lo creas me s[i]ento contento en grado superlativo[.]" "[C]omo tardaste en contestarme . . . piensa con cuanto gusto resivi tu carta y tu invitación." "Hoy todo el dia pensava en ti te imaginava o sea que te veia en mi pensamiento muy contenta."

59. MCA to JCE, 9 July 1964, CFP. "Quería pedirte un consejo respecto a el estudio tu que piensas ¿me convendría seguir estudiando? si piensas que si me dises que te gustaría que estudiara[.]" "[C]reo que tu que tienes mas experiencia y conoces mejor la vida me podras orientar, lo dejo a tu criterio[.]"

60. JCE to MCA, 17 July 1964, CFP. "Shelly Me da alegria de que me preguntes de tu estudio y te quiero decir que lo que tu quieras o sea la carrera que te guste si puedes seguirla hazlo, que aunque en mi egoismo me siento confuso pues comprende de que puedo imaginar si tu sigues estudiando. No hagas caso a esto ultimo y mucho menos a lo que diga la gente." "Lo que si deseo con todo el corazon es que no salieras del pueblo pero en fin como dice el dicho que sea lo que Dios quiera[.]"

61. Ibid. "Ojalá y pueda ir pronto para allá para platicar de ésto." "[S]aves tengo ganas de estar allá unos meses pues . . . siempre que voy me quedo muy poco tiempo pero creo es decir pienso que la proxima voy a estarme cuando menos unos 3 meses ojalá y sean mas."

62. JCE to MCA, 1 August 1964, CFP. "Shelly Si tengo muchas ganas de ir pero por ahorita no puedo por motivo a que tengo bastante trabajo y no quiero dejarlo porque entonces pondrian a otro en mi lugar[.]" "[A]horita en este mes comensamos a preparer los siembros de 'Betabel' ('Remolacha azucarera') y yo creo que como tengo planeado el viaje pues creo que esta bién[.]"

63. *Necesidades esenciales en México*, 25, 46.

64. Gerber, *Authors of Their Lives*; and Siems, *Between the Lines*.

65. MCA to JCE, 13 April 1964, CFP. "Te extrañaré que te escriba en papel sin ralla pero sabes ya me estaba dando envidia al ver que tu asi lo haces y haces la letra muy derecha, pero por mas que me esfuerzo ya bes que no consigo irme derecha, unos renglones van al cielo otros será al infierno y en fin todo un desastre, pero me he propuesto a no dejar que me ganes aunque sea en eso." For an image of the letter, see page 81.

66. Ibid. "[Q]uiero hacerte un cuestionario haber que tan bien estas en ingles, no te enfades si tienes tiempo me lo contestos y si no no es compromiso." "Cada palabra bale un punto me las contestas en español y . . . te mando la calificación. Ah! y tu me mandas otro, fáciles asi como yo te los hice, ¿he?"

67. JCE to MCA, 22 April 1964, CFP. "[B]ueno tu califica como lo has estudiado ya que aqui se habla el idioma íngles modificado[.]"

68. Ibid. "Saves que comenzó ha haber classes aqui en el barrio . . . pero no he ido mas que un dia no me gustó mucho pero haber si sigo llendo[.]" "No creo que este bién escrito pues lo que se lo he aprendido lericamente unicamente lei 2 leccio-nes de La National Schools cuando todavia no me venia para aca asi que si no fuera por eso creo que ni siguiera supiera decir 'yes.'" The institute advertised in Mexico and other parts of Latin America through print magazines and newspapers. See, for instance, *Selecciones de Reader's Digest* 42, no. 248 (July 1961), 4; and *El Tiempo*, Bogotá, Colombia, 7 March 1943, 6, 8.

69. JCE to MCA, 10 May 1964, CFP. "[T]e voy a decir los que no supistes asi que ¡Atención! 10 I really = yo realmente. Wish = deso y Mariagge [*sic*] es matrimonio asi que yo creo tener buena calificación[.]"

70. JCE to MCA, 17 July 1964, CFP. "Saves ahora que comiense la clase en el prox-imo curso voy a ir par aver si aprendo algo y luego te mando cuestionarios he!"

71. MCA to JCE, 13 April 1964, CFP. "Realmente me tenias intrigada con la tar-danza de tu contestación hasta llegué a pensar que te habías ofendido con algo de lo que te digo, o no sabía que pensar pero . . . creo que valió la pena pues me encantó la foto[.]"

72. Cancian, *Families, Lovers, and Their Letters*, 116–17.

73. JCE to MCA, 21 May 1966, CFP. "[U]na cosa que te va a parecer simple es que escribo unos renglones y volteo a ver tu retrato el grande lo tengo frente a mi y me parece que estoy platicando contigo al fin que si puede ser sierto porque el pensam-iento y el alma pueden vencer la distancia asi que cuando leas esta imaginate que estamos juntos[.]"

74. Personal communication with David A. Gerber, 12 April 2013.

75. JCE to MCA, 14 May 1965, CFP. "[T]us retratos los tengo aqui enfrente en el radio fijate en uno estás tu y Chifis sentadas enfrente a la cosina en mi casa y el otro

estás tu con las manos juntas y sonriendo no se que estarias diciendo pero te miro muy contenta ¿recuerdas cuando te retrataron que decia?"

76. MCA to JCE, 3 May 1964, CFP. "[M]i caricatura no te la mando porque no he podido ir a aguas. y aqui salen mas feos que como son las personas habersi pronto boy si tienes tu mándame unos, ¿he?"

77. JCE to MCA, 17 July 1964, CFP. "Me gustó mucho tu retrato no se por que ati no te gusta[.]" "Fijate para caricature esta y no la tuya, no es que sea defecto del fotografo si no que asi estoy de feo cuando no sea peor[.]"

78. JCE to MCA, 8 June 1965, CFP. "[A]si que si a ti no te gustan a mi si y mucho por eso no dejes de regresarmelos."

79. For more on Spanish-language music, radio, and braceros, see D. Cohen, *Braceros*, 118–39; and in the United States more generally, see F. Gutiérrez and Reina Schement, *Spanish-Language Radio*; and "How to Win with Juan," *Sponsor: The Buyers of Broadcast Advertising*, 4 June 1951, 25–27, 50.

80. JCE to MCA, 6 April 1964, CFP. "Saves te queria platicar de una canción que está de nueva y cuando la oigo pienso mucho en ti se llama 'Me regalo contigo' la cantan los 'Impala' si no la has oido ojalá y cuando la escuches te guste."

81. For Conchita's interest in "youthful bands," see MCA to JCE, 4 June 1966, CFP. "[M]e dices que te platique de la fiesta como veras me la pasé bien para que me quejo vinieron dos conjuntos juveniles con lo que me gusta esá música[.]" English translation: "You ask me to tell you about the party as you will see I had a good time why should I complain? we had two youth bands I really like that music[.]"

82. MCA to JCE, 13 April 1964, CFP. "La canción si me gusta, no mucho pero ahora que se que te gusta trataré de hacer porque me guste mas, a mi me gusta 'Laverinto' con Sonia Lopez y 'el Cartero.'"

83. JCE to MCA, 2 June 1964, CFP. "Desde la otra carta te iva a platicar que ya tengo el disco ese que te gusta está bonito lo compre hace como un mes[.]"

84. Ibid. "Saves que voy a preguntar si puedo mandarte unos discos para comprarlos y si me dejan te voy a mandar unos con Cony Francis[.]"

85. MCA to JCE, undated, ca. October 1964, CFP. "[A] propósito ahorita estoy oyendo una canción que hace tiempo te quería preguntar si te gustaba se llama 'Invierno Triste' con Conie bueno no se como se escribe pero tu me entiendes de quien se trata puesto que es tu favorita[.]"

86. The references to Connie Francis in the correspondence as well as the 45 rpm record among family memorabilia explain why her music occupied such a central role in our household. My father played her records on Saturday mornings, on long car trips to Mexico, and during family gatherings. Doubtless the music conjured fond memories of the courtship and of his days in Imperial Valley.

87. JCE to MCA, 20 October 1964, CFP. "[T]odavia no he oido esas canciones que dices aqui llegan un poco retardadas los discos que están de moda en el interior[.]" "[P]or lo regular los 'hits' musicales los tocan en el dia y yo no tengo tiempo de oir el radio hasta en la noche[.]"

88. F. Gutiérrez and Schement, *Spanish-Language Radio*, 7, 11.

89. JCE to MCA, 20 October 1964, CFP. "[T]al vez por eso no las he oido ojalá y pronto las oiga y ya te avisaré si me gustan o no, tienen el titulo algo sugestivo por eso

creo que si me van a gustar ademas 'Conny Francis' canta muy bonito tiene una voz muy bonita."

90. JCE to MCA, 20 October 1964, CFP. "Yo aqui he oido una que no se lo que dice pues la he oido pocas veces y me gustó voy a poner atencion al titulo y lo que diga y luego te cuento lo unico que le he aprendido es 'on the mis[s]ing moon light' no puedo traducirlo, pero creo que la van a traducir pues asi ha pasado con muchas canciones que a mi me han gustado desde nuevas[.]"

91. JCE to MCA, 28 January 1965, CFP. "[F]ijate un detalle que me hayuda a sentirme allá pongo el radio en la XEW de México pues es la unica estación de radio de por allá que alcansa a llegar hasta aca[.]"

92. JCE to MCA, 22 August 1965, CFP. "Ahorita estoy oyendo el disco aquel de Conny F[rancis] te acuerdas es Quiereme mucho una de las canciones que mas me gusta[.]" "[Y]o me acuerdo mucho de aquel dia que estuvimos en el rancho . . . oyendo el disco . . . recuerdas es uno de los dias mas bonitos que he vivido y me es muy grato recordarlo."

93. F. Gutiérrez and Schement, *Spanish-Language Radio*, 7.

94. JCE to MCA, 16 December 1964, CFP. "[P]ues saves que en la noche oigo solo difusoras de aqui pues hay unas programas muy bonitos[.]"

95. JCE to MCA, 14 May 1965, CFP. "Queria mandarte dedicar unas canciones en la XELO de Cd. Juarez yo la oigo aqui muy bién y tiene un programa que se llama serenata Internacional[.]" "[D]ime si la puedes oir para de[d]icarte algo asi las oímos al mismo tiempo."

96. MCA to JCE, undated, ca. June 1965, CFP. "Ya nos trajeron el radio ahora si sí quieres nada mas me dices a que hora y que día y en que estación."

97. JCE to MCA, 28 June 1965, CFP. "[E]l martes habla un locutor que solo lo hace los Martes y a el quiero mandarle pedir que te dedique unas canciones[.]"

98. JCE to MCA, 8 July 1965, CFP. "Yo creo que ese Locutor estará de Vacaciones bién despues mas delante será eso[.]"

99. JCE to MCA, 8 July 1965, CFP. "Cuentame que peliculas has visto yo hace tiempo que no voy al cine el motivo es que ahorita son las dias tan largos y creo que es por eso también que no he encontrado peliculas que me gustan."

100. JCE to MCA, 7 March 1965, CFP. "Cuentame que peliculas hasa visto. [Y]o aqui vi 55 dias en Pequin . . . también vi La Noche de la Iguana que filmaron en Puerto Vallarta[.]"

101. EH Interview, Calvillo, Aguascalientes, 23 September 2015.

102. PCE Interview, San José, California, 12 December 2016.

103. MCA to JCE, undated letter, ca. March/April 1965, CFP.

104. De Usabel, *The High Noon of American Films*, 150. Films were rarely, if ever, dubbed in English because of the difficulties with regional variations in dialect and accents as well as the power of the Mexican film actors' union, which sought to protect its market from Hollywood's unfair practices. See ibid., 182–90.

105. MCA to JCE, undated letter, March/April 1965, CFP. "Fijate que me estoy santificando . . . ya tenemos que andar muy honestos y con tanto calor que esta hacienda himajinate que sacrificio y tampoco podemos ir al cine con lo que me gusta a

proposito no he visto muchas peliculas . . . 'En la vieja California' 'El Americano feo' y muchos mas como casi todos los dias boy mas bien hiba."

106. JCE to MCA, 10 April 1966, CFP. "Conchita si vieras que contento me vine esta vez ahora no fue como la otra que me vine muy triste, quisiera que los dias se hacieran segundos para ir y ya no separarnos cuantas cosas quisiera decirte pero no puedo porque quisiera decirlos todos a una sola ves y creo que una sola palabra los puede decir y esa palabra es 'te quiero[.]' "

107. JCE to MCA, 22 May 1966, CFP. "Mis mayores temores han sido de que tu no me llegues a querer y que me llegaras a terminar pero ahora todo se me afigura distinto y le doy gracias al Cielo por tener una ilusión un cariño tan bonito y esa ilusión y ese cariño eres tu y no tienes una idea que feliz me siento y mas ahun cuando me pongo a pensar en que pronto se realizará mi sueño . . . sea como sea tenemos que casarnos pronto."

108. MCA to JCE, 23 June 1966, CFP. "[S]i vieras como me da miedo que me digas de esas cosas se que es necesario pero no se lo que me pasa quisiera que todo pasara como un sueño para no tener que pasar por eso, no se si a ti te pasa lo mismo pero nomás de pensar en tanto lio hasta me pongo nerviosa[.]"

109. JCE to MCA, 6 July 1966, CFP. "[Y]o también me pongo a pensar de cómo le vamos ha hacer pero al fin de un modo u otro tendria que ser."

110. Ibid. "No te puedo decir ahora con exactidud para cuando me voy pues todavia tengo que ir a San José donde esta mi Mamá y mi papá y preparar la ida haber que como siga mi papá."

111. JCE to PCE, 25 August 1966, CFP. "Yo me vine el 3 de Agosto y voy a casarme en estos dias y creo que me voy luego."

112. JCE to PCE, 18 December 1966, CFP. "[B]ueno ya no hallo la puerta y quiero decirte que si tu o Jesus tienen chansa de ayudarme con unos $20.00 para pagar la compostura porque en esta semana no tengo chansa de conseguir porque tu saves es Navidad el savado y todos tienen necesidad de comprar sus regalos[.]"

113. JCE to PCE, 27 December 1966, CFP. "[A]hora tendré que rentar casa pues no es posible vivir de arrimado tu saves que es dificil y no habia hecha la lucha por conseguir casa[.]"

114. AA Interview, Modesto, California, 14 June 2008.

Chapter Two

1. MCA to JCE, 16 September 1964, CFP. "Estoy muy triste porque no me boy a ir a estudiar tu no te puedes himajinar lo que siento por el estudio que creo que me boy a volver loca (un poco mas de lo que estoy) nada me consuela y todo me parese mas feo no creas que exajero pues no tengo motivos para hacerlo."

2. JCE to MCA, 29 September 1964, CFP. "Siento mucho que estés triste por no haber seguido estudiando yo también quise estudiar cuando terminé la primaría pero no pude bueno lo que yo queria estudiar era una carrera un poco dificil y costosa[.]" "[A]hora quisiera estudiar algo de probecho rapido pero no hayo que."

3. MCA to JCE, 23 July 1964, CFP. "[M]e da mucho gusto que te hayas desidido a venir a estarte mucho digo mucho a comparación de lo que te estas estas otras veces pero

quisiera saber mas o menos para cuando vienes porque había pensado ir para el rancho[.]"

4. MCA to JCE, 16 September 1964, CFP. "Te comunico que ya estoy de regreso y con ganas de escribir muchas cartas asi es de que contéstame rápido[.]"

5. Crummett, "A Gendered Economic History"; Crummett, "Agrarian Class Structure"; and Hernández López, *Monografía*.

6. For poverty in Calvillo, see González Esparza, *Estado de bienestar*, 57, 85–86. For the lack of primary schooling, see Aguascalientes, *Recorridos*.

7. Rojas et al., *Breve historia*, 183–93.

8. Crummett, "A Gendered Economic History," 106.

9. Ibid., 109.

10. Rojas et al., *Breve historia*, 186.

11. Ibid., 188–210.

12. For population, see Hernández López, *Monografía*, 141.

13. Noriega-Verdugo, "Economic Overview," 117.

14. JA Interview, San José, California, 19 January 2009.

15. AA Interview, Modesto, California, 14 June 2008.

16. Ibid.; and JA Interview, San José, California, 19 January 2009.

17. JA Interview, San José, California, 19 January 2009.

18. JGD Interview, Calvillo, Aguascalientes, 13 February 2009.

19. JA Interview, San José, California, 19 January 2009.

20. Ibid.; and AA Interview, Modesto, California, 14 June 2008.

21. Aguascalientes, *Recorridos*, [5].

22. DSR Interview, Calvillo, Aguascalientes, 19 September 2015.

23. AA Interview, Modesto, California, 14 June 2008.

24. Ibid.

25. MCA to JCE, 16 September 1964, CFP. "[S]i vieras que feliz me la pasé en el rancho está tan hermoso que hasta a ti te hubiera gustado, bueno supongo que a ti no te a de gustar mucho el rancho puesto que nunca has vivido en el pero yo como quien dice soy mas bien campecina."

26. Ibid. "[F]íjate que todos los dias ibamos a diferentes partes entre barrancas y serros en una ocasión bajamos una barranca tan inclinada y trabajosa que hasta ganas me daban de llorar nada mas cerraba los ojos y el caballo desidia y cuando estubimos de regreso ay tienes que no podia mover ni un musculo y como te has de imaginar se empezaron a reir de mi mis primos y me desian que no que no que era tan buen jinete."

27. MCA to JCE, 16 September 1964, CFP. "![Q]uisiera contarte muchas cosas pero no ti[e]nen ninguna importancia cuando menos para ti a comparacion de las diferentes disberciones que tendras tu por aqui."

28. Played by Gloria Iturbe, Doctora Corazón was a popular radio personality who provided advice on affairs of the heart on radio station XEW based in Mexico City. Women, presumably, would write in anonymously with their secrets, and the doctora answered them. Later it was revealed that the radio station fabricated most of the letters. Granados, *XEW*, 237. For more on rock and roll in Mexico, see Schmidt, "Making It Real," 49.

29. MCA to JCE, 9 December 1964, CFP. "La coronación fue en el cine . . . anoche estuvo lloviendo toda la noche y como has de suponer no tuvo chiste después de la coronación nos fuimos al jardín y como estaba lloviendo fuimos a una refresqueria nos invitó Paco."

30. GGD Interview, 13 February 2009, Calvillo, Aguascalientes.

31. MCA to JCE, undated, ca. April 1964, CFP. "Fíjate que me estoy santificando estoy en los ejercicios y con estas cosas creo que boy progresando, ya tenemos que andar muy honestos y con tanto calor que esta hacienda himajinate que sacrificio y tampoco podemos ir al cine con lo que me gusta[.]" "[C]omo casi todos los dias boy mas bien hiba."

32. MCA to JCE, 24 May 1965, CFP. "[A] proposito de Lola tengo muchas ganas de verla pero mas de ir al cine fijate que aqui no he ido ni una vez como estan los cines lejos y no puedo irme sola y menos escondidas como lo hacia allá[.]"

33. MCA to JCE, 28 February 1964, CFP. "[Y]o no soy bonita como dices soy bastante horrible, pero te concedo razón en que te espreses asi pues me vistes en la noche, creo que si me vieras de dia creo que no dirias lo mismo[.]"

34. MCA to JCE, 25 June 1964, CFP. "[B]oy a parecer mosca en leche, es gracioso no crees[?]"

35. JCE to MCA, 30 June 1964, CFP. "¿Shelly porque dices que ivas a pareser mosca en leche? No creo que estes 'prieta' para decir eso bueno quizas sea que eres segun mi concepto algo Modesta Realmente Shelly eres de un character de miedo; no se como decirlo si temperamento de mucha personalidad cosa que no va con tu edad."

36. MCA to JCE, 9 July 1964, CFP. "[M]e atribuyes muchos cualidades que no existen en mi, que si me creyera me sentiria mas ancha que un rinocerante."

37. MCA to JCE, 25 June 1964, CFP. "[M]e retrate para el certificado pero no me hicieron el favor quedé enteramente como soy . . . no me decido a mandartelo me cae muy mal y a demas no es grande es como el que te dí, asi quieres que te lo mande aunque sea asi en la otra te lo mando, fijate que mando sacar uno grande de 50 cm de largo por 48 de a.[ncho] que te parece, que estoy loca[?]"

38. MCA to JCE, 11 March 1965, CFP. "Fíjate que hace algunos días Paco le mando a Chifis unas fotos . . . si vieras que horribles quedamos como unas brujas (asi como Chifis y Concha) las conoces?" "[T]e dije que tu hiba a dar de unos cuando tenía catorce 14 años pero siempre me arrepentí porque se me hice muy gorda mejor después te mando un montón para que asustes los ratones . . . (no te enojes es broma)."

39. MCA to JCE, 28 February 1964, CFP. "[Q]uiero decirte que sabe como se te haran mis cartas no me se expresar hago la letra bastante fea, en fín ya no digo mas porque creo que llanaré el papel y no acabo de decir todos los defectos."

40. Conchita disparaged her intellect and letter writing in thirteen of the thirty-five letters she sent, while José did the same in two or three of the forty-five he sent.

41. MCA to JCE, undated, ca. September/October 1964, CFP. "[D]ime cuantas cartas tienes mías si es que no las has quemado, porque estan tan mensas que es lo único que se merecen."

42. JCE to MCA, 20 October 1964, CFP. "[T]engo y son 12 ademas la invitación de tu graduacion todas las guardo ademas con un detalle que te va a parecer 'simple' los recortes de el sobre . . . lo[s] guardo en la misma carta ¿crees tu que merecen quemarse si guardo hasta los recortes?"

43. JCE to MCA, 14 December 1965, CFP. "[B]ueno queria decirte en una forma especial que siento feo que escribas al final Dispensa los garabatos. No quiero que los repitas mi letra está de no entendersele y casi nunca te digo eso asi que no mas he?"

44. RSM Interview, Calvillo, Aguascalientes, 14 February 2009.

45. PM Interview, Calvillo, Aguascalientes, 12 February 2009.

46. MCA to JCE, undated, ca. September/October 1964, CFP. "José fíjate que me desconcierta tu carta al principio porque dice Concepcion como siempre escribes Conchita pensé que por algo estabas disgustado pero después leí que no era así, es un detalle sin importancia pero como te dije me desconcertó."

47. MCA to JCE, 23 July 1964, CFP. "Yo creo que a tu mamá no le caígo muy bien ni a Maura porque cuando me ben nada mas un a Dios desos descortéz bueno a tu mamacita casi nunca la veo, fíjate que a Chifis le hacen mas honores que ni se los merece . . . . no creas que estoy selosa . . . esto nada mas te lo platico para llenar el papel."

48. JCE to MCA, 1 August 1964, CFP. "Shelly Lo que me platicas al ultimo te dire que la que está celosa es Maura pues cuando fui me pregunto acerca de ti y le dije que eras mi novia y estoy casi seguro que si esta celosa ojalá y tu tambien lo estes eso me hace sentir como pudiera explicarte si feliz o contento porque si es asi es señal que puedes llegar a quererme como lo deseo."

49. MCA to JCE, 11 August 1964, CFP. "[H]ace poquito fuí a tu casa es decir fuimos Chifis y yo tu mamá nos trató muy bien, y me di cuenta que te llama mi 'lindo' a [mi] me dice Concha a Chifis Chonita pero no me apuro tu si me dices Conchita[.]"

50. JCE to MCA, 5 February 1965, CFP. "Creo que si se llevaran mejor ustedes con José E. creo que eso influencia en favor de su salud de tu mamá[.]"

51. MCA to JCE, 11 March 1965, CFP. "No te hiba a decir nada de lo de José E. porque es una cosa muy larga de explicar de todos modos te agradesco tus consejos y siento mucho no poder seguirlos porque jamás estaría dispuesta a hacer una cosa que no sintiera, o crees tu que podría hacerlo si lo odio como a nadie en el mundo por tanto mal que de el hemos recibido que es la causa de nuestra desgracia y mas cosas que no te puedo decir espero me comprendas que al cabo estoy segura que aunque lo tratáramos de lo mejor no cambiría al contrario se sentirá mas seguro de si y seriá peor."

52. RSM Interview, Calvillo, Aguascalientes, 14 February 2009.

53. PM Interview, Calvillo, Aguascalientes, 12 February 2009.

54. JCE to MCA, 3 March 1965, CFP. "Mira cuando nos veamos hablaremos de ésto porque es dificil decir estas cosas asi por carta. Si quieres puedes contarme tus problemas no tengas pena talvez te pueda hayudar siquiera un poco y para mi me dará gusto en hayudarte[.]"

55. JA Interview, San José, California, 19 January 2009.

56. Rojas et al., *Breve historia*, 185–211.

57. González Esparza, *Estado de bienestar*, 57–67

58. MCA to JCE, 30 January 1965, CFP. "Creo que siempre nos vamos a Ags." "[N]o me hiba pero si vieras la pobre de mi mamá como a seguido de mal que no me atrevería a quedarme[.]"

59. JA Interview, San José, California, 19 January 2009.

60. MCA to JCE, 30 April 1965, CFP. "[S]i vieras como estoy de triste . . . se me hace imposible que pueda aguantar. Luego que llegué encontré trabajo en un taller pero casi no me gusta, me ofrecieron otro de contadora en una tienda de ropa donde se gana buen dinero pero tampoco me gustó porque los dueños son puros hombres y hay ai muchos y unos muchachos muy creídos será que quiero ver como en Calvillo fuera gente cencilla o no se pero lo que si te digo que va hacer muy difícil que pueda trabajar agusto aveces me dan ganas de irme otra vez a Calvillo pero luego pienso también que que boy hacer ahí[.]"

61. JCE to MCA, 8 May 1965, CFP. "No se que desirte . . . no se si tenga celos o miedo a el cambio[.]" "Confió en ti que se que eres buena y cincera creo que nunca me engañaras ademas tengo puesta mi fe en ti y en Dios que sea lo que Dios quiera Yo te quiero a la Buena y con todo mi corazón por eso confio en ti."

62. JCE to MCA, 8 May 1965, CFP. "Ojalá y te acostumbres al ambiente yo se que no es igual que en Calvillo yo vivi un año y se como es todo allí hasta me imagino la casa donde viven pues conosco esa calle solo que ya olvidé el nombre de las tiendas que hay cerca pues saves que cuando vivi alli trabajé en la Pepsi Cola y conoci todos las calles, asi que deseo cinceramente que te acostumbres a la ciudad que vivas contenta. ¿Saves porque te digo esto? es que yo he vivido muy triste y se lo feo que es por eso no quiero que tu también sufras como yo."

63. JCE to MCA, 14 May 1965, CFP. "Caray Conchita creo que a ésto es a lo que te decia que tenia miedo o algo asi parecido a venirme y tu quedarte alla y tener que recordarte y estar tan solo, si no fuera por la esperanza que tengo de pronto verte creo que no tendria objeto vivir."

64. MCA to JCE, 14 May 1965, CFP. "[S]i vieras no tengo tiempo para esas cosas porque entro al trabajo a las 7 de la mañana y nada mas salgo a comer y otra vez hasta las 7 de la noche, mi patrona es como un chamuco todo el dia nos da unas buenas regañadas muy feas si vieras como estoy de flaca he bajado 16 k. cosa increible." "[P]ero si vieras el quihacer que tenemos cuando llego en la noche no se si ponerme a lavar que hay serros de ropa sucia o arreglar mi ropa o a coser . . . y tan cansada que queciera mejor estar acostada[.]"

65. JCE to MCA, 1 June 1965, CFP. "Conchita me da tristeza que no estés agusto y que te mortifiques . . . (aunque por otra parte quisiera que hasta te pusieras fea para que nadie se fijara en ti) Celos verdad? es que como nunca me han querido tengo la impresión de ser celoso[.]"

66. MCA to JCE, 23 July 1965, CFP. "No te habia escrito porque nos hi[bamos] a cambiar de casa y asi para m[andarte] la nueva dirección, es una lat[a] tremenda andar de aqui par[a allá] y mas no estando uno aco[stumbrado] pero en fin que le vamos h[acer?]" "[F]ijate que me gusta mas aqui a donde nos cambiamos porque esta muy [cerquitas] el templo de la Purisima y un jardinsito . . . sabras es junto al

parque Hidalgo una que esta muy de moda ahorita haber cuanto duramos aqui." (The letter is torn, and the remainder is difficult to read. The insertions are my best interpretations based on what remains and the context.)

67. AA Interview, Modesto, California, 14 June 2008.

68. Pointing to the recording device, Juan indicated, "Don't put that [the information] in there." JA Interview, San José, California, 19 January 2009.

69. MCA to JCE, 23 October 1965, CFP. "Mira estamos Chifis y yo en Fresnillo nadie sabe donde estamos exepto mi mamá y San Juana ésta ultima carta que me henviaste me la mando mi mamá con el jefe fue a Ags. y llegó a la casa porque mi mama tampoco sabia la dirección de nos. y nada mas he recibido una como te digo pero ya le enviamos la dirección a mi mamá para que me las remita porque no tiene caso que tu me los envies hasta aca porque no se cuando nos vamos yo creo a ver pronto ... hestoy muy agusto nada mas que la comida me cae muy mal digamos demaciado ... es una casa de huéspedes que de categoría."

70. MCA to JCE, 1 November 1965, CFP. "José quiero que me disculpes por no haberte dicho la verdad en la otra carta pero creo tu comprenderas me da verguenza decirtelo no porque sea una cosa vergonzosa si no que no se como lo tomaras tu creo no me jusgaras mal al conocer mas o menos los problemas que tenemos en la casa[.] Sabes ya no le aguantavamos a ese señor Escalera y Chifis y yo nos fuimos de la casa claro que con permiso de mi mamá y estamos trabajando aqui en Fresnillo somos agentes yo creo que mañana Dios mediante nos vamos a Tepetongo yo creo que todo este mes o no se yo tengo muchísimas ganas de ver a mi mamá ya ves como está la pobre de henferma y yo creo que ahora el Sr. se aprobecha ahora que no estamos[.]"

71. Ibid. "Mira no hay que ser pesimistas hay que creer que nuestro sueño es realidad asi nos sentiremos menos tristes[.]"

72. MCA to JCE, undated, ca. November 1965, CFP. "Desde hace algún tiempo para aca me siento terriblemente triste yo nunca lloraba por nada y ahora soy tan sentimental que nomas porque se muere un Chucho me pongo a llorar, no es para menos creo yo con tanta cosa ya mas o menos te himajinaras fuera uno de su casa y trabajando que es lo peor para mi con lo 'liviana' que soy que quisiera pasármela acostada eso no me da verguenza desírtelo ... los patrones caen gordos yo al mío quisiera mandarlo aya donde tu sabes el mio es un ogro pero tiene sus ratos buenos que son muy pocos[.]"

73. JCE to MCA, 17 November 1965, CFP. "[S]aves que me sentía triste tengo unos días que me siento triste tal parece que voy de acuerdo con el tiempo pues éstos dias hesta nublado y ha llovido un poco al mismo tiempo hace algo de frio ... estava triste y pensando en ti quería escribirte pero con eso de la tristeza (otra vez) no hallaba que decirte ... o que si tal vez te acordarás de mi[.]" "[Q]ue largo se me hacen los dias esperando pronto ir yo no se ni como le iré hacer pero tengo que ir pronto[.]"

74. MCA to JCE, 10 December 1965, CFP. "[E]stoy aqui con San Juana cociendo tengo muchisima costura ... ahora no puedo escribirte mucho pero siquiera ya sabes que me encuentro en Calvillo ahora si te voy a escribir seguido y espero que tu también[.]"

75. JCE to MCA, 14 December 1965, CFP. "Resivi tu carta la cual contesto con mucho gusto ya tenia muchas ganas de saver de ti si vieras cuanta tristesa tenia y pendiente a la vez pero hoy que se que estás en Calvillo me siento tranquilo[.]"

76. MCA to JCE, undated, ca. January 1966, CFP. "Fresnillo, Sombrerete, Durango, y muchas partes mas[.]"

77. Ibid. "[Y]o me la pase muy aburrida bueno no lo pacé aqui en Calvillo me fui a . . . Ags. hubo pachanga fueron los frenética del ritmo se puso suave nada mas que empesaron los borrachos (aguafiestas) y luego nos fuimos a la casa."

78. Ibid. "[D]iras que siempre te digo que me la paso aburrida pero . . . aunque valla a fiestas no se lo que me pasa que en ninguna parte me encuentro bien y nada me alegra, y fijate una cosa he notado que desde que vine de donde handava como que todo a cambiado y ya ne me gusta soñar como antes ahora si ví la vida esactamente como es y para mi no tiene ningún sentido, bueno ya boy a dejar de mensadas."

79. MCA to JCE, 4 November 1964, CFP. "[F]ijate que ahora que me fuí al rancho soñé que me habías escrito y que Chifis habia abierto la carta y asi que efectivamente y me regaño porque no te mandava saludos de ella pues en cada vez que te escribo te manda saludar. sabes será porque soy muy egoista porque se me olvida no te lo digo pero ahora recibe mil saludos de ella."

80. Ibid. "Sabes tengo gusto porque vas a ir y al mismo tiempo susto o no se como llamarlo porque pienso que al verte de nuevo cambian mis sentimientos . . . ahora no se cuáles son a veces pienso que te quiero pero otras veces lo contrario en fin no saco nada en tiempo, no te puedo explicar por carta quizas cuando vallas y hablemos pueda hacerlo."

81. MCA to JCE, 30 January 1965, CFP. "Sabes el dia que te fuiste me quede muy triste primeramente porque crei que hibas a ir a la casa después y segundo porque te vi como que tu no estabas triste[.]"

82. Ibid. "[S]abes me dio mucho gusto al recibirla, pero luego que vi un papel tan chiquito no te niego que me dio un poco de coraje, espero que a la próxima sea un periódico[.]"

83. MCA to JCE, undated, ca. April 1965, CFP. "Sin mas quien te quiere."

84. For the closing salutations, see MCA to JCE, 30 April 1965, CFP. "[E]n espera de la tuya[.]"; MCA to JCE, 24 May 1965, CFP. "[T]odo el cariño[.]"; MCA to JCE, undated, June 1965, CFP. "[T]u peor es nada[.]"; and MCA to JCE, 23 July 1965, CFP. "[S]in mas[.]"

85. MCA to JCE, 23 October 1965, CFP. "[Q]uien no te olvida[.]"; and MCA to JCE, undated, ca. November 1965, CFP. "[Q]uien te quiere[.]"

86. MCA to JCE, 10 December 1965, CFP. "[Q]uien no te olvida[.]"

87. For the letters she sent in 1966 and their closing statements, see MCA to JCE, undated, ca. January 1966, CFP. "[Q]uien no te olvida[.]"; MCA to JCE, 3 March 1966, CFP. "[Q]uien te quiere[.]"; MCA to JCE, 4 April 1966, CFP. "[Recibe . . . el cariño de quien desea verte pronto[.]"; MCA to JCE, undated, ca. April 1966, CFP. "[Q]uien te quiere y no te olvida[.]"; MCA to JCE, 4 June 1966, CFP. "Recibe . . . el cariño[.]"; MCA to JCE, 23 June 1966, CFP. "[Q]uien te quiere[.]"; and MCA to JCE, undated, ca. July 1966, CFP. "[Q]uien desea verte pronto[.]"

88. MCA to JCE, 4 April 1966, CFP. "[Q]uisiera que no pensaras que te lo cuento porque quiero obligarte a que te cases con migo haveces pienso que te sentiras como comprometido y como nunca nos hemos disgustado me has podido como te diré bueno safarte de mi[.]" "[S]i vieras que de chismes que eres casado y que se yo no te ofendas no creas que dudo de ti; pero ya van muchas personas que me dan esa noticia como comprenderás los chismes son lo de menos pues la gente nomas está inventando lo único que me importa es lo que me digas tu[.]" "P.D. Salúdame a tu esposa."

89. "Consignaron a un ladrón de ganado," *El Heraldo de Aguascalientes*, 3 June 1966, 6, section 2, Hemeroteca Nacional, Universidad Nacional Autónoma de México (UNAM), Mexico City.

90. AA Interview, Modesto, California, 14 June 2008.

91. Ibid.

92. Ibid.

93. JCE to MCA, 14 June 1966, CFP. "Cuando tengas tiempo escribe una carta al Consulado de Guadalajara pidiendo información . . . de la pasada[.]"

94. AA Interview, Modesto, California, 14 June 2008.

Chapter Three

1. PCE Interview, San José, California, 20 April 2008.

2. Letters from the three eldest siblings, Jesús, Juan, and José, to Paco indicate that their father, José Chávez Torres, wrote to them often but that they responded infrequently.

3. JCT to PCE, 14 February 1963, CFP. "[Y]o espere y espere la venida de ustedes y nada, está bien no se puede ni modo, yo lo que tengo pendiente es que Maura no he ido por ella está en Guadalajara, y con eso de que ya vienen y que ya vienen y nomás de tonto esperando, yo lo que les he pedido es que me desengañen si es que vienen o no asi para ir por la muchacha o mandarle dinero para que regrese a la casa[.]"

4. Levitt defines social remittances as the "ideas, behaviors, identities, and social capital that flow from receiving- to sending-country communities." Levitt, "Social Remittances."

5. This overview comes primarily from Sánchez, *Becoming Mexican American*; D. Gutiérrez, *Walls and Mirrors*; Guerin-Gonzales, *Mexican Workers*; Ruiz, *From out of the Shadows*; Cross and Sandos, *Across the Border*, 10; and Gamio, *El inmigrante mexicano*.

6. Sánchez, *Becoming Mexican American*, 40–41, 49, 135. For more on the role of the U.S. government in regulating Mexican labor and immigration, or what is called the "rotating door" of immigration policies and practices, see sources cited in note 5; and Mae Ngai, *Impossible Subjects*; and Granados Alcántar and Pizarro Hernández, "Paso del Norte."

7. For more on circular or return migration, see Lowell, "Circular Mobility, Migrant Communities, and Policy Restrictions."

8. A. Rosas, *Abrazando el Espíritu*.

9. BCT Interview, Aguascalientes, Aguascalientes, 10 February 2009.

10. PCE Interview, San José, California, 20 April 2008; and receipt for international money orders."

11. M. Smith, "Beyond the Borderlands," 240–41. For more on traqueros, see Garcilazo, *Traqueros*; and C. Rodríguez, "Health on the Line."

12. For more on the rebellion, see Mayer, *The Cristero Rebellion*.

13. MCE Interview, Calvillo, Aguascalientes, 12 February 2009; and MCE Interview, Calvillo, Aguascalientes, 19 September 2015; and PCE Interview, Calvillo, Aguascalientes, 19 September 2015.

14. BCT Interview, Aguascalientes, Aguascalientes, 10 February 2009.

15. JCE Interview, Calvillo, Aguascalientes, 13 February 2009.

16. PCE Interview, 20 April 2008, San José, California. For his municipal posts, see "Nombramiento, Juez Menor de Calvillo, Aguascalientes," *Supremo Tribunal de Justicia, Aguascalientes, 10 de Enero de 1943*, in author's personal collection; Hernández López, *Monografía del Municipio de Calvillo*, 168; receipt for international money order, Portola, California, August 31, 1944; and [Nombramiento] Legislatura del estado de Aguascalientes, Enero 10 de 1951, in author's personal collection.

17. For the value of the peso in relation to the dollar from 1954 to 1976, see Banco de Mexico, Sistema de Información Economica, "U.S. Dollar—MXN Exchange Rate since 1954," http://www.banxico.org.mx/SieInternet/consultarDirectorioInternetA ction.do?accion=consultarCuadro&idCuadro=CF373&sector=6&locale=en. The peso held steady at 12.50 to the U.S. dollar until 1976, when the exchange rate fell to nearly 20 pesos. http://www.banxico.org.mx/SieInternet/consultarDirectorioInter netAction.do?accion=consultarCuadro&idCuadro=CF373&sector=6&locale=en.

18. For more on the gendered expectations of Mexican men to migrate to support their families, see C. Rosas, "El desafío de ser hombre y no migrar."

19. PCE Interview, San José, California, 20 April 2008.

20. PCE Interview, San José, California, 26 July 2015.

21. PCE Interview, San José, California, 20 April 2008.

22. AGT Interview, Aguascalientes, Aguascalientes, 10 February 2009.

23. PCE Interview, San José, California, 20 April 2008.

24. PCE Interview, San José, California, 2 September 2014; MCE Interview, Calvillo, Aguascalientes, 12 February 2009. Evidence of remittances (sent through money orders or *giros postales*) is scarce but does exist. Nota de giros sobre el extranjero vendidos al Banco Mercantil del Bajío, S.A., 26 April 1955, in author's personal collection.

25. PCE Interview, San José, California, 20 April 2008.

26. Ibid.

27. Ibid.

28. Ibid.

29. MCE Interview, Calvillo, Aguascalientes, 21 September 2015; PCE Interview, Calvillo, Aguascalientes, 21 September 2015; and EH Interview, Calvillo, Aguascalientes, 23 September 2015.

30. Gerber, *Authors of Their Lives*, 64–65, 101–2.

31. JCT to PCE, 11 January 1963, CFP; and JCT to PCE, 13 March 1963, CFP.

32. See, for instance, JCT to PCE, 24 September 1962, CFP. "[D]inos para cuando viene José si es que pueda venir. Contestame . . . y dime para cuando te puedes venir."

33. JCT to PCE, 5 October 1962, CFP. "[Y] si no ya ustedes sabrán como le hacen." JCT to PCE, 15 October 1962, CFP. "Dime . . . si vienen se pueden venir juntos sempre que puedan y si no ni modo."

34. JCE to PCE, 2 September 1962, CFP. "[S]i voy es solo por 2 semanas tengo que sembrar pronto y luego la lluvia se pone muy duro por el camino y que apenas acabo de salir de las drogas y si tu asunto se tarda tendré que sostenerte aqui y para diciembre tengo chansa de estarme un mes . . . dile a mi papá que no no me esperen que no fui."

35. JCT to PCE, 5 December 1962, CFP. "Aqui está Juan y la señora mamá del Juan José vinieron hace unos dias."

36. JCT to PCE, 20 November 1962, CFP. "[M]e contestas pronto y haber que dice José si es que viene o no lo mismo Jesús, quiero llevar a tu madre que la vea el D[octo]r."

37. Insight on Jilda's health comes from MCE Interview, 11 February 2009, Calvillo, Aguascalientes; and AA Interview, 14 June 2008, Modesto, California.

38. JCT to PCE, 4 November 1963, CFP. "Nosotros seguimos lo mismo con tu madre que no es posible el que pueda andar sin las Muletas, sea por Dios."

39. JCT to PCE, 13 March 1963, CFP. "Sabes que llevamos a tu mama a León con un Oculista y a Guadalajara con Riebeling, sobre la otra enfermedad."

40. JCT to PCE, 6 June 1963, CFP. "Tocante al Ojo de tu mamá, con la medicina que se puso le sirvió mucho y sobre la operación si es de hacerse, nada más que será cuando tu vengas, entonces haremos eso."

41. JCT to PCE, 29 October 1964, CFP. "[S]abes que yo quiero llebar a tu madre a Guadalajara a los primeros días de diciembre, a que la examine el Dr."

42. MCE, Interview, San Francisco, California, 30 September 2015.

43. JS to MCE, 15 January 1963, CFP. "[F]ijate que yo no se como se dieron cuenta de las fotos y ya traen un arguende que para que te cuento. [M]ira quiero que agas exactamente lo que yo te digo[.]" "[D]iles que si te los mande con todo y negativos y que tu los quemaste para que se acabara todo el lio."

44. For more on sex and sexuality in Mexico, see Lispett-Rivera and Johnson, *The Faces of Honor*; Lavrin, *Marriage and Sexuality*; and Twinam, *Public Lives, Private Secrets*.

45. Ruiz, *From out of the Shadows*, 51–71.

46. JCT to PCE, 18 May 1963, CFP. "[Q]uiere ir para alla haber si le pueden arreglar tu y Jesús."

47. JCT to PCE, 6 June 1963, CFP. "Mira yo quisiera que alguno de ustedes le gestionara el modo de que fuera Maura para con ustedes o con Cuca mi prima, he sabido que están por pedirla para matrimonio . . . y yo con ese hijo de su pelona no quisiera y por eso yo le sugerí a Jesús que le gestione Con Cuca el que ella nos ayude para que se la lleven una temporada, ya tu me dirás que es lo que opinas por que tu tienes distinto modo de penzar de tus demás hermanos, ya te digo me contestas lo más pronto que puedas sobre este asunto."

48. JCT to PCE, 21 June 1963, CFP. "Dime si y compraste el carro y haber si puede ir Maura para ese Pais."

49. JCE to PCE, 11 November 1963, CFP. "Paco Saves que hace dias me escribió mi papá y parece o está muy sentido con todos nosotros quizá tenga razón yo me tardo en escribirle por motive a no tener nada para mandarle y también muy poco que decirle." "[Y]a has de saver lo de Maura pues según me da entender mi papa ella se fue con el José Soto[.]"

50. JCT to PCE, 26 September 1963, CFP. "[S]e me hace muy lejos hasta mayo, asi me llevan, yo quisiera que les fuera possible venir a lo mas para diciembre proximo por que tengo un asunto que tratar con ustedes, y hasta mayo se me hace lejos."

51. In her research on Italian migrants and their epistolary practices, Cancian has found that repeated letter writing was a sign of growing powerlessness in the relationship, as I have found it was for José, the patriarch. See Cancian, *Families, Lovers, and Their Letters*, 112.

52. JCT to PCE, 19 October 1963, CFP. "[M]ira quiero que le digas a Jesús que haga el ánimo y vengan tu y el ya hace muchos años que no se dá una vuelta y quiero tener una entrevista con ustedes[.]" "[Y]a te digo vé a Jesús y le enseñas ésta carta para que se dé cuenta que necesito que venga y ya te digo si te es posible venir al principio del mes bueno . . . te repito dile a Jesús que haga el sacrificio y venga[.]" "[T]u y Jesús si quisiera que vinieran por que me urge que nos veamos."

53. JCT to PCE, 4 November 1963, CFP. "Mira Paco quiero que veas a Jesús y le digas que que pasa que haga el animo y se de una vuelta, alcabo you creo que no los molestamos, ya mucho tiempo debido a nuestra edad, y que quuiero tratar un asunto con casi con todos, ustedes haber que opinamos, por que saves que acaba de pasar un caso algo duro para mi, referente a Maura, ya vendrás y te daras cuenta de lo sucedido pero ya Dios dirá, asi es que si ves a Jesús haber si le es posible[.]"

54. JCT to PCE, 15 January 1964, CFP. "Ta aviso que ya se casó Maura por la Iglecia y ya estamos solos, yo y tu madre, sea por Diós a lo que uno no espera llegar llega pero hay se vá ya no es tanto el tiempo que les hemos de dura."

55. PCE Interview, 1 August 2015, San José, California.

56. JCT to PCE, 27 August 1964, CFP. "[R]eferente a lo de tu mamá tocante a su santo lo pasó sin pena y sin gloria, nadie se acordó de ella mas que tu tio Pablo y Susana le mandaron unas tarjetas y fué todo, de sus hijos ninguno se acordó de ella."

57. MCA to JCE, 23 July 1965, CFP. "[T]u sabras lo que haces pero yo creo que deverías escribirle mas seguido[.]"

58. JCE to MCA, 27 July 1965, CFP. "Me alegro de que hayas ido a mi casa y no creas que dejo tanto tiempo sin escribirles lo que pasa es que me tardo si acaso una semana en contestarles[.]"

59. JCE to PCE, 11 November 1963, CFP. "Saves que yo no se como decirte . . . pero saves que nuestra familia ya está por los suelos[.]"

60. JCT to PCE, 25 December 1962, CFP. "Me preguntas del dinero, lo vine sacando batayando pero me lo pagaron y le dí a Maura $100.00. cien pesos y lo demáslo tengo con el fin de poner la luz."

61. JCT to PCE, 13 March 1963, CFP. "Mira Paco escribele a Jesús y dile que me ayude con algo para acabar de pagar la casa." JCT to PCE, 22 March 1963, CFP.

"[E]stoy muy gastado tube que conseguir tres mil pesos para completer el pago de los diez mil pesos que era el saldo[.]"

62. JCT to PCE, 6 April 1963, CFP. "[Y]a le dije a Jesús que me ayudara con algo por que me quedé sin centavos y ustedes me ayudaron con mucho y no pueden seguirme ayudando, y estoy esperando que me conteste haber si me puede mandar algo para poder hacer ese gasto . . . todo está muy caro material y mano de obra."

63. JCT to PCE, 18 May 1963, CFP. "[T]e diré a mi no megusta taparle a nadie, no me ha llegado a mandar nada ya tiene casi dos años que no me manda ni un centavo hizo más Juan me acaba de mandar Ciento cincuenta Dollars."

64. JCT to PCE, 9 July 1963, CFP. "Mira Jesús no me ha ayudado ni con un cinco hace ya más de tres años, no se que pensará y necesito para ver si arreglo la casa, que se ésta cayendo."

65. JCT to PCE, 29 December 1963, CFP. "Paco que paso con el dinero que te iba a mandar Jesús aqui no ha llegdo nada dime si siempre no manda nada, para saber . . . ya te digo he estado esperando esos centavos que Jesus te prometio y nada."

66. JCT to PCE, 11 January 1963, CFP. "Juan aqui está en la casa, y quiero que le ayuden arreglar su entrada por eso quiero ir a Guadalajara, a ver si me apalabro con el Lic. Vergara y si no tu tio Pablo dice nos consigué una carta de trabajo o lo que se necesite para la tramitación del Pasaporte de parte de los Estados Unidos, nada más quiero que me ayuden con dinero, haber si es possible arreglarale a Juan por que aqui tu saves que no trabaja en nada y necesita dinero, yo es imposible darle todo lo que necesita, por eso yo les pido que me ayuden para el."

67. JC to PCE, 23 January 1963, CFP.

68. A thorough search of contemporary Aguascalientes newspapers demonstrates that they offered little information on immigration policies and practices. As José admitted on occasion, he gained his insight from word of mouth. See *El Heraldo de Aguascalientes* and *El Sol del Centro*.

69. See, for instance, Rubén Salazar, "Four Farm Groups Sue Wirtz over Mexican Labor," *Los Angeles Times*, 11 December 1963, A1, 8; and Rubén Salazar, "Controversy on Bracero Program Stirs Fear of 'Grapes of Wrath' Era," *Los Angeles Times*, 19 July 1964, F1, 2.

70. JCT to PCE, 29 December 1963, CFP. "Paco no dejes de gestionar con Emanuel Braude el asunto, ya te mandare el Domicilio y el Num. de Telefono."

71. JCT to PCE, 7 May 1964, CFP. "Referente el asunto para Juan tu hermano, he sabido que parece que ya hay más chanza de arreglar, siempre te encargo haber y si se le puede arreglar, ya nos estaremos comunicando."

72. For more on the Immigration Act of 1965 generally, see Ngai, *Impossible Subjects*, 258–64. For how it applied to people of Mexican origin, see Johnson, "The Beginning of the End."

73. Reichert and Massey, "History and Trends," 479; and Cerrutti and Massey, "Trends in Mexican Migration," 25.

74. JCT to PCE, 26 April 1965, CFP. "[T]e aviso, que según una carta que le escribió Braude a un sujeto de aqui, parece que pronto van a quitar la famosa forma 320, le dice al fulano, que el que tenga en los Estados Unidos algún pariente, hermano o padre a cualquier pariente, cercano, y que este legalmente en los Estados

Unidos, o sea Nacional, con much facilidad le puede arreglar al pariente que quiera tomar Visa, you mismo vi la carta de Braude, ojalá y sea cierto."

75. JCT to PCE, 15 June 1964, CFP. "[D]espués de que tanto que batalla uno para arreglar, ojalá y que quiten esa forma, que es la que dá lata, conforme la quiten, tienes que hacer la lucha para ver si es posible arregle tu hermano."

76. JCT to PCE, 6 August 1964, CFP. "[N]o quiere trabajar, él lo sabe yo ni modo de exigirle."

77. JCT to PCE, 15 January 1964, CFP. "[L]e mandé cuatro cientos pesos que me pidió para venirse para la casa."

78. JCT to PCE, 27 August 1964, CFP. "[S]aves que Juan tu hermano se vá para Mexicali, parece que tiene el huevo quebrado no me afloja con sacarme dinero, a tal grado que ya casi me quebró, porque para todo es de puro dinero, pero yo creo que es lo último que le doy."

79. JCT to PCE, 6 April 1963, CFP. "Paco dile a José que si son afectos a que le juguemos a Loteria para el 5 de mayo me Mandan para comprar un Cachito 'pero pronto.'" JCT to PCE, 18 April 1963, CFP. "[M]e dices que mande comprar dos cachitos para el Sorteo del día cinco de mayo, hasi lo hice y cuestan cien pesos los dos o sea cincuenta pasos cada cacho[.]" JCT to PCE, 6 June 1963, CFP.

80. JCT to PCE, 15 June 1964, CFP. "Mira mandame, siquiera un Dolarito para la Vacuna de Pichirilo y el Duque."

81. JCT to PCE, 25 December 1962, CFP. "Me informas que ya arreglaste tu entrada, ahora a trabajar y juntar centavos, por que es como se hace algo en la vida."

82. JCT to PCE, 9 July 1963, CFP. "Paco me dices que tienes Carro y que es usado, ésta bueno nada más que esté de buen uso[.]"

83. JCT to PCE, 15 January 1964, CFP. "[M]e dices que ya estas trabajando, cuida tu trabaja y lo que ganas cuida[.]"

84. JCT to PCE, 9 March 1965, CFP. "Referente que esta llendo a la escuela, haces bien de instruirte, y si puedes estudiar la Mecánica, está bien."

85. JCT to PCE, 20 November 1962, CFP. A perusal of *Selecciones* from the early 1960s indicates that the articles were Spanish translations of selected articles from U.S. magazines such as *Life*, *Parents*, and *Redbook*, short stories, and news from a variety of outlets.

86. JCT to PCE, 9 March 1965, CFP. "Paco ya tenia mucho pendiente de ti por motivo a que no me contestabas, ya teniamos cuidado, pero ya recibí tu carta y ya nos consolamos." "[N]o dejes de contestar aunque sea nada más el sobre con eso sabemos que estas bien."

87. Gerber, "Acts of Deceiving," 323.

88. JCT to PCE, 26 September 1963, CFP. "[A]caba de vender toda la propiedad, yo creo que viene llendo."

89. JCT to PCE, 27 August 1964, CFP. "Te aviso que ya servicio de Telegrafo aqui en Calvillo . . . se puede ofrecer a la nada."

90. For when José realizes that his father is ill, see JCE to MCA, 27 July 1965, CFP. "Yo lla sabia de que mi papa estaba enfermo desde cuando tu me platicaste de tu mama."

91. Goldstein, *Genes and Disease*, 22.

92. Ibid., 36, 64–66. For more on Parkinson's, see Querejeta Villagómez, *Historia de la enfermedad*; Sharma, *Parkinson's Disease*; and Parkinson's Disease Information, Parkinson's Disease History, http://www.parkinsons.org/parkinsons-history.html.

93. Villagómez, *Historia de la enfermedad*, 215.

94. JCT to PCE, 9 March 1965, CFP. "[E]n tu casa seguimos mal, . . . mi mano ya no me sirve tengo un fuerte Neuritis, y nomás me está temblando, me estoy haciendo la lucha haber si es posible el que me componga, si no Dios sabrá."

95. Goldstein, *Genes and Disease*, 70–72.

96. JCT to PCE, 26 March 1965, CFP. "[H]e ido a Guadalajara, por unas tres o cuatro veces, y me dijo el Dr, un Neurologo, que es necesidad de operación y debe ser en la cabeza, y yo no me resuelvo no me duele ni nada, nada más que no me sirve mucho."

97. JCE to MCA, 22 August 1965, CFP. "[H]e handado poco triste pues mí papá está enfermo y casi sin esperanza de aliviarse según me dice fue a Mexico y no se mejora."

98. JCE to PCE, 6 March 1963, CFP. "Sali de Mex. el domingo a las 12 . . . y llegue aqui el lunes a las 12 de la noche, hice 30 horas has aquí; dormi 6 horas en el camino[.]"

99. JCT to PCE, 25 August 1965, CFP. "[S]igo algo malo, yo sea por Diós. Mira Paco no hayo que hacer con esta enfermedad si me vieras no me conoces como me encuentro de agotado, y estoy confin ir a Guadalajara haber si me es posible conseguir mi salud, y conforme puedan no dejen de venir para vernos." "Ya te seguiré avisando conforme siga de mi enfermedad."

100. Goldstein, *Genes and Disease*, 16, 45–47, 53–54.

101. Pasaporte Provisional Núm. 72, Visitante . . . los veintidos días del mes de Marzo del año de mil novecientos sesenta y seis [22 de Marzo de 1966], in author's personal collection.

102. Goldstein, *Genes and Disease*, 40–42, 58–61. For more on the role of pesticides, see Stetka, "Parkinson's Disease and Pesticides."

103. JCE to MCA, 14 June 1966, CFP. "[H]ace 8 dias le llame por telefono a mi mama y dice que no saven ahun que tiene mi papá no han encontrado nada, solo le estan controlando el 'Diabetis [.]'"

104. JCE to PCE, 25 August 1966, CFP. "[C]reo que ya no tiene azucar en la sangre solo . . . [la] queja es el estomago hace poco lo llevé a La Chona a ver una enfermera que es muy buena para curar y le dió unas gotas pero creo que sigue igual[.]"

105. LE to PCE, 18 September 1966, CFP. "[Q]ue le vamos a ser nimodo[.]"

106. JCE to PCE, 5 November 1966, CFP; JCE to PCE, 27 December 1966, CFP; and JCE to PCE, 28 February 1967, CFP.

107. JCT to PCE, 31 December 1966, CFP.

108. LE to PCE, 5 November 1966, CFP. "Pues tu papa sigue igual de su comida come vien nomas no allamos que darle mira se toma 4 huevos y 3 jelatina y leche galletas y un jacecui quiere puro vueno y de todos modos dise que no queda agusto y todo tan caro asi es que no allo que aser."

109. Parkinson's Disease Dementia, http://www.alz.org/dementia/parkinsons -disease-symptoms.asp; and Hamilton, "Can a Cancer Drug Reverse Parkinson's and Dementia?"

110. LE to PCE, 10 March 1967, CFP. "[H]ijo quiero decirlé que tu Papa ya tiene dias que esta mas enfermo y ay ratos en que no sabe ni lo que dice ni lo que quiere, en una palabra, ay ratos que parece que pierde todo conocimiento." "[Y]o te digo esto para que estes prevenido por si algo llegara a pasar pero no quiero que te destantees en tu trabajo por venir nada mas por que esté enfermo[.]"

111. AST to LE, 18 February 1967, CFP. "[D]ile a Jose que . . . siempre pido a Diosito por el . . . te mando 4 dolares para que te que alludes en algo."

112. JCT to PCE, 16 July 1967, CFP. "[A]qui en Mexicali hay una mujer que cura muchas enfermedades[.]" "[C]on esta señora viene gente desde muy lejos y ha curado a muchos, yo dijiera que seria bueno traer a mi papa al fin que no cobra caro[.]"

113. Ibid. "Paco si puedes mandar a mi papa unos 10—a 15 Dls porque me manda decir que necesita dinero yo voy a mandarle aunque sea unos 10 Dls y mas delante como pueda lo ayudaré[.]"

114. PS Interview, Calvillo, Aguascalientes, 12 February 2009.

115. MCE Interview, Calvillo, Aguascalientes, 12 February 2009.

116. PCE Interview, San José, California, 1 August 2015.

Chapter Four

1. AA to PCE, 6 April 1963, CFP. "Mira Paco no creas que estoy desesperada o impaciente por que no vienes simplemente te lo digo porque en algunas cartas dices que vienes pronto y a la otra ya que no vienes, no lo niego tenia ganas de que vinieras ahora para la fiesta pero ya que no puedes ní modo de que lo hagas no quiero pedirte un impocible . . . [o] contajiarte con mi tristeza[.]"

2. Ibid. "[P]or lo que veo tú lo que haz tratado siempre es buscar la forma de que manera puedes erirme y reirte de mi, pero esto se acabó no dejaré que me sigas tratando en la forma que lo haces, siempre me das a entender que solo yo tengo interes en lo nuestro y por lo tanto no quiero ser una rogona, y creo que hasta te hago la vida pesada . . . no creas que estoy enojada te lo digo sin rencor solo creo que esto es lo mejor para bien de los dos[.]" "(A Dios Paco)[.]"

3. Osorio, "Postcards in the Porfirian Imaginary"; and Stampa, "El correo en Mexico," 17. For more, see, for instance, Bose, "Origenes del correo terrestre"; and Gojman de Backal and Bonilla, *Historia del correo en México.*

4. For studies on the mail, telephone, and telegraph systems in Mexico in the twentieth century, see Muñoz Gómez, *El correo, el teléfono y el telégrafo*; and Cardenas de la Peña, *El teléfono.*

5. Hernández López, *Monografía del Municipio del Calvillo*, 141; and MCE Interview, Calvillo, Aguascalientes, 19 September 2015.

6. For more on the Mexican economy's collapse in the 1980s and 1990s, see, for instance, Haber and Klein, *Mexico since 1980*; and the introduction to this book.

7. For more on the decline of the mail service, see Consumer Postal Council, "Index of Postal Freedom, Mexico."

8. United States Postal Service, *The United States Postal Service*, 3–6, 10–11.

9. Ibid., 11–16.

10. Ibid., 19–31.

11. Ibid., 33, 41. For calls for privatization, see Hudgins, *Mail at the Millennium*.

12. For more on José and Conchita's relationship, see chapters 1 and 2.

13. For more on masculinity and migration, see C. Rosas, "El desafío de ser hombre y no migrar"; Pérez, "Crossing the Border"; and D. Cohen, *Braceros*.

14. Gerber, *Authors of Their Lives*, 317, 321.

15. AA to PCE, 22 November 1962, CFP. "Me habías dicho que regresabas el mes anterior[.]" "Por favor me contestas lo mas pronto que puedas para que me digas cuando te vienes aunque no lo creas tengo deseos de bolverte a ver por aquí[.]"

16. AA Interview, Modesto, California, 14 June 2008.

17. AA to PCE, 22 November 1962, CFP. "[V]ueno creo que me estoy poniendo sentimental . . . no habia por que me mintieras al desirme que te ivas a venir el mes pasado puedes desirme si es que ya no quieres que te escriva por favor dimelo te prometo no molestarte mas."

18. Ibid. "[T]e ruego me perdones mis tonterias." "Creeme que me da pena con tigo por que creo que te cuesta trabajo entenderle a mi letra que no es letra son puros garavatos y tanta falta de octagrafia y lo mal dictados que ago las cartas pero espero me perdones todos mis errores por que como tu sabes soy una ignorante[.]"

19. Ibid. "[C]reo que ya te estoy haciendo un periodico a todo esto no creo que te interese mucho todo lo que de mi dependa ya que ni siquiera me dijiste la verdad de cuando te víenes[.]" "[S]e despide de ti quíen te estima. Y no me agas caso son bromas[.]"

20. AA to PCE, 2 December 1962, CFP. "[N]o tengas pendiente de que me consiga otro no hay quien se ocupe de mi en cambio tu dime cuantas te has conquistado[.]"

21. Ibid. "[M]ira mis melodias favoritas son con la Sonora Santanera 'que te valla bien' y con Paco Cañedo 'que Hinumano[.]'" "[F]ijate que estubieron los tres Diamantes en Guadalajara el sabado yo los estaba escuchando[.]"

22. Ibid. "No se te olbide mandarme tu foto o solo que no quieras que te conteste no lo hagas[.]" "[S]e despide de ti tu peor es nada que tonto dicen verte mejor que escribírte."

23. PCE to AA, 24 December 1962, CFP. "[E]n realidad creo que me siento muy solo, ojalá y si quiere Dios, pronto estaré en Calvillo, te extraño mucho, y siento no haberte mandado ni una tarjeta, pero la presente es portadora de mis sentimientos asia ti."

24. Ibid. "Tal vez tu creas que soy muy falso en mis promesas, pero si no voy este año a allá es que en realidad me lo impidan mis problemas economicos, y creeme que quisiera estar contigo, principalmente este dia 24[.]"

25. Ibid. "Quiero decirte como la última vez, que tú eres la única, y si por suerte el destino nos tiene otro rumbo, que sea bueno, ya que mi cariño ha sido para ti, y si tu llegaras a no tomarme en cuenta creemelo que seria el fin para mi, pues como tu ves, eres la unica que ha sido mi felicidad, y es lo único que me alienta a seguir viviendo, y si Dios no disponse otra cosa, mi felicidad estará contigo."

26. Ibid. "Creo que me he hecho demasiadas ilusiones contigo, pues creo que tu estuviste traicionandome con uno de mis amigos, y creo que fue algo breve lo qe me engañaste, pues al poco tiempo te convenciste de que era algo dificil entender otro cariño que para ti era diferente, y que lo que queria era tan solo probar su tiro en el amor y la tración, yo sabre cuidarme de esas cosas, pues en mi corta vida e visto que quién más aprecia uno es el primero que lo traíciona[.]"

27. Ibid. "[R]ecuerda a el Pinole que quiso hacer una canallada, que afortunadamente fuiste los suficiente fuerte para sobreponerte a la tentación y te conservaste integra para mi, tan solo, y es lo que me dio fuerzas para seguirte queriendo y poder confiar en ti." "Soy tuyo hasta que el destino lo quiera."

28. AA to PCE, 25 December 1962, CFP. "[Y]a no te escribo mas por que si me pongo a desirte todo lo que te tengo que desir . . . no cave en el papel[.]"

29. AA to PCE, 13 January 1963, CFP. "No te de pena dejarme de contestar haslo a la hora que tu quieras no me tengas lastima que según veo es lo que quieres." "No te gastes tu dinero para un simple recado digamos, esto te lo digo por que los mios son periodicos[.]"

30. AA to PCE, 26 January 1963, CFP. "[N]o es cosa que no me importes pero creo que no es justo lo que haces mandarme dos o tres letras cuando yo te escribo hasta el hultima renglon[.]"

31. In the nineteenth and early twentieth centuries in the United States, neurasthenia, a form of "nervousness" but with links to physical exhaustion, emerged as a health concern among the upper classes. See Bederman, *Manliness and Civilization*. Among Latinas and Latinos, some scholars view nervios as a "folk illness." See, for instance, Dresp, "Nervios as a Culture-Bound Syndrome."

32. PCE Interview, San José, California, 20 April 2008. Paco also fell victim to los nervios. He described an attack as a state of anxiety followed by intense itchiness over his entire body. That attack came on soon after migrating to San José, California, from Brawley, California, and not knowing his future economic state.

33. AA to PCE, 26 January 1963, CFP. "[P]erdoname si en algo to ofendi en la otra pero no fue mi intención, creo que estoy muy nervioza por eso cometo tanto error pero tu eres bueno y sabras perdonarme."

34. Ibid. "[B]ueno ya no te escribo mas por que mamá me vio haciendo la carta y nomas me esta regañando y no se ni lo que estoy haciendo."

35. AA to PCE, 27 March 1963, CFP. "Contestame mejor a mi casa si me haces favor[.]"

36. AA to PCE, 26 January 1963, CFP. "Es todo por ahora se despide de ti tu novia que no te olbidara jamas."

37. For more on gender ideologies in Mexico, see, for instance, Porter, *Working Women in Mexico City*; Arrom, *The Women of Mexico*; Lispett-Rivera and Johnson, *The Faces of Honor*; Lavrin, *Marriage and Sexuality*; and Twinam, *Public Lives, Private Secrets*.

38. AA to PCE, 20 February 1963, CFP. "Con el que platico algunas veces es con el maldito Che (digo Perico) pero supe que dijo que se va ha casar con migo y poreso ya casi no platico con el porque me da pena tu sabes como soy de chiviada." "Asi es de que no te fies mucho porque anda tras mis huesos[.]"

39. Ibid. "Por tus cartas ní te preocupes las tengo debajo de el colchon, no te aseguro que esten completos por que ya se los an llevado las chinches[.]" "[N]o estaba enojada porque no me habias contestado pensé que no te había llegado la mia por que me parece que no le puse tu nombre y estaba pensando que se me iba a regresar, con el cuento de que nomas me estaban regañando no me acorde hasta despues[.]" "[L]a canción que me dices te gusta cada vez que boy a la paletería la marco[.]"

40. AA to PCE, 18 March 1963, CFP. "Paco no entiendo porque dices que you no ise la otra quiero pensar que estabas muy borracho para salirme con eso[.]" "[S]eguro fue porque ise la letra mas chiquita para que me cupieran los mentados poemas[.]" "[Y]a no pienses que pongo quien me los aga."

41. Ibid. "[M]ira te voy a decir lo que casi estoy seguro ya te mandaron decir que me ven platicando con un gorrudo . . . esto te lo digo porque tu hermano me vio, es tan terco que ya no puedo salir ni a la puerta porque ya me esta esperando y el error estubo en que le dije que no me gusta tener novio y que no puedo querer a nadie y me va saliendo con que algún dia puedo llegar a quererlo yo pence que con ésto no me molestaría mas y creo que cada dia es peor . . . le doy buenos cortones y sigue en la misma dice que me tengo que casar con el realmente no se como quitárme esta plaga . . . me pone de nerbios."

42. AA to PCE, 27 March 1963, CFP. "Tenia una pequeña esperanza de que al fin pudieras venir pero creo que me voy a quedar esperando toda la vida, espero no molestarte mas[.]" "[D]etodos modos te digo que dia es la fiesta es el 23[.]"

43. Ibid. "[C]uaquier dia voy a ir nomas no digas que soy presumida pero yo tambien ya tengo enque viajar no creas que nomas tu tienes[.]" "[M]e despido de ti y me quedo esperando que algun dia puedas venir aunque te dije que ya no te hablaria mas de esto[.]"

44. Dreby, "Gender and Transnational Gossip."

45. Lispett-Rivera and Johnson, *The Faces of Honor*; Lavrin, *Marriage and Sexuality*; and Twinam, *Public Lives, Private Secrets*.

46. ALE to PCE, 15 September 1962, CFP. "Mira en primer lugar te voy a platicar de Chona ella está triste y desconzolada pués le falta su teporocho y aquí esta ahorita en mi casa que tambien es la tuya y dice que ojalá vengas para Diciembre."

47. ALE to PCE, 25 December 1962, CFP. "En cuanto a Tú: Lombricienta te voy a decir que la verdad yo no he visto que te haga de Vil Chivo los Tamales y es la pura verdad."

48. PM to PCE, 30 December 1962, CFP. "Fijese que ahora en la fiesta un dia estaba yo parado platicando con la raza en el jardin cuando pasó su TEPOROCHA acompañada pero al tiempo que la vi el se quito y no dió chance de decirle que me la iva a pagar pues me dijo ¡SANGRON VIEJO NO QUERIA IRSE! asi que eso indica que todavia la sigue siendo fiel, no vaya Ud. a ser el que le juege rudo."

49. ALE to PCE, undated, ca. March 1963, CFP. "[M]ira está bueno que si todavía le escribes a Chona y si es tú jiotosa le mandes decir que no sea tan . . . de leona pues todas las noches se la pasa platicando con el sangrón ese que te cai tan gordo y a veces pienso que te está haciendo los tamales de vil Chivo con el batito sangrepesao ese que también a mi me cai bién gordo el hijo de su tarata."

50. ALE to PCE, 5 March 1963, CFP. "Mira Paco, Chona te quiere en verdad pero se halla entra la espada y la pared, y es que tú ya sabes como son las hermanas de ella que nada más burlándose de la gente y en ellas no se fijan, como dicen por hay la Zorra no se ve su cola y le dicen que nosea taruga y que se consiga otro por hay y que si te quiere mucho por que no te manda decir que vengas por ella y te matrimonies, y así se acaban las dificultades."

51. ALE to PCE, 8 May 1963, CFP. "Yo me di cuenta cuando tu canija Espátula te empezó a hacer 'Guey' y desde entonces no me ha vuelto a dirijir la palabra[.]"

52. Ibid. "[S]e hacia del rogar pero luego que toda la bola de Dráculas perdón de hermanas le dijeron que ese si le convenía ya ni se hizo del rogar[.]" "[H]ay tienes al pelao bién parao con toda la familia. El se llama, bueno el nombre creo que no te interezará pero es hijo de [*&^%] Antonio Flores."

53. ALE to PCE, 26 May 1963, CFP. "Mira compadre, sabe que a mí me gusta decir la verdad respecto de las teporochas y pienso que tal vez el señorito . . . tenga muchas ganas de 'cazarse' pero francamente ella no parece que se le olvide por un momento su pior es nada y tal vez tenga la leve esperanza de que cuando vengas le digas que . . . bueno tú ya sabes que . . . ¿o no?" "Y a mí hasta ahorita no me ha vuelto a dirijir la palabrosia ni siquiera mi tía doña Nata—lía, así es que ya no me doy cuenta de lo que piense tú ex-Jiotosa respecto de tí." "[P]rocura no aguitarte tanto consiguete una jiotosa cuando tengas chanza y así te olvidas de cosas tristes[.]"

54. ALE to PCE, 12 July 1963, CFP. "Pués sabes mano que, tal parece que a tú ex-jiotosa no se olvida ni un momento de su pior es naranjas porque a mí ya me saluda . . . y me preguntó que cuando ibas a venir y le dije que del mes de Septiembre en adelante y se puso a reparar como una mula de puro gusto y dijo que te quiere tal vez más que antes[.]" "[M]e dice que le enseñe las cartas que tú me mandes, para ver como te expresas tú de su respetable perzona."

55. ALE to PCE, 26 July 1963, CFP. "Pués sabes que ahorita le acabo de enseñar la carta a tú exteporocha y dijo que habías quedado muy bien en las fotos, solamente que te le hacías mas flaco pero que estabas igual de guapo que antes y dice que tiene unas ganas locas de verte y me dijo te preguntara si vas a venir de cierto del mes de Sep."

56. Ibid. "[D]ice que te quiere mucho que ojalá y tú no la olvides nunca que ella aunque lejos siempre está junto de tí y cerca pero muy cerca de tú corazón, aunque tú no la quieras."

57. MSS to PCE, 16 July 1964, CFP. "Paco me preguntas en tu carta que si Chona tíene novio pues sí, sí tíene per es nadamas para pasar el rato porque ella me lo dijo. [S]abes que por fin ella lloro por tí cuando le dijo un hermano tuyo que te híbas o te bas a casar con una de la Chona es síerto o no es síerto."

58. Ibid. "[F]ijate que anoche cuando salimos del cine le preguntamos a Toño que si hera síerto y nos dijo que el no se daba cuenta, pero yo creo que tu nos sacas de dudas 'o no[.]' "

59. MSS to PCE, 21 September 1964, CFP. "[F]ijate que esta Chona se corto el pelo, y se be mas guapa, y dice que sí quieres le escribas tu y que si te contesta con mucho gusto y dice que recibas un abrazo de su parte eso es, fue lo que me dijo que tu le escríbas primero."

60. IH to PCE, 5 June 1964, CFP. "[O]yes Paco 'ya conoces sus mujeres malas de San José a poco no conoses los secretos como en san Luis Sonora te acuerdas de cuando fuiste pues a eso me refiero mandame decir[.]"

61. A. Rosas, *Abrazando el Espíritu*; and D. Cohen, *Braceros*, 118–42.

62. MCA to JCE, 28 January 1964, CFP. "P.D. Saludeme a Paco y dígale por favor que si no es mucha molestia me escriba. Si me hace favor[.]"

63. JCE to MCA, 2 February 1964, CFP. "P.D. Paco no está aqui si no con gusto le dava tu recado, él está en San José, Calif se fue pará allá desde Julio del año pasado."

64. JCE to MCA, undated, ca. April 1964, CFP. "Saludos con mucho afecto para Chonita y dile que si yo pudiera hacer que Paco y ella se reconciliaran con mucho gusto lo haria dile que no pierda las esperansas pues yo se que Paco la quiere al menos cuando estuvo aqui se lo dijo a una persona que le tiene mucha confiansa."

65. MCA to JCE, 13 April 1964, CFP. "Dice 'Chifis' que gracias por tus palabras de aliento que espera que sea asi como tu lo dices."

66. JCE to MCA, 22 April 1964, CFP. "[T]ell Chifis I really wish some day she and my brother get togother and get mariage."

67. MCA to JCE, 3 May 1964, CFP. "[S]erá mejor que le digas que llo te mando preguntar o haber como inventas porque creo que mi hermanita desconfía demasiado de esa niña."

68. JCE to MCA, 10 May 1964, CFP. "Queria decirte que siento mucho no poderle decirle a Paco lo que Chifis quiere pues no se como hacerle y creeme que deberas lo siento y saves porque porque pienso que si le escribo a Paco y le pregunto creo que va a pensar que como yo . . . me intereso en el y Chifis pues . . . entre nosotros muy pocas veces nos hemos tratado de estos asuntos[.]"

69. MCA to JCE, 24 May 1964, CFP. "[M]il disculpas y tambien te pido olvidemos eso ¿quieres?"

70. JCE to MCA, 26 August 1964, CFP. "No quiero ni mensionar de eso que dices que mi hermano me calló muy mal y ojalá y no sepa Paco que ya quiesiera Juan ser como el."

71. MCA to JCE, 3 March 1966, CFP. "[F]ijate que la chifis tiene un novio del Ojo Caliente bien que nos reimos de él porque le dice ay te huacho y arriendate no es cosa para dar risa pero en fin que le vamos hacer pero dice que siquiera para no pasárcela tan triste[.]"

72. MCA to JCE, 4 June 1966, CFP. "[A] por sierto que la mujer se me hace que es la del forestal la que fue a Malpaso el día del paseo andava bien cuete y me dijo que lo hiba a saber mi novio porque estábamos tomando refresco en la carpa donde estaban un conjunto se me hiso muy chistosa y luego Chona que le va diciendo que quien la habia comisionando para que nos cuidara se le puso media enojada."

73. AA to PCE, 6 September 1966, CFP. "Pues como tu ya haz de estar enterado de la estupidez que acaban de cometer nuestros hermanitos me ciento sumamente abatida porque como tu haz de saber Conchita aparte de ser mi hermana era para mi la única hamiga . . . con quien yo contava aúnque siempre hayamos vivido . . . como las bolas del billar peleando y ciempre juntas[.]"

74. AA Interview, Modesto, California, 14 June 2008.

75. AA to PCE, 6 September 1966, CFP. "[E]ncuanto los veas me escribas porque tambien me he quedado muy preocupada por Concha pues cuando salio de aqui estava en un estado de animo muy lamentable y mucho me temo que hasta pueda enfermar por el golpe tan duro que ha resibido hal tener que dejar todo lo que era parte de si misma." "[T]u sabes mamá que es lo que más le a dever dolido dejar[.]"

76. AA to PCE, 6 September 1966, CFP. "[A]busando de tu confianza quisiera que habersi te hes posible ir pronto para donde ellos viven para que me informes de como se encuentran pues estoy segura que si le escribo a concha o ella escribe no va ha decirme la verdad es poreso que acudo a ti y sabiendote lo alegre que eres estoy segura que la dara mucho gusto que tu bayas a visitarlos para que se distraiga un poco más, no creas que píenso que José no íra ha poner todo lo que este de su parte para que no este tan aguitada tu sabes asi le ara sentir un poco más que no está tan sola[.]"

77. Ibid., "[Y]o creo que con tanta remendación ya pensaras que me gustaste para niñera pero tu sabes, estas en tu derecho de no hayudarme en lo que te pido, de ser asi te ruego que te olbides de que te he molestado y agas de cuenta que no te he escrito y mandandote decír tanta mensada detodos modos no olbides que si algun dia necesitaras de mi alluda ya que es poco en lo que puedo serbirte no basiles un momento que yo estoy para serbirte a ti y a los tuyos[.]"

78. AA to PCE, 9 October 1966, CFP. "*Chulopon* no sabes el gusto que resibo siempre que escribes y aun más ahora que me mandaste tú foto en la cual estas muy bien[.]"

79. Ibid. "[Q]uiero preguntarte algo si no es mucha indiscreción ¿que es lo que estas estudíando?" "Claro que si no quieres decir por algun motive ni modo me resignare a quedarme en hayunas[.]" "[S]abes me daría mucho gusto que todos tus sueños de grandeza se te cumplieran sería motivo de satisfacción para ti y para todos los tuyos, no puedo más que admirarte por se tan estudioso y a la vez trabajador y . . . el de ser tan buen hijo[.]"

80. Ibid. "[E]ncambio yo voy de mál en peor cada dia yo creo que jamas en mi cochína vida voy a salir de nada siempre he sído una ignorante cómo tú ya lo sabes pero ni modo, confio en que tú algun día me paces un poco de siencía y eso si es que me la tome cómo medícamento para ber si mejoro un poco."

81. PCE to AA, 1 November 1966, CFP. "I'm studing English and Welding, how do you like that; is good; don't you think so skinny? that's the way I think I'm going to make you happy and don't ask me questions like that, It makes me feel so bad, tha I think we are strangers[.]" "[Q]uiero que me hables con confianza no como si fueramos nada más amigos[.]" "[P]or eso que quiero que todas las cartas las detruyas y que nadie las vea, asi para que lo que tu digas sea lo que tu sientas y nadie malinterprete mis palabras quiero que tengas confianza conmigo y que me quieras mas de lo que ahorita me quieres, y si algún dia no me quieres o no te agrado sea por decision tuya no por la de otra persona que lo puede hacer unicamente con el fin de burlarse de ti[.]"

82. AA to PCE, 24 November 1966, CFP. "[N]o se que me pasa cada vez que resibo notícias tuyas es como si de pronto todo cambíara veo todo de colores mas vivos, el sol mas lumínoso los árboles más hermosos bueno todo me parece más lindo aún

en los dias que estoy más fatigada y mas fastidiada con solo pensar en ti o ponerme a releer tu cartas todo desaparece al momento 'a' por que sabes no he quemado las cartas las he esto guardando pero no te preocupes nadie las be que no sea yo." "¿Vaz a venir para dic.? me gustaria mucho que lo hicieras tengo tantas ganas de bolverte a ver que yo creo que jamas te vere[.]"

83. The insight on powerlessness among migrants and letter writers left behind comes from Cancian, *Families, Lovers, and Their Letters*, 112.

84. PCE to AA, 19 December 1966, CFP. "Pues hay tienes que se vino Navidad y le he pedido a Santa Claus qe me haga el fabor de dejarme como regalo un carro nuevo para ir a verte pronto, pero dada la casualidad que me porte tan mal que dudo y me lo traiga y dime tu que le pediste, casi creo advinar y se me me imagine que es un chamacón casi como yo, o no?"

85. Ibid. "Ayer o antier me fuí a un baile que hacen para navidad para todos los estudiantes malos como yo y me diverti en cantidad solo que tu no veniste, pues que pasa que me hiciste esperar y esperar, como lo hubiera gozado pero te pusiste tus moños y no veniste ... pero ni modo tal vez un dia no muy lejano nos veamos otra vez."

86. Ibid. "Cuando salgo del trabajo me encuentro una muchacha que se parece a ti y me dan ganas de hablarle pensando que tu eres pero luego pienso que tu no eres y pues no le hablo."

87. AA to PCE, 20 March 1967, CFP. "Ahora que me dices que ibas a venir no sabes cuanto me hubiera gustado que así hubiera sucedido."

88. AA to PCE, 23 June 1967, CFP. "[T]e voy a pedir un ultimo fabor en el nombre del cariño que un dia dijiste tenerme y espero que al menos eso no me lo negaras porque tu sabes que mil veces un desengaño que estar con la incertidumbre y te haceguro que despues que digas la ultima palabra jamas bolvere a molestarte[.]"

89. Cancian, *Families, Lovers, and Their Letters*, 112.

Chapter Five

1. Cybelle Fox, "Unauthorized Welfare," 1052–53.

2. RMS to PCE, 24 August 1962, CFP. "[E]stoy esperando carta tulla y nomás no. ¿[Q]ue pasa? ... [A]qui la pasa uno chevere." "[L]lo me acomode por lo pronto en un restaurat aqui en el centro de los angeles no estoy de planta trabajo 3- o 4 dias a la semana gano 1.25 la hora[.]" "P.D. dime si resiviste la tarjeta que te mandé aqui jalo en el [H]ilton[.]" "[F]ijate que el dia que llegué aqui consegui jale de Bas Boy [bus boy] en WooliWod [Woolworth's] pero no pude por falta del seguro social y ahora lla lo saqué puedo trabajar donde quiera es lo unico que piden, el SS pues[.]" "[A]qui vieras ay millones y todas jalan más que parejo."

3. Ibid. "[L]lo me vine por Tijuana como tu saves y no uvo vorlote ni mucho menos, te voy a desir mira si tus papeles no estan algo aventajados mejor vente a Tijuana ay sacas tu mica local y lla estas aqui en [L]os [A]ngeles." "Fijate que aqui la migra no te molesta nunca porque casi puro Chicano ay aqui[.]" "[A]nimate paco aqui esta la movida más que buena ... aqui es grandisisimo como no te imaginas[.]"

4. Levitt, "Social Remittances."

5. RMS to PCE, 24 August 1962, CFP. "[P]aco espero me contestes luego y que sean unas 5 hojas de carta para saver como esta allá la movida[.]"

6. Pérez, "Crossing the Border"; D. Cohen, *Braceros*; and C. Rosas, "El desafío de ser hombre y no migrar."

7. Gamio, *El inmigrante mexicano*; Sánchez, *Becoming Mexican American*; Ngai, *Impossible Subjects*, 237; Lytle Hernández, *Migra!*; Stern, "Buildings, Boundaries, and Blood"; Stern, "Nationalism on the Line"; Calavita, *Inside the State*; and D. Gutiérrez, *Walls and Mirrors*.

8. For more on repatriation and banishment of Mexicans and Mexican Americans, see Balderrama and Rodríguez, *Decade of Betrayal*; and M. Ramírez, "Contested Illegality."

9. Mitchell, *They Saved the Crops*.

10. Ngai, *Impossible Subjects*, 237.

11. Ibid., 238–39.

12. RMS Interview, Calvillo, Aguascalientes, 5 February 2017.

13. RMS to PCE, 2 February 1963, CFP. "[L]a paso más o menos suave." "[F]ijate que lla metí mi solicitud al consulado y lla me mandaron el primer aviso nada más espero que me llamen para ir a presentarme, aunque no tengo las cartas ní la de sostenimiento ní la de trabajo." "[O]jalá y tu me dieras un norte más o menos donde conseguirlas, mejor si es para jalar en el campo."

14. RMS to PCE, undated, ca. March 1963, CFP. "[A]qui como tu saves vienen muchos residentes y les e encargado las cartas, pero tu saves sin conocerlos."

15. RMS to PCE, undated, ca. January 1963, CFP. "[F]ijate nomás lla quisiera tener mis papeles para andar juntos por allá varias partes de los E.U.A. pero fijate nomás lastima llo creo que de perdido 2 o 3 meses más[.]"

16. Population figures come from the 1960 U.S. Census.

17. RMS to PCE, undated, ca. January 1963, CFP. "[P]laticame como esta todo aqui en Brawley calif, bueno lla me imagino[.]"

18. ALE to PCE, 25 December 1962, CFP. "Espero que me mandes decir que tan suave está el norte[.]"

19. JL to PCE, 20 July 1963, CFP. "[S]abes que tengo ganas de hir a Mexicali pero no me animo tu que me aconsejas que aga[.]"

20. For evidence that he communicated about his work, see PCE to ALE, 22 July 1965, CFP.

21. Personal communication with the Mexican film scholar Sergio de la Mora, 12 December 2016. See also De Usabel, *The High Noon of American Films*, 150–51; and Amador and Blanco, *Cartelera cinematográfica digital*, which provides a list of all films screened in Mexico from the silent era through the 1980s.

22. PCE Interview, San José, California, 12 December 2016. Gamio, *El inmigrante mexicano*, 98, 112, 160.

23. AH to PCE, 18 February 1964, CFP; IH to PCE, 29 March 1964, CFP; IH to PCE, 2 May 1964, CFP. "[S]i puedes prestarme 30.00 o 40.00 dolares aunque sea tu la mitad y Jesús la otra mitad dile a Jesús que si me quiere hacer el favor"; and IH to PCE, 24 May 1964, CFP. "¿[E]s justo eso?"

24. IH to PCE, 5 June 1964, CFP. "[R]ecibi los centavos con los 20 los que tengo ahorrados y los poquitos que junte con eso llego al final de lo que necesito gracias [P]aco pero muchas gracias[.]"

25. IH to PCE, 17 August 1964, CFP; IH to PCE, 20 September 1964, CFP.

26. PS to PCE, undated, ca. December 1962, CFP. "He sabido que le ha ido a todo dar, no sabe cuanto me allegro . . . P.D. Platiqueme en que chambea y si es sierto que la ha ido vien."

27. ALE to PCE, 15 November 1963, CFP. "[E]sperando que al recibirla gozes de Buena salud y tengas tus bolsillos llenos de $$$$$$$$$$$$$$$."

28. JLV to PCE, 17 October 1966, CFP. "[F]ijate que ahorita tengo un apuro y como tu me dijiste ase mucho que cuando tubiera algun apuro te escribiera y ahoralo tengo . . . de perdis unos $100 pesos o 150 pues Chela se enfermo y ni modo[.]"

29. JLV to PCE, 17 December 1962, CFP. "Bueno My Good Forieen [Friend] Good Bay . . . Saludame a the girls." JLV to PCE, 17 February 1964, CFP. "Platicame c[u]antas jiotosas tienes por alla, si ya hisiste tu primera communion o todavia no[.]"

30. ALE to PCE, 5 June 1963, CFP. "[E]spero que cuando vengas para acá nos tengas la sorpresa que ya no les tienes miedo a las Jiotosas y que llegues bién aventado para todo . . . pero no te apures ni digas que eres muy tarugo para las cucarachas[.]"

31. For Mexican immigrants' views of North American women, see Gamio, *El inmigrante mexicano*, 114, 115, 119, 206, 207, 231, 235, 240, 259.

32. ALE to PCE, 3 December 1966, CFP. "[P]latícame si tienes algún detalle, novia o de perdida alguna garbanza, porque se que abundan las piojosas de la nueva ola por allá, de esas que les dicen a Go-Go y que son muy aventadas, asi que debes de tener siquiera una para ruletear."

33. IH to PCE, 5 June 5 1964, CFP. "[O]yes Paco 'ya conoces sus mujeres malas de San José a poco no conoses los secretos como en san Luis Sonora te acuerdas de cuando fuiste pues a eso me refiero mandame decir[.]"

34. RMS to PCE, 6 September 1963, CFP. "[E]spero que tu traes tus chamaconas por aqui pues ojalá y traigas unas 15 o mas."

35. RMS to PCE, 4 August 1964, CFP. "[T]e felisito y ojalá así se porte de vien unos 15 o 20 years."

36. PCE to ALE, 22 July 1965, CFP. "[M]e aventé uno con tu tio Juan echale echale Mendoza el merito y de Julio, fijate nomás que artistas, tambien vi a Irma Serrano[.]"

37. Ibid. "Es lo que me dá coraje con estos chicanos de aqui que la musica buena no les gusta[.]" For more on tensions between Mexican immigrants and U.S.-born Mexican Americans, see Gamio, *El inmigrante mexicano*; and D. Gutiérrez, *Walls and Mirrors*.

38. IH to PCE, 6 March 1964, CFP. "Cal[v]is, Ranch a ver a Juanita."

39. IH to PCE, 29 March 1964, CFP. "[T]u con un carrito mas facil sera ir a ver a los chavalas tu ya te me adelantaste pero ni modo y entonces hasta vamos juntos a 'Calvis, Ranch.' [Y] aver si me traigo de ese pueblito una Cherita alcabo ya me comi a mi novia . . . asi es que ay que probar por otro lado aver que suerte tengo[.]" A few months later, Alfonso again referred to the car, telling Paco to take care of it:

"[D]on't mistreat it for when we go to 'Calvis, Ranch.'" IH to PCE, 20 September 1965, CFP.

40. ALE to PCE, 12 July 1963, CFP. "[Y]o quiero conocerlo y además verte a tí a ver como estás de ponchado con el ejersicio[.]"

41. RMS to PCE, 4 August 1964, CFP. "[F]ijate que hoy amesió [*sic*] el cachetón ponchado ni hablar, habra que arreglar esa llantoa[.]"

42. RMS to PCE, 13 August 1964, CFP. "Saludos a tu super carr y ojalá se siga portando cada dia mejor."

43. ALE to PCE, 11 July 1967, CFP. "Lo felicito por estar estudiando más que por los diplomas y trofeos que puedas sacar en él studio, yo tambien quisiera estudiar, pero no te imaginas los problemas que origina poder realizer tal deseo aqui en la capital . . ."

44. RM to PCE, 26 August 1964, CFP. Original wording in English, along with strikeout and spelling errors, has been transcribed verbatim.

45. RM to PCE, 3 October 1964, CFP. "Te escribo de prisa porque yo creo que al rato salgo con un amigo en su carro a Tijuana, para dilapidar una 100,000,000.00 parte de mi cuantiosa fortuna en las mujeres de la street."

46. RM to PCE, 11 November 1964, CFP. "Fijate que en Lindsay me consegui 2 novias y con las 2 echaba mucho beso; una de ellas tiene 18 floridas primaveras y la otra va a cumplir 15 y la de 15 es maestro en el arte del beso, me daba puros de lenguita. Tengo un chorro de movidas de que platicar contigo; pero ahorita no me acuerdo de más. Es todo por now."

47. MLL to PCE, 29 July 1963, CFP. "Paco me dice que se incuentra solo y triste pues mire aga el animo y deberas benga para aca."

48. RMS Interview, Calvillo, Aguascalientes, 5 February 2017.

49. For more on caló and its use and reception in Mexico, see Mraz, "Today, Tomorrow and Always," 132; and Monsiváis, "Cantinflas and Tin Tan," 51. For more on its gendered meaning and use among Mexican Americans in the United States, see C. Ramírez, "Saying 'Nothin.'"

50. RMS to PCE, 30 July 1963, CFP. "Dime Paco si me podrias conseguir las cartas para en caso de que llamen, mas que yo a ti despues te dispare unas cahuamas[.]"

51. RMS to PCE, 6 September 1963, CFP. "[L]lo aqui estoy muy íngrido (whit my girly frend) y no se que aser, casarme no, pues estoy en la vil chilla[.]" "[L]lo creo que lo mejor fuera irme de aqui legisillos, dime como esta por aqui donde tu estas, si abria chansa de caerte por aqui[.]"

52. Ibid. "[P]ues de lo contrario me pelaria para los angeles, nada más que en los angeles uno solo se síente medio tristón vieras y ase falta alguien con quien basilar y pasar el rato, para no sentirse uno tan lejos del terre bueno tu me entiendes."

53. Ibid. "[M]ira paco si me aviento y logro pasar con favor de Dios, es para hecharnos una temporadita buenisilla y luego pos salirme yo, lla que a todo dar con tus papeles, saves que mi pasaporte todavia lo llevo largo pues ni me an contestado, pues ay mucha gente dioquís aqui en el paso y vecindad." "[E]ntonces en serio [P]aco si vez tu que se pueda que fuera yo pues nomás me dises, por que de plano Juárez lla no me save a nada en las condisiónes que me encuentro[.]" "I see you my fine and good friend . . . p.d. contestame luego paco please[.]"

54. RMS to PCE, 25 September 1963, CFP. "[M]ira [P]aco lla compre carro para falluquiar aqui boy a pasar fruta del otro lado aqui al Mercado ojalá y le agarre el modo al jale este."

55. Ibid. "[A]quí en Juárez lla esta casi todo Calvillo vieras cuante jente ay de por allá el terre."

56. Cross and Sandos, *Across the Border*, 33–34.

57. RMS to PCE, 28 October 1963, CFP. "[M]i carro se jodio y mi fui a la lona peor que K.O.T."

58. RMS to PCE, 24 January 1964, CFP. "[P]ero llo de todos modos me voi a abentar aver como me ba."

59. Ibid. "[F]ijate que llo fracase con mi carro en la fayuca pues se me desbielo el carajo y a la lona me fui . . . ahora estoy aqui de empleado en la peluqueria de mi tio pero no sale ni pa tamales de miercoles esta muy sobado el negosio." "[F]ijate que lla cumpli un año con mi solisitud → y no me dan ni la más leve esperanza . . . no ay mas que entrarle de mojado si me toca suerte paso pues a jalar y si no ni modo."

60. RMS to PCE, 5 February 1964, CFP. "[A]ndo de bala perdida aquí en Juariles[.]" "[V]oi a ver si jalo aqui, para alivianarme y entrarle por la mera puerta."

61. RMS to PCE, undated, ca. February 1964, CFP. "[P]ues mi pasaporte ní modo no se pudo me venden las cartas a 300.00 dolares así tu crees cuando paso." "[C]uentame como esta aquí el ambiente, y ahora si si Dios quiere por aquí nos vimos. A y ademas ay tienes que lla se murió mí novía. [N]i modo, en paz descanse."

62. RMS to PCE, 18 February 1964, CFP. "[F]ijate que tengo aqui en Culiacan 10 dias chocamos de este lado de Durango a 100 k[ilo]m[etro]s no huvo muertos pero si heridos de gravedad llo solo me desloqué el brazo derecho[.]"

63. Ibid. "[S]í te contara el desmadre que me paso todo el camino, llorabas mejor no te lo cuento."

64. RMS to PCE, 12 March 1964, CFP. "[P]ude pasar pero no te imaginas como batalle estuve en Tijuana como 12 dias sufriendo la pena negra."

65. Sources consulted for this brief history of border enforcement in the 1960s and 1970s include Lytle Hernández, "Crimes and Consequences"; Lytle Hernández, *Migra!*; Andreas, "Transformation of Migrant Smuggling"; Calavita, *Inside the State*; and Nevins, *Operation Gatekeeper*. For more on the unprecedented increased policing and budgetary expansions of the 1990s and beyond, see also Andreas, *Border Games*; Dunn, *The Militarization of the U.S.-Mexico Border*; Donato, Wagner, and Patterson, "The Cat and Mouse Game." For studies on the social impact of those policies and practices, see Regan, *The Death of Josseline*; Urrea, *The Devil's Highway*; and Ibarra, "Buscando La Vida."

66. RMS Interview, Calvillo, Aguascalientes, 5 February 2017.

67. RMS to PCE, 12 March 1964, CFP. "[L]lo jalo en la que salga asta de jerente tengo una semana aqui casi pescando fresas pero jalamos 7–6—o 8 horas y nos las pagan a 1.00 . . . asi es que llo creo q no es justo mira paco please contestame[.]" "[N]o ando aquí agusto por la migra que cada rato viene este lunes fuí a los angeles a sacar un Seguro Social y como suerte vino la migra cuando llo andaba en los angeles y me escape como gato."

68. RMS to PCE, 18 March 1964, CFP. "[M]ira paco ojalá y uviera jale aqui en Sn José llo jalo en lo que sea pues fijate que estoy vien endrogado y asta ay tienes que me quiero casar sin manis ni piri." "[O]jalá aya jale llo con una poco de machetiada al Ingles me ago entender[.]" "[P]d tengo ganas de verte para que nos hechemos unas platícadonas de a 100 horas 'you know[.]' "

69. RMS to PCE, undated, ca. April 1964, CFP. "Dime si aún jalas de dishuaser. Llo conosco vien ese rama y houseman, y Bosboy pues es mi mero fuerte[.]"

70. RMS to PCE, 6 April 1964, CFP. "[S]i viera su mercé que ri jarto trabajoso y feo ista aquí Juárez qui pus la verda mijor mi quiero ir pal ranchu."

71. RMS to PCE, 23 June 1964, CFP. "[P]ues aquí me tienes en Tíjuas estoy jalando y ahorrando lo poquito que se puede para aventarme ay te encargo jale vueno dijo sí logro llegar sino pues en el nombre de Dios[.]" "[S]i Dios quiere the next week por aqui te caigo si Dios."

72. RMS to PCE, 27 July 1964, CFP. "Mr [P]aco espero te ayes a.t.m. que aquí nos pues lla no se sí somos de carne y hueso o de agua."

73. RMS to PCE, 29 July 1964, CFP. "[O]jalá y lla al resivir tu contestación lla tengas jale for me pues creo que es mucho mejor aquí en San Chepo [San José], que aquí donde estamos[.]"

74. RMS to PCE, 4 August 1964, CFP. "[A]quí nos pues piscando mas que sea re-frios esta jodidón el 'dura'-sno[.]"

75. RMS to PCE, 29 July 1964, CFP. "[M]i nuevo apedillo you know[.]"

76. RMS to PCE, 4 August 1964, CFP. "[F]ijate que el otro dia me sacaron un frijol tamaño durasno, la migratoria pues nos agarro en el baño y eso fue lo que me balentió[.]" "[L]la saves paco en cuanto aya jale nos pelamos en 1ero que ojalá fuera pronto pues llo aquí estoy con el 'chico' en la mano[.]" According to informal discussions with family members, the expression "con el 'chico' en la mano" means "holding one's behind."

77. RMS to PC, 13 August 1964, CFP. "[L]la no sirve esto[.]"

78. PCE Interview, San José, California, 20 April 2008.

79. RMS to PCE, 6 January 1965, CFP. "[P]orque veo que es la unica forma de poder juntar algo para luego venir a establecernos a Chihuahua[.]"

80. RMS to PCE, 25 January 1965, CFP. "[P].d. Paco dime plis si viste a Mr Rocky lla me imagino que a de estar vien enojado contestame luego por favor."

81. RMS to PCE, 6 January 1965, CFP. "[O]jalá paco tu que eres el unico que pu-edes alludar en esta cosa me pudieras conseguir en una parte u otra trabajo por favor, dime si aún estas con don nazario en el Restaurant[.]"

82. RMS to PCE, 25 January 1965, CFP. "[M]e dises que no estas trabajando pues que caray presisamente de eso te desia en mi anterior de Mr Rocky . . . para chamba para mi[.]" "[E]l pasaporte que te desia si encontré a los que los venden y fuí y asta les dí el enganche pero no tuve lla para pagar los 40 dollars que me faltan[.]" "[P]ues not te imaginas que no e completado ni para mí seremonia pero pues en el nombre de Dios aver como salgo[.]"

83. RMS to PCE, 19 March 1965, CFP. "[P]ues aqui no te creas es duro y no se gana tanto[.]"

84. RMS to PCE, 1 April 1965, CFP. "[L]lo . . . anduve en las nueces pero se acabarón y ahora estoy en la peluqueria pero esta poco dificil la chamba pero ay vamos mas o menos[.]" "[L]lo en la 1er oportunidad me voi con todo y mata a jalar una temporada[.]"

85. RMS Interview, Calvillo, Aguascalientes, 5 February 2017.

Conclusion

1. Abrams, *Oral History Theory*, 1.

Bibliography

Manuscript Collections

Ben Yellen Papers, MS 193, Mandeville Special Collections Library, UCSD
Chávez Family Papers (Correspondence), 1962–1971

Personal Interviews

Asunción Alvarado
Juan Alvarado
José Guadalupe "Paco" Francisco Chávez Esparza
Juan Chávez Esparza
Maura Chávez Esparza
Baudelio Chávez Torres
Guillermina Gallegos Díaz
Alicia González Torres
Eligio Hernández
Raúl Jaramillo
Rogelio Martínez Serna
Steve Reeves
Dolores "Lola" Salazar Rodríguez
Pedro "Perico" Sánchez
Rebeca Serna Macías

Newspapers, News Services, and Magazines

Associated Press
El Heraldo de Aguascalientes, Universidad Nacional Autónoma de Mexico,
    Mexico City
El Sol del Centro de Aguascalientes, Universidad Nacional Autónoma de Mexico,
    Mexico City
El Tiempo
Holtville Tribune
Imperial Hometown Review
Imperial Valley Press
La Opinión
La Voz de la Frontera
Los Angeles Times
Selecciones de Reader's Digest

Dissertations and Reports

Brown, Robert Michael. "The Impact of U.S. Work Experience on Mexican
Agricultural Workers: A Case Study in the Village of Jacona, Michoacán,
Mexico." PhD diss., University of Colorado, 1975.
Crummet, María de los Angeles. "Agrarian Class Structure and Migration:
A Comparative Regional Analysis from Aguascalientes, México." PhD diss.,
New School for Social Research, 1984.
Fernández, Leah. "Race and the Western Frontier: Colonizing the Imperial Valley,
1900–1948." PhD diss., University of California, Santa Barbara, 2012.
Ramírez, Marla A. "Contested Illegality: Three Generations of Exclusion through
Mexican Repatriation and the Politics of Immigration Law, 1920–2005." PhD
diss., University of California, Santa Barbara, 2015.
Rodríguez, Chantel Renee. "Health on the Line: The Politics of Citizenship and
the Railroad Bracero Program of World War II." PhD diss., University of
Minnesota, 2013.
Schantz, Eric M. "From the Mexicali Rose to the Tijuana Brass: Vice Tours of the
United States–Mexico Border, 1910–1965." PhD. diss., UCLA, 2001.

Documentaries

Harvest of Loneliness. Directed by Vivian Price, Gilbert González, and Adrian
Salinas. New York: Films for the Humanities and Sciences, 2011. DVD.
Maquilapolis. Directed by Vicki Funari and produced by Sergio de la Torre. San
Francisco: California Newsreel, 2006.
"Not a Drop to Drink." *The Border*. Directed by Mathew Snedden and Paul
Espinosa. Albuquerque: KNME/PBS, 1999. VHS.

Published Sources

Abrams, Lynn. *Oral History Theory*. New York: Routledge, 2011.
Abrego, Leisy. *Sacrificing Families: Navigating Laws, Labor, and Love across Borders*.
Stanford, CA: Stanford University Press, 2014.
Acevedo-Muñoz, Ernesto R. *Buñuel and Mexico: The Crisis of National Cinema*.
Berkeley: University of California Press, 2003.
Aguascalientes, Aguascalientes. *Recorridos: La vida educativa en los municipios de
Aguascalientes, Calvillo*. Boletín Municipal de Información Educativa,
Aguascalientes, December 2008. http://www.iea.gob.mx/webiea/comunicacion
/archivos/recorridos/CALVILLOF1.pdf. Accessed 6 June 2016.
Alamillo, José I. *Making Lemonade out of Lemons: Mexican American Labor and Leisure
in a California Town, 1880–1960*. Urbana: University of Illinois Press, 2006.
Alarcón, Rafael. "U.S. Immigration Policy and the Mobility of Mexicans (1882–
2005)." *Migraciones Internacionales* 6, no. 1 (January-June, 2011): 185–218.
Amador, Luisa María, and Jorge Ayala Blanco. *Cartelera cinematográfica digital, 1912–
1989*. Mexico City: UNAM Dirección General de Publicaciones, 2011.

Amuchástegui, Ana, ed. *Sucede que me canso de ser hombre: Relatos y reflexiones sobre hombres y masculinidades en México*. Mexico City: Colegio de México, 2007.

Andreas, Peter. *Border Games: Policing the U.S.-Mexico Divide*. Ithaca, NY: Cornell University Press, 2000.

———. "Transformation of Migrant Smuggling across the U.S.-Mexican Border." In *Global Human Smuggling: Comparative Perspectives*, edited by David Kyle and Rey Koslowski, 107–25. Baltimore: Johns Hopkins University Press, 2001.

Andrés, Benny J. "Invisible Borders: Repatriation and Colonization of Mexican Migrant Workers along the California Borderlands during the 1930s." *California History* 88, no. 4 (2011): 5–21, 63–65.

———. *Power and Control in the Imperial Valley: Nature, Agribusiness, and Workers on the California Borderland, 1900–1940*. College Station: Texas A&M University Press, 2014.

Arredondo, Gabriela F. *Mexican Chicago: Race, Identity, and Nation, 1916–39*. Chicago: University of Illinois Press, 2008.

Arreola, Daniel, and James R. Curtis. *The Mexican Border Cities: Landscape Anatomy and Place Personality*. Tucson: University of Arizona Press, 1994.

Arrom, Sylvia. *The Women of Mexico, 1790–1857*. Stanford, CA: Stanford University Press, 1992.

Bachelor, Steven J. "Toiling for the 'New Invaders': Autoworkers, Transnational Corporations, and Working-Class Culture in Mexico City, 1955–1968." In *Fragments of a Golden Age: The Politics of Culture in Mexico since 1940*, edited by Gilbert M. Joseph, Anne Rubenstein, and Eric Zolov, 273–326. Durham, NC: Duke University Press, 2001.

Bailey, Beth. *From Front Porch to Back Seat: Courtship in Twentieth-Century America*. Baltimore, MD: Johns Hopkins University Press, 1988.

Balderrama, Francisco E., and Raymond Rodríguez. *Decade of Betrayal: Mexican Repatriation in the 1930s*. Albuquerque: University of New Mexico Press, 1995.

Banco de México, Sistema de Información Economica, "U.S. Dollar—MXN Exchange Rate since 1954." http://www.banxico.org.mx/SieInternet/consultarDi rectorioInternetAction.do?accion=consultarCuadro&idCuadro=CF373&sector =6&locale=en. Accessed 23 June 2014.

Bederman, Gail. *Manliness and Civilization: A Cultural History of Gender and Race in the United States, 1880–1917*. Chicago: University of Chicago Press, 1996.

Bender, Steven. *Run for the Border*. New York: New York University Press, 2012.

Berg, Charles Ramírez. *The Classical Mexican Cinema: The Poetics of the Exceptional Golden Age Films*. Austin: University of Texas Press, 2015.

Berland, Lauren, ed. *Intimacy*. Chicago: University of Chicago Press, 2000.

———. "Intimacy: A Special Issue." *Critical Inquiry* 24, no. 2 (Winter 1998): 281–88.

Blackwell, Maylei. *¡Chicana! Contested Histories of Feminism in the Chicano Movement*. Austin: University of Texas Press, 2011.

Boehm, Deborah. *Intimate Migrations: Gender, Family, and Illegality among Transnational Mexicans*. New York: New York University Press, 2013.

———. "'Now I Am a Man and a Woman!': Gendered Moves and Migrations in a Transnational Mexican Community." *Latin American Perspectives* 35, no. 1 (January 2008): 16–30.

Bolton, Herbert E. *Anza's California Expeditions.* 5 vols. Berkeley: University of California Press, 1930.

Borges, Marcelo J., and Sonia Cancian. "Reconsidering the Migrant Letter: From the Experience of Migrants to the Language of Migrants." *History of the Family* 21, no. 3 (July 2016): 281–90.

Bose, Walter B. L. "Origenes del correo terrestre en México: Los Correos Mayores (1579–1765)." *Revista de Historia de América* 23 (June 1947): 55–103.

Bracero History Archive. http://braceroarchive.org. Accessed 12 May 2017.

Breckenridge, Keith. "Love Letters and Amanuenses: Beginning the Cultural History of the Working Class Private Sphere in Southern Africa, 1900–1933." *Journal of Southern African Studies* 26, no. 2 (2000): 337–48.

Broughton, Chad. "Migration as Engendered Practice: Mexican Men, Masculinity, and Northward Migration." *Gender and Society* 22, no. 5 (October 2008): 568–89.

Cabana, Gabriela S., and Jeffery J. Clark. "Introduction: Migration in Anthropology; Where We Stand." In *Rethinking Anthropological Perspectives on Migration*, edited by Gabriela S. Cabana and Jeffery J. Clark, 3–15. Gainesville: University Press of Florida, 2011.

Calavita, Kitty. *Inside the State: The Bracero Program, Immigration, and the I.N.S.* New Orleans: Quid Pro, 2011.

Camín, Héctor Aguilar, and Lorenzo Meyer. Translated by Luis Alberto Fierro. *In the Shadow of the Mexican Revolution: Contemporary Mexican History, 1910–1989.* Austin: University of Texas Press, 1993.

Cancian, Sonia. *Families, Lovers, and Their Letters: Italian Postwar Migration to Canada.* Winnipeg: University of Manitoba Press, 2010.

Cárdenas de la Peña, Enrique. *El correo.* Mexico City: Secretaría de Comunicaciones y Transportes, 1987.

———. *El teléfono.* Mexico City: Secretaría de Comunicaciones y Transportes, 1987.

Castellanos, M. Bianet. "Building Communities of Sentiment: Remittances and Emotions among Maya Migrants." *Chicana/Latina Studies* 8, no. 1/2 (Spring 2009): 140–71.

Castellanos, M. Bianet, and Deborah A. Boehm. "Introduction: Engendering Mexican Migration; Articulating Gender, Regions, Circuits." *Latin American Perspectives* 35, no. 1 (January 2008): 5–15.

Cerrutti, Marcela, and Douglas S. Massey. "Trends in Mexican Migration to the United States, 1965 to 1995." In *Crossing the Border: Research from the Mexican Migration Project*, edited by Jorge Durand and Douglas S. Massey, 17–44. New York: Russell Sage Foundation, 2004.

Cohen, Deborah. *Braceros: Migrant Citizens and Transnational Subjects in the Postwar United States and Mexico.* Chapel Hill: University of North Carolina Press, 2011.

———. "From Peasant to Worker: Migration, Masculinity, and the Making of Mexican Workers in the U.S." *International Labor and Working-Class History* 69, no. 1 (Spring 2006): 81–103.

Cohen, Rina. "'Mom Is a Stranger': The Negative Impact of Immigration Policies on the Family Life of Filipina Domestic Workers." *Canadian Ethnic Studies Journal* 32, no. 3 (2000): 76–88.

Collins, Kimberly. "The Imperial Valley and Mexicali: An Introduction to the Region and Its People." In *Imperial-Mexicali Valleys: Development and Environment of the U.S.-Mexican Border Region*, edited by Kimberly Collins et al., 3–14. San Diego: San Diego State University Press, Institute for Regional Studies of the Californias, 2004.

Consumer Postal Council. "Index of Postal Freedom, Mexico." http://www .postalconsumers.org/postal_freedom_index/Mexico_-_Sepomex.shtml. Accessed 1 October 2015.

"Correos de Mexico." http://www.correosdemexico.gob.mx/English/Paginas /History.aspx. Accessed 1 October 2015.

Cross, Harry E., and James A. Sandos. *Across the Border: Rural Development in Mexico and Recent Migration to the United States*. Berkeley: Institute of Governmental Studies, 1981.

Crummet, María de los Angeles. "A Gendered Economic History of Rural House-holds: Calvillo, Aguascalientes, México, 1982–1991." *Frontiers* 22, no. 1 (2001): 105–25.

Davidson, Miriam. *Lives on the Line: Dispatches from the U.S.-Mexico Border*. Tucson: University of Arizona Press, 2000.

De Genova, Nicholas. "The legal production of Mexican/migrant 'illegality.'" *Latino Studies* 2, no. 2 (2004): 160–85.

De Usabel, Gaizka S. *The High Noon of American Films in Latin America*. Ann Arbor, MI: UMI Research Press, 1982.

Donato, Katherine M., Donna Gabaccia, Jennifer Holdaway, Martin Manalansan IV, and Patricia R. Pessar. "A Glass Half Full? Gender in Migration Studies." *International Migration Review* 40, no. 1 (February 2006): 3–26.

Donato, Katherine M., Brandon Wagner, and Evelyn Patterson. "The Cat and Mouse Game at the Mexico-U.S. Border: Gendered Patterns of Recent Shifts." *International Migration Review* 42, no. 2 (June 2008): 330–59.

Doss, Erika. "Affect." *American Art* 23, no. 1 (Spring 2009): 9–11.

Dreby, Joanna. *Divided by Borders: Mexican Migrants and Their Children*. Berkeley: University of California Press, 2010.

———. "Gender and Transnational Gossip." *Qualitative Sociology* 32, no. 1 (March 2009): 33–52.

Dresp, Christine S. Wolf. "Nervios as a Culture-Bound Syndrome among Puerto Rican Women." *Smith College Studies in Social Work* 55, no. 2 (1985): 115–36.

Dunn, Timothy. *The Militarization of the U.S.-Mexico Border, 1978–1992: Low-Intensity Conflict Doctrine Comes Home*. Austin: Center for Mexican American Studies, University of Texas at Austin, 1996.

Durand, Jorge, and Douglas S. Massey. "Mexican Migration to the United States: A Critical Review." *Latin American Research Review* 27, no. 2 (1992): 3–42.

Durand, Jorge, Douglas S. Massey, and Emilio Parrado. "The New Era of Mexican Migration to the United States." *Journal of American History* 86, no. 2 (September 1999): 518–36.

Durazo, Norma Fimbres. "Capitalist Development and Population Growth in the County of Imperial, California and Mexicali, Baja California." In *Imperial and Mexicali Valleys: Development and Environment of the U.S.-Mexican Border Region*, edited by Kimberly Collins et al., 43–54. San Diego: San Diego State University Press, Institute for Regional Studies of the Californias, 2004.

Earle, Rebecca. "Letters and Love in Colonial Spanish America." *The Americas* 62, no. 1 (July 2005): 17–46.

Echols, Alice. "Orphans in the Storm: The Building and Loan Crisis of the 1930s." In *Shortfall: A Hidden History of 20th-Century American Capitalism*. New York: The New Press, 2017.

Elliott, Bruce S., David A. Gerber, and Suzanne M. Sinke, eds. *Letters across Borders: The Epistolary Practices of International Migrants*. New York: New York University Press, 2006.

Fein, Seth. "From Collaboration to Containment: Hollywood and the International Political Economy of Mexican Cinema after the Second World War." In *Mexico's Cinema: A Century of Film and Filmmakers*, edited by Joann Hershfield and David R. Maciel, 123–64. Wilmington, DE: Scholarly Resources, 1999.

———. "Myths of Cultural Imperialism and Nationalism in Golden Age Mexican Cinema." In *Fragments of a Golden Age: The Politics of Culture in Mexico since 1940*, edited by Gilbert M. Joseph, Anne Rubenstein, and Eric Zolov, 159–98. Durham, NC: Duke University Press, 2001.

Fernández-Kelly, María Patricia. *For We Are Sold, My People and I: Women and Industry in Mexico's Frontier*. Albany: State University of New York Press, 1984.

Flores, Lori. *Grounds for Dreaming: Mexican Americans, Mexican Immigrants, and the California Farmworker Movement*. New Haven, CT: Yale University Press, 2016.

———. "A Town Full of Dead Mexicans: The Salinas Valley Bracero Tragedy of 1963, the End of the Bracero Program, and the Evolution of California's Chicano Movement." *Western Historical Quarterly* 44, no. 2 (Summer 2013): 124–43.

Fox, Claire F. *The Fence and the River: Culture and Politics at the U.S.-Mexico Border*. Minneapolis: University of Minnesota Press, 1999.

Fox, Cybelle. "Unauthorized Welfare: The Origins of Immigrant Status Restrictions in American Social Policy." *Journal of American History* 102, no. 4 (2016): 1051–74.

French, William E. *The Heart in the Glass Jar: Love Letters, Bodies, and the Law in Mexico*. Lincoln: University of Nebraska Press, 2015.

Galarza, Ernesto. *Merchants of Labor: The Mexican Bracero Story; An Account of the Managed Migration of Mexican Farm Workers in California, 1942–1960*. Charlotte, NC: McNally and Loftin, 1964.

Gamio, Manuel. *El inmigrante mexicano: La historia de su vida, entrevistas completas, 1926–1927*. Mexico City: Instituto Nacional de Migración, 2002.

García, Juan R. *Operation Wetback: The Mass Deportation of Mexican Undocumented Workers in 1954*. Westport, CT: Greenwood Press, 1980.

García y Griego, Manuel. "The Importation of Mexican Contract Laborers to the United States, 1942–1964." In *Between Two Worlds: Mexican Immigrants in the*

United States, edited by David Gutiérrez, 45–85. Wilmington, DE: Scholarly Resources, 1996.

Garcilazo, Jeff. *Traqueros: Mexican Railroad Workers in the United States*. Denton, TX: University of North Texas Press, 2012.

Gerber, David A. "Acts of Deceiving and Withholding in Immigrant Letters: Personal Identity and Self-Presentation in Personal Correspondence." *Journal of Social History* 39, no. 2 (Winter 2005): 315–30.

———. *Authors of Their Lives: The Personal Correspondence of British Immigrants to North America in the Nineteenth Century*. New York: New York University Press, 2006.

Gitter, Seth R., Robert J. Gitter, and Douglas Southgate. "The Impact of Return Migration to Mexico." *Estudios Económicos* 23, no. 1 (January–June 2008): 3–23.

Gojman de Backal, Alicia G., and Laura Edith Bonilla. *Historia del correo en México*. Mexico City: Servicio Postal Mexicano, 2000.

Goldstein, Natalie. *Genes and Disease: Parkinson's Disease*. New York: Chelsea House, 2009.

González Esparza, Victor M. *Estado de bienestar: Familia y pobreza en México; Reflexiones sobre el caso de Aguascalientes, 1940–1995*. Mexico City: Grupo Impresor, 1998.

Granados Alcántar, José Aurelio, and Karina Pizarro Hernández. "Paso del norte, qué lejos te vas quedando: Implicaciones de la migración de retorno en México." *Estudios Demográficos y Urbanos* 28, no. 2 (May–August 2013): 469–96.

Granados, Pável. *XEW: 70 años en el aire*. Mexico City: Editorial Clío, 2000.

Green, Allison. "Cablevision(nation) in Rural Yucatan: Performing Modernity and *Mexicanidad* in the Early 1990s." In *Fragments of a Golden Age: The Politics of Culture in Mexico since 1940*, edited by Gilbert M. Joseph, Anne Rubenstein, and Eric Zolov, 415–51. Durham, NC: Duke University Press, 2001.

Guerin-Gonzales, Camille. *Mexican Workers and the American Dream: Immigration, Repatriation, and California Farm Labor, 1900–1939*. New Brunswick, NJ: Rutgers University Press, 1994.

Gutiérrez, David. *Walls and Mirrors: Mexicans, Mexican Americans, and the Politics of Ethnicity*. Berkeley: University of California Press, 1995.

Gutiérrez, Felix, and Jorge Reina Schement. *Spanish-Language Radio in the Southwestern United States*. Austin: University of Texas Press, 1979.

Gutmann, Matthew. *The Meanings of Macho: Being a Man in Mexico City*. Berkeley: University of California Press, 1996.

Guzmán, Romeo. "The Transnational Life and Letters of the Venegas Family, 1920s to 1950s." *History of the Family* 21, no. 3 (July 2016): 457–82.

Haber, Stephen, and Herbert S. Klein. *Mexico since 1980*. New York: Cambridge University Press, 2008.

Hamilton, Jon. "Can a Cancer Drug Reverse Parkinson's and Dementia?" http://www.npr.org/sections/health-shots/2015/10/17/448323916/can-a-cancer-drug-reverse-parkinsons-disease-and-dementia. Accessed 19 October 2015.

Hernández López, Toribio. *Monografía del Municipio del Calvillo*. Aguascalientes: Gobierno del Estado de Aguascalientes, Instituto Cultural de Aguascalientes, 2002.

Herrera, Carlos. "Before the Waters . . . the Desert: An Early History of the Imperial Valley." In *Imperial and Mexicali Valleys: Development and Environment of the U.S.-Mexican Border Region*, edited by Kimberly Collins et al., 17–32. San Diego: San Diego State University Press, Institute for Regional Studies of the Californias, 2004.

Hoffnung-Garskof, Jesse. *A Tale of Two Cities: Santo Domingo and New York after 1950*. Princeton, NJ: Princeton University Press, 2010.

Hondagneu-Sotelo, Pierrette, ed. *Gender and U.S. Immigration: Contemporary Trends*. Berkeley: University of California Press, 2003.

———. *Gendered Transitions: Mexican Experiences of Immigration*. Berkeley: University of California Press, 1994.

Hondagneu-Sotelo, Pierrette, and Ernestine Avila. " 'I'm Here but I'm There': The Meanings of Latina Transnational Motherhood." *Gender and Society* 11, no. 5 (October 1997): 548–60.

Hudgins, Edward L., ed. *Mail at the Millennium: Will the Postal Service Go Private?* Washington, DC: Cato Institute, 2001.

Huebner, Andrew J. "Writing History with Emotion." *American Historian* (August 2014): 14–15.

Ibarra, María de la Luz. "Buscando La Vida: Mexican Immigrant Women's Memories of Home, Yearning, and Border Crossings." *Frontiers* 24, nos. 2 and 3 (2003): 261–81.

Irwin, Robert, and Maricruz Ricalde. *Global Mexican Cinema: Its Golden Age*. London: British Film Institute, 2013.

Jamieson, Lynn. *Intimacy: Personal Relationships in Modern Societies*. Cambridge: Polity Press, 1998.

Johnson, Kevin R. "The Beginning of the End: The Immigration Act of 1965 and the Emergence of the Modern U.S.-Mexico Border State." In *The Immigration and Nationality Act of 1965: Legislating a New America*, edited by Gabriel J. Chin and Rose Cuison Villazor, 116–72. New York: Cambridge University Press, 2015.

———. "The Forgotten 'Repatriation' of Persons of Mexican Ancestry and Lessons for the 'War on Terror.' " Fifteenth Annual Dyson Distinguished Lecture, Pace Law School, March 2005. UC Davis Legal Studies Research Paper No. 64. http://ssrn.com/abstract=862905.

———. "The New Nativism: Something Old, Something New, Something Borrowed, Something Blue." In *Immigrants Out! The New Nativism and the Anti-Immigrant Impulse in the United States*, edited by Juan F. Perea, 165–89. New York: New York University Press, 1997.

Joseph, Gilbert M., and Timothy J. Henderson. *The Mexico Reader: History, Culture, Politics*. Durham, NC: Duke University Press, 2003.

Joseph, Gilbert M., Anne Rubenstein, and Eric Zolov, eds. *Fragments of a Golden Age: The Politics of Culture in Mexico since 1940*. Durham, NC: Duke University Press, 2001.

Lavrin, Asunción, ed. *Marriage and Sexuality in Colonial Latin America*. Lincoln: University of Nebraska Press, 1992.

Levitt, Peggy. "Social Remittances: Migration Driven Local-Level Forms of Cultural Diffusion." *International Migration Review* 32, no. 4 (Winter 1998): 926–48.

Light, Alison. *A Common People: A History of an English Family.* London: Penguin / Fig Tree Press, 2015.

Lispett-Rivera, Sonya, and Lyman L. Johnson, eds. *The Faces of Honor: Sex, Shame, and Violence in Colonial Latin America.* Albuquerque: University of New Mexico Press, 1998.

Lowell, B. Lindsay. "Circular Mobility, Migrant Communities, and Policy Restrictions: Unauthorized Flows from Mexico." In *Migration, Population Structure, and Redistribution Policies*, edited by Calvin Goldscheider, 137–57. Boulder, CO: Westview Press, 1992.

Loza, Mireya. *Defiant Braceros: How Migrant Workers Fought for Racial, Sexual, and Political Freedom.* Chapel Hill: University of North Carolina Press, 2016.

Lutz, Helma. "Gender in the Migratory Process." *Journal of Ethnic and Migration Studies* 36, no. 10 (2010): 1647–63.

Lystra, Karen. *Searching the Heart: Women, Men and Romantic Love in Nineteenth-Century America.* New York: Oxford University Press, 1989.

Lytle Hernández, Kelly. "The Crimes and Consequences of Illegal Immigration: A Cross-Border Examination of Operation Wetback, 1943 to 1954." *Western Historical Quarterly* 37, no. 4 (Winter 2006): 421–44.

———. *Migra! A History of the U.S. Border Patrol.* Berkeley: University of California Press, 2010.

Maciel, David. *El Bandolero, El Pocho, y La Raza: Imagines cinematograficas del chicano.* Mexico City: Siglo XXI Editores/CONACULTA, 2000.

Martínez, Oscar. *Border Boom Town: Ciudad Juárez since 1848.* Austin: University of Texas Press, 1978.

Martínez Rodríguez, José Luis. *El correo en México.* Mexico City: Servicio Postal Mexicano, 2000.

Massey, Douglas. "The Social Organization of Mexican Migration to the United States." *Annals of the American Academy of Political and Social Science* 487 (September 1986): 102–13.

Massey, Douglas, et al. *Return to Aztlan: The Social Process of International Migration from Western Mexico.* Berkeley: University of California Press, 1987.

Matsumoto, Valerie. "Courtship in American History." *OAH Magazine of History* 18, no. 4 (July 2004): 27–29, 34.

Mayer, Jean A. *The Cristero Rebellion: The Mexican People between Church and State, 1926–1929.* Cambridge: Cambridge University Press, 2008.

McGinn, Noel F. "Marriage and Family in Middle-Class Mexico." *Journal of Marriage and Family* 28, no. 3 (August 1966): 305–13.

McKay, Deirdre. "Sending Dollars Shows Feeling: Emotions and Economies in Filipino Migration." *Mobilities* 2 (2007): 175–94.

Mejía Barquera, Fernando. *La industria de la radio y la televisión y la politica del estado mexicano.* Mexico City: Fundación Manuel Buendia, 1989.

Mitchell, Don. *They Saved the Crops: Labor, Landscape, and the Struggle over Industrial Farming in Bracero-Era California*. Athens: University of Georgia Press, 2012.

Molina, Natalia. *How Race Is Made in America: Immigration, Citizenship, and the Historical Power of Racial Scripts*. Berkeley: University of California Press, 2014.

Monsiváis, Carlos. "Cantinflas and Tin Tan: Mexico's Greatest Comedians." In *Mexico's Cinema: A Century of Film and Filmmaking*, edited by Joanne Hershfield and David R. Maciel, 49–80. Lanham, MD: Rowman and Littlefield, 1999.

Montes, Veronica. "The Role of Emotions in the Construction of Masculinity: Guatemalan Migrant Men, Transnational Migration, and Family Relations." *Gender and Society* 27, no. 4 (August 2013): 469–90.

Mraz, John. "Today, Tomorrow and Always: The Golden Age of Illustrated Magazines in Mexico, 1937–1960." In *Fragments of a Golden Age: The Politics of Culture in Mexico since 1940*, edited by Gilbert M. Joseph, Anne Rubenstein, and Eric Zolov, 116–57. Durham, NC: Duke University Press, 2001.

Muñoz Gómez, Daniel. *El correo, el teléfono y el telégrafo en Guadalajara*. Jalisco, Mexico: Gobierno de Jalisco Secretaría General Unidad Editorial / Guadalajara, 1988.

Nail, Thomas. *The Figure of the Migrant*. Stanford, CA: Stanford University Press, 2015.

Navarro, Moisés González. *Los extranjeros en México y los mexicanos en el extranjero, 1821–1870*. Vol. 3. Mexico City: Colegio de México, 1994.

Necesidades esenciales en México: Situación actual y perspectivas el año 2000. 2 Educación. Mexico City: Siglo XXI Editores / Complamar, 1982.

Nevins, Joseph. *Operation Gatekeeper and Beyond: The War on "Illegals" and the Remaking of the U.S.-Mexico Boundary*. New York: Routledge, 2001.

Ngai, Mae. *Impossible Subjects: Illegal Aliens and the Making of Modern America*. Princeton, NJ: Princeton University Press, 2005.

Niblo, Stephen R. *Mexico in the 1940s: Modernity, Politics, and Corruption*. Lanham, MD: Rowman and Littlefield, 2000.

Noriega-Verdugo, Sergio. "Economic Overview: Employment Patterns in Mexicali." In *Imperial and Mexicali Valleys: Development and Environment of the U.S.-Mexican Border Region*, edited by Kimberly Collins et al., 113–31. San Diego: San Diego State University Press, Institute for Regional Studies of the Californias, 2004.

Orozco, José. *Receive Our Memories: The Letters of Luz Moreno, 1950–1952*. New York: Oxford University Press, 2017.

Osorio, Alejandra. "Postcards in the Porfirian Imaginary." *Social Justice* 34, no. 1 (2007): 141–54.

Parkinson's Disease Dementia. http://www.alz.org/dementia/parkinsons-disease-symptoms.asp. Accessed 19 October 2015.

Parkinson's Disease Information. Parkinson's Disease History. http://www.parkinsons.org/parkinsons-history.html. Accessed 20 August 2015.

Parrado, Emilio A., and Chenoa A. Flippen. "Migration and Gender among Mexican Women." *American Sociological Review* 70 (2005): 606–32.

Parrado, Emilio A., and René M. Zenteno. "Gender Differences in Union Formation in Mexico: Evidence from Marital Search Models." *Journal of Marriage and Family* 64, no. 3 (August 2002): 756–73.

Parrenas, Rhacel. *Children of Global Migration: Transnational Families and Gendered Woes.* Stanford, CA: Stanford University Press, 2005.

———. "Long-Distance Intimacy: Class, Gender, and Intergenerational Relations between Mothers." *Global Networks* 5, no. 4 (2005): 317–36.

Pérez, Ramona L. "Crossing the Border from Boyhood to Manhood: Male Youth Experiences of Crossing, Loss, and Structural Violence as Unaccompanied Minors." *International Journal of Adolescence and Youth* 19, no. 1 (September 2014): 67–83.

Perry, Elizabeth Mary. "Finding Fatima: A Slave Woman of Early Modern Spain." *Journal of Women's History* 20, no. 1 (Spring 2008): 151–67.

Pilcher, Jeffrey M. *Cantinflas and the Chaos of Mexican Modernity.* Lanham, MD: Rowman and Littlefield, 2001.

———. "Mexico's Pepsi Challenge: Traditional Cooking, Mass Consumption, and National Identity." In *Fragments of a Golden Age: The Politics of Culture in Mexico since 1940*, edited by Gilbert M. Joseph, Anne Rubenstein, and Eric Zolov, 71–90. Durham, NC: Duke University Press, 2001.

Porter, Susie S. *Working Women in Mexico City: Public Discourses and Material Conditions, 1879–1931.* Tucson: University of Arizona Press, 2003.

Querejeta Villagómez, Enrique. *Historia de la enfermedad de Parkinson.* Mexico City: Instituto Politécnico Nacional, 2008.

Quilodrán, Julieta. "México: Diferencias de nupcialidad por regiones y tamaños de localidad." *Estudios Demográficos y Urbanos* 4, no. 3 (1989): 595–613.

Raat, W. Dirk, and Michael M. Brescia. *Mexico and the United States: Ambivalent Vistas.* 4th ed. Athens: University of Georgia Press, 2010.

Ramírez, Catherine. "Saying 'Nothin': Pachucas and the Languages of Resistance." *Frontiers* 27, no. 3 (2006): 1–33.

Rapport, Nigel, and Andrew Dawson, eds. *Migrants of Identity: Perceptions of "Home" in a World of Movement.* Oxford, UK: Bloomsbury Academic Press, 1998.

Regan, Margaret. *The Death of Josseline: Immigration Stories from the Arizona Borderlands.* Boston: Beacon Press, 2010.

Reichert, Josh, and Douglas S. Massey. "History and Trends in U.S. Bound Migration from a Mexican Town." *International Migration Review* 14, no. 4 (Winter 1980): 475–91.

———. "Patterns of U.S. Migration from a Mexican Sending Community: A Comparison of Legal and Illegal Migrants." *International Migration Review* 13, no. 4 (Winter 1979): 599–623.

Rodríguez, Gerardo. *Ondas nada más: Voces de la radio aguascalentense.* Aguascalientes, Aguascalientes: Instituto Cultural de Aguascalientes, Unidad Estatal de Culturas Populares, 2009.

Rojas, Beatríz, Jesús Gómez Serrano, Andrés Reyes Rodríguez, Salvador Camacho, and Carlos Reyes Sahagún. *Breve historia de Aguascalientes.* Fideicomiso Historia de las Americas, Fondo de Cultural Economico, Mexico. 2nd ed. Mexico City: Colegio de México, 1995.

Rosas, Ana E. *Abrazando el Espíritu: Bracero Families Confront the U.S.-Mexico Border.* Berkeley: University of California Press, 2014.

Rosas, Carolina. "El desafío de ser hombre y no migrar: Estudio de caso en una comunidad del centro de Veracruz." In *Sucede que me canso de ser hombre: Relatos y reflexiones sobre hombres y masculinidades en México,* edited by Ana Amuchástegui, 275–308. Mexico City: Colegio de México, 2007.

Round, Phillip H. *The Impossible Land: Story and Place in California's Imperial Valley.* Albuquerque: University of New Mexico Press, 2004.

Rubenstein, Anne. *Bad Language, Naked Ladies, and Other Threats to the Nation: A Political History of Comic Books in Mexico.* Durham, NC: Duke University Press, 1998.

Ruiz, Vicki L. *From out of the Shadows: Mexican Women in the Twentieth Century.* New York: Oxford University Press, 1998.

Salzinger, Leslie. *Genders in Production: Making Workers in Mexico's Global Factories.* Berkeley: University of California Press, 2003.

Sánchez, George J. *Becoming Mexican American: Ethnicity, Culture, and Identity in Chicano Los Angeles, 1900–1945.* New York: Oxford University Press, 1995.

Sanders, Nichole. *Gender and Welfare in Mexico: The Consolidation of a Postrevolutionary State.* University Park: Pennsylvania State University Press, 2011.

Sassen, Saskia. *Expulsions: Brutality and Complexity in the Global Economy.* Cambridge, MA: Belknap Press of Harvard University Press, 2014.

Schmidt, Arthur. "Making It Real Compared to What? Reconceptualizing Mexican History since 1940." In *Fragments of a Golden Age: The Politics of Culture in Mexico since 1940,* edited by Gilbert M. Joseph, Anne Rubenstein, and Eric Zolov, 23–68. Durham, NC: Duke University Press, 2001.

Schmidt Camacho, Alicia. *Migrant Imaginaries: Latino Cultural Politics in the US-Mexico Borderlands.* New York: New York University Press, 2008.

Segura, Denise, and Pat Zavella, eds. *Women and Migration in the U.S.-Mexico Borderlands.* Durham, NC: Duke University Press, 2007.

Sharma, Nutan. *Parkinson's Disease.* Westport, CT: Greenwood Press, 2008.

Siems, Larry. *Between the Lines: Letters between Undocumented Mexican and Central American Immigrants and Their Families and Friends.* Tucson: University of Arizona Press, 1995.

Sifuentez, Mario. *Of Forests and Fields: Mexican Labor in the Pacific Northwest.* New Brunswick, NJ: Rutgers University Press, 2016.

Smith, Michael M. "Beyond the Borderlands: Mexican Labor in the Plains States, 1900–1930." *Great Plains Quarterly* (1981): 239–51.

Smith, Robert. *Mexican New York: Transnational Lives of New Immigrants.* Berkeley: University of California Press, 2005.

Smith-Rosenberg, Carol. *Disorderly Conduct: Visions of Gender in Victorian America.* New York: Oxford University Press, 1985.

Sorensen, Nina. "Narratives of Longing, Belonging, and Caring in the Dominican Diaspora." In *Caribbean Narratives of Belonging: Fields of Relations, Sites of Identity,* edited by Jean Besson and Karen F. Olwig, 222–42. London: Macmillan Caribbean, 2006.

Stampa, Manuel Carrera. "El correo en Mexico: The Mail in Mexico." *Artes de México*, no. 96 (1967): 14–21.

Stern, Alexandra M. "Buildings, Boundaries, and Blood: Medicalization and Nation-Building on the U.S.-Mexico Border, 1910–1930." *Hispanic American Historical Review* 79, no. 1 (February 1999): 41–81.

———. "Nationalism on the Line: Masculinity, Race, and the Creation of the U.S. Border Patrol, 1910–1940." In *Continental Crossroads: Remapping U.S.-Mexico Borderlands History*, edited by Samuel Truett and Elliott Young, 299–322. Durham, NC: Duke University Press, 2004.

Stetka, Bret. "Parkinson's Disease and Pesticides: What's the Connection?" *Scientific American*, 8 April 2014, https://www.scientificamerican.com/article /parkinsons-disease-and-pesticides-whats-the-connection/. Accessed 4 May 2017.

Stoler, Anne. *Haunted by Empire: Geographies of Intimacy in North American Histories*. Durham, NC: Duke University Press, 2006.

Twinam, Ann. *Public Lives, Private Secrets: Honor, Sexuality, and Illegitimacy in Colonial Spanish America*. Stanford, CA: Stanford University Press, 1999.

United States Census Bureau. "Poverty Thresholds 1962." http://www.census.gov /hhes/www/poverty/data/threshld/thresh62.html. Accessed 5 May 2015.

United States Postal Service. *The United States Postal Service: An American History, 1775–2006*. Publication 100. November 2012. https://about.usps.com/publications /pub100.pdf. Accessed 1 October 2016.

Urrea, Luis Alberto. *The Devil's Highway: A True Story*. Reprint, New York: Little, Brown, 2004.

Vollmann, William T. *Imperial*. New York: Penguin Press, 2010.

Waldinger, Roger. *The Cross-Border Connection: Immigrants, Emigrants, and Their Homelands*. Cambridge, MA: Harvard University Press, 2015.

Weise, Julie M. *Corazón de Dixie: Mexicanos in the U.S. South since 1910*. Chapel Hill: University of North Carolina Press, 2016.

Wilkerson, Isabel. *The Warmth of Other Suns: The Epic of the Great Migration*. New York: Vintage Books, 2010.

Zelizer, Viviana A. *The Purchase of Intimacy*. Princeton, NJ: Princeton University Press, 2005.

Zolov, Eric. "Discovering a Land 'Mysterious and Obvious': The Renarrativizing of Postrevolutionary Mexico." In *Fragments of a Golden Age: The Politics of Culture in Mexico since 1940*, edited by Gilbert M. Joseph, Anne Rubenstein, and Eric Zolov, 234–72. Durham, NC: Duke University Press, 2001.

Zong, Jie, and Jeanne Batalova. "Mexican Immigrants in the United States." Migration Policy Institute, 17 March 2016. http://www.migrationpolicy.org /article/mexican-immigrants-united-states?gclid=CjwKEAiAmdXBBRDohZCV kYHTl2oSJACWsZj9xZbP6CMo_n19i_7j08QHLihlgt1olD_jG1x4O2dhoBoCW63w _wcB. Accessed 23 November 2016.

Index

Women: and absence of family
members, 102–3, 115, 129, 138, 159;
and bracero program, 39; and
domestic chores, 47, 67, 74, 75, 143,
161; gender norms and expectations
about, 20–21, 51, 74, 86, 88–90, 144;
jobs for, 14, 87, 88–91, 189; migrants'
dreams about, 174–75, 190; and sexual
double standard, 147, 152; surveillance of male sexuality by, 21, 131–32,
152–54; surveillance of sexuality of,
21, 23, 86, 112, 131–32, 144, 145–46,
147–52, 195. *See also* Gender norms
and conventions
Working conditions, 15, 42, 48–59
World War II, 2, 5, 6, 8, 105, 168

Zapata, Emiliano, 8
Zelizer, Viviana A., 21
Zolov, Eric, 9–10, 12